# Madeline Smith, Bond Girl

This work is of non-fiction and is based on extensive research around individuals and events. To the best of the co-author's ability, events have been portrayed accurately and as a result of numerous interviews with the person who is the subject of the book. The views and opinions regarding individuals or events are those of the person who is the subject of the book and do not necessarily represent those of Philip Kay-Bujak. All information used in this book is used with no guarantee of absolute accuracy.

# Madeline Smith, Bond Girl

## From 60s Fashion Model to Half a Century on Stage and Screen

Philip Kay-Bujak with Madeline Smith

First published in Great Britain in 2026 by
White Owl
An imprint of Pen & Sword Books Limited
Yorkshire – Philadelphia



ISBN 9781036148669



A CIP catalogue record for this book is available from the British Library.



Typeset by Mac Style
Printed in the UK by CPI Group (UK) Ltd, Croydon, CR0 4YY.

The Publisher's authorised representative in the EU for product safety is Authorised Rep Compliance Ltd., Ground Floor, 71 Lower Baggot Street, Dublin D02 P593, Ireland.
www.arccompliance.com

For a complete list of Pen & Sword titles please contact:

PEN & SWORD BOOKS LIMITED
47 Church Street, Barnsley, South Yorkshire, S70 2AS, England
E-mail: enquiries@pen-and-sword.co.uk
Website: www.pen-and-sword.co.uk
or
PEN AND SWORD BOOKS
1950 Lawrence Road, Havertown, PA 19083, USA
E-mail: uspen-and-sword@casematepublishers.com
Website: www.penandswordbooks.com

*For Emily*

# Contents

# Introduction

> 'Books are not about passing the time. They're about other lives. Other worlds. Far from wanting time to pass, one just wishes one had more of it. If one wanted to pass the time one could go to New Zealand.'
>
> Alan Bennett

This is a book about a life spent in an industry designed for one purpose only – to entertain us. The devotion required to want to bring joy to others is immeasurable, which makes the task of a biographer trying to chart such a life, but to also understand it, a considerable challenge. There are so few professions where someone is totally dedicated to service of others – education and health are two, but the performing arts are a third.

I hope that this is not a book, in Alan Bennett's words, to 'pass the time' but one that also adds to our understanding of 'other worlds' – one in which a slight, anorexic young teenage girl was taken on a magic-carpet ride through the rapidly changing world of the 1960s and who, almost overnight, became a world-famous model. It is also a book about the growth of television and films throughout the 1970s and how production companies simply devoured whatever new proposal they could get their hands on, found the funding and created series after series that gave life to many of the television and film stars whom we remember from our childhoods. These were halcyon days for new and up-and-coming talent to elbow their way alongside those who had spent generations practising their craft – it would not be without friction between the old and the new, but both had to find an accommodation with each other and adapt to maximize the new opportunities that lay before them. So this is also a book about determination, guts, courage and often wobbling self-belief, a struggle to get on to the first rung and fight to climb the ladder of success – not knowing just how many steps there might be.

When the camera in a cold Pinewood studio leads us very slowly panning from right to left across the king-sized bed which pretends to be James Bond's London apartment, how are we to know where Roger Moore's first 'Bond Girl' had come from? Our imagination wants her to be a cultured Italian secret agent who has been with our British hero in a night of passion and love. But just as the so-called apartment is actually made of chipboard in the corner of a huge cold building, so our Italian secret agent had arrived by grubby taxi from Kew three hours earlier on this cold January morning. The arts are all about illusion, and this book tries to sweep away some of the smoke and mirrors and show how Madeline Smith climbed her own ladder, despite the many slips and pitfalls along the way. Madeline would never claim to be a star – but she has twinkled nevertheless, from the night-sky of her 1960s modelling shots, through to supporting roles in films, sexual exploitation in dark horror films and on to children's television and short films with Peter Cook and Eric Morecambe. What is more remarkable is that Madeline Smith is still twinkling today as she performs and narrates through her repertoire of Bond movie theme evenings and her Frankenstein shows.

The majority of this book relies on what Maddie – as she is known to friends – remembers. Our research interviews were really discussions about aspects of her career and the huge roll-call of talented actors and stars that she met on her journey. I have tried to record these many talented professionals in the footnotes which act as an A–Z of people we should not forget and who added so much to our own lives and the entertainment of a nation, and these should be referred to as you move through the book to get a sense of the wonderful people whom Maddie worked alongside. Where Maddie is speaking to us directly, her narrative is indented in a different font in the hope that you can hear her voice speaking directly to you.

That iconic and hopeful, pleading look that personified the fashion and carefree abandon of the 1960s and then went on to television and stage success in the 1970s and 1980s remains etched in Maddie's face, and is as hopeful as ever. It was a long climb on her own ladder, and she is still climbing – hoping that the rungs will never end. Finally, if this is a good book, then it is my sincere hope that when you have read Maddie's story, you will feel that you have 'looked into other lives and other worlds' and not want to go to New Zealand, as Alan Bennett suggests, but you 'will just want more of it'.

# Acknowledgements

Biographical writing, by its very nature, is a responsibility not to be taken lightly, and this is a book that could not have been written without the support and commitment given by Madeline Smith herself. So to Maddie, I say a deep and sincere thank you for trusting me to write a book about her life, and for her patience while it all came together.

If it had not been for the kind invitation to talk about one of my books at my local bookshop in East Grinstead, I would never have met the charming and inspirational Madeline Smith, so my enduring thanks go to the equally inspirational John Pye. Not only did John facilitate the early introductions, he also supplied a discreet corner of his shop where Maddie and I could talk about her life – and share in some delicious fruit cake to keep us going during some long afternoons.

While there will inevitably be omissions and errors in any book, I would also like to thank Brian Elliott and Geoffrey Kay for their painstaking proof reading and guidance on elements of this story. Any remaining errors should be laid at my door. Thanks also need to go to Julia Muirhead from Our Lady of Loreto & St Winefride Catholic Church, the archive section of the Victoria & Albert Museum and innumerable contacts around the globe who provided insights and information on Maddie's career.

The time it takes to prepare and then write any book necessarily impacts upon family life. So thank you to my wife, Helena, and my children, Skye and Cameron, for yet again being so patient with me during the dozens of telephone conversations that held up dinner, and the many hours where Dad was lost to them in some part of this story.

Finally, this book would not have been possible without the constant support and encouragement of Madeline Smith herself. It takes courage to allow someone to delve into one's past and to make observations – and at times judgements – on one's decisions. I am deeply grateful that Maddie put her trust in me to complete the project and gave me so much of her personal time, making the process fun so that this part of her life – and the times in which she lived, the people she met and the world that we have lost – is at least preserved and passed on to future generations.

PKB
East Sussex
Autumn 2025

Part One

# From Birth to Biba

# Chapter 1

# 'I should have been Nicky'

'I was born in a thunderstorm…'

Madeline Smith

Any conversation with Madeline Smith will, at some point, lead to her family. Madeline is not only securely connected to her past but also her experiences of early family life – so much of which has shaped her character far more than is usual. Like many people, she treasures her many positive memories of childhood but also remembers every detail of times when things did not go so well. She is very much the sum of the parts of her past.

> 'My earliest memories connect to my father's mother – I feel I am a mixture of my grandmother and my father. She had a passion for gardening and so do I – I love my little garden and I can recall my earliest memories still being looking up at the branches of trees floating overhead as I was pushed flat on my back in my pram. I know I am more connected to my grandmother as my mother hated gardening and I feel I share less with my mother, who was very quiet and unassuming. Nellie was also fun loving and full of joy whereas my mother had a tough life, starting in a new country and finding it difficult to live the life she so much wanted.'

Maddie, as I shall now call her, has always seen her life against the backdrop of her roots and what she experienced as a child. While she looks back at her grandmother as a very positive influence, Maddie also shared and shares a good connection with her mother and regards the difficult challenges that she faced through a philosophical prism of understanding and reality. In the post-war world of the 1950s, where so many lives had become displaced and where a new society was being built, many of the established social patterns of society had been broken, new relationships were everywhere and people needed to rush to get married and build a family in ways that were unusual.

So much had been taken away by the war, including room to grow up and build relationships, and Maddie reflects upon the way that her mother and father, without the impact of the war, would never have met and perhaps had very little in common. But this was far from unusual in a post-war world of social dislocation, displaced persons and a desire to recover quickly from the years of lost peace.

Regardless of how and why Maddie's parents met, they did and they quickly married. Having moved to rural Hartfield in East Sussex in 1948, Maddie was born the following year in a large Victorian house that had been converted into a wartime nursing home. Her father, Robert, and mother, Ursula, were determined that she should have the best place that was available for her birth – the date was 2 August 1949, the same day on which actor Peter O'Toole had been born seventeen years earlier. For years after, Maddie would often be reminded that, when local GP Dr Dennison arrived for the birth, a huge, savage thunderstorm raged overhead – perhaps a premonition of the times ahead in the Hammer horror films that were only twenty years distant, or maybe a portent of the Irish temper that Maddie admits she inherited from the Irish roots of her father, Bob.

The grand and spacious new family home had been requisitioned by the British Army during the Second World War before reverting back to a large family house. Remembering those days, Maddie always sensed that her mother had wanted a boy, probably to be called Nicholas; the small seeds of a sense of inadequacy were thus sown very early in Maddie's life – whether real or imagined.

The weather at the time of her birth remains in Maddie's mind as a prophetic statement about her character. From personal experience, the benign, often beguiling and charming Maddie Smith can also rumble like the early echoes of a distant thunderstorm. If you don't want it passing right over your head, it's a good idea to either physically move to shelter from the rainstorm and reach for the safety of a metaphorical oak tree, or try to avoid the clouds passing overhead by nimble distraction in conversation. Just like an English thunderstorm, the clouds pass exceptionally quickly and the sunshine of Maddie's personality beams like the sun breaking through the rain – but do be careful to listen.

Maddie is certain that her mother, Ursula, was an intelligent woman, a musician whose marriage to her father was often fraught with tension. In some ways they fitted together well, but in others they seemed to have little in common or be 'not of the same world'. Maddie has always been aware that her memories reflect the challenges that her grandparents and parents had to face in building new lives against a post-war background of a disconnected society.

> 'My grandfather worked for a dairy and washed bottles in his early life before making his way to becoming a manager in the north of England for the Express Dairy, and that's when we moved to East Sussex, where he was able to buy his own dairy. We lived above the Brockhurst Dairy, London Road, East Grinstead, where my earliest childhood memories come from. Early-morning starts and quite a bit of time on my own with everyone working long hours.'

Maddie has shared a quiet love-affair with East Grinstead that seemed to become stronger as she ventured along her life's journey, and the town represents an abundance of memories for her. Recollections of some of the happy but disfigured and bandaged faces of ex-Royal Air Force crews, who had been treated at the local hospital by Archibald McIndoe, the pioneering plastic surgeon, stand out in her early memories.

Long hours of childhood play were quite a feature of Maddie's early life as her father purchased a thriving newspaper shop in nearby Forest Row when she was of pre-school age. Maddie feels joy in this period of her very early life, despite her father's very early-morning runs to collect newspapers from the train station, carrying bundles through the kitchen and out into the yard to be prepared for sale. Worthy of note is that one of Maddie's first toys was a dressing-up box full of clothes and ribbons, which presaged her love of drama and pretending to be another person. She remembers that a tube of Smarties was needed to help her start walking! Anyone meeting Maddie today would never guess that she felt she was an overweight child and a slow starter, but the mixture of encouragement from her father and a sweet chocolate treat clearly did the trick as she took her first steps on the thick grass of her home in Forest Row.[1]

Maddie's relationship with her father was and still is a little complex; they were and remain very alike. They share not only an Irish temperament and temper, but an impulsive nature, creativity on a level that would burst the average imagination and a great love of questioning everything. Maddie proudly admits her mind never stops whirring as she thinks about everything and nothing, with an imagination that burns up calories like a stream train.

> 'I'm definitely my father's child. Dad and I were over-thinkers, living far too much in the solitary world of our imaginations. I did not want to be like him but I have to admit being the very spitting image.'

To get to know the real Maddie, hiding under the mirage of the natural talent of an actress, is like following a trail of breadcrumbs. One of her endearing characteristics is a desire to be discovered, but Maddie does not give away too many pieces of bread. Within those deep but wide-eyed looks that her fans are so aware of, we have a small clue as to why she seems so beguiling: it's not that nobody is home, it's that the occupant is endlessly busy thinking and working behind the windows. To the innocent observer, it resembles a naïve wonderment at the world, an innocence that drags you into her look in the early years of her career. But really, she is naturally overwhelmed by so many emotions that it becomes a sort of trance that we witness in that moment. It is this that creates the wide-eyed and overwhelmed look that entranced so many millions in her career as a model and became one of the defining images of the 1960s.

In 1952, the family moved north-west from the rural, quiet and quirky Forest Row to the bustle of the emerging middle-class suburb of Kew and a rather nice house near Kew Gardens in Taylor Avenue. It would be here that Maddie would spend the formative and most difficult years of her young life. Looking back now, Maddie will tell you quite bluntly that growing up in Kew was a mixture of innumerable memories but also missed opportunity, hope and trauma. All of these play into what even today makes Maddie Smith so endearing to so many.

As one matures one becomes more aware that life can be tough for most and impossible for some. In her career that lay ahead, Maddie introduced us to large quantities of both, where emerging talent was destroyed by either fate or suicide, where happy days were followed by disaster. Her life reminds us that the 1960s, and to a lesser extent the 1970s, were a potent and visible mixture of the masks of comedy and tragedy.

From the age of 4 in 1953, Mrs Silverman's Nursery School was a daily walk with Mum. Then from 1954 onwards, Maddie attended Broomfield School, where she loved reading, tumbled happily in gym classes and felt a love of drama, with any chance of putting on an act at home or at school seized upon by a happy little girl.

> 'I had a dressing up box and created my own little theatre in the bottom of my wardrobe, and here I could put on my own imaginary plays. Sometimes pals would join me and we played with the dolls house that every little girl wanted. I could spend hours in my room on my own, locked away in my imagination.'

Up to the age of 8, education at private preparatory school was supplemented by weekly Sunday School classes, then Maddie was sent to Queen's Primary School on Kew Green to prepare her for senior school. It was Sunday School that really began to cement Maddie Smith's commitment to a Christian life, her spirituality developing from a very early age. Sunday School was quite something in the 1950s. Very often taken seriously and well supported, it was a place where the values of the Church were reinforced and where families could feel its love and support in their daily lives. This was especially so in the Catholic church at Our Lady of Loreto and St Winefride in Kew Gardens.[2] Often at odds with the pace of the emerging world outside, the teachings of the church gave a solid foundation for Maddie to rely upon in the life that lay ahead.

Situated just a few minutes' walk south-east of the National Archives and on the eastern edge of the Royal Botanic Gardens in Kew, an area riddled with Polish Catholic émigré families who had remained in Britain after the war, the 8-year-old Madeline Smith looked forward with elation every Sunday to seeing what she still refers to as the first love of her life in the person of Father John Maceneny. The impact that Father John had on Maddie is hard to underestimate.

> 'When he came to visit my family, I would run down the path and wrap myself around his legs and cling on – and I was only as high as his knee! He was such an influential figure in my life and I hung onto his every word. I mourn his passing to this very day.'

What good fortune it is when someone is lucky to have such positive formative influences on them when they are very young. It is sadly rare for most, but for Maddie, the messages that she took in at that tender age would last a lifetime. Father John Maceneny had started at St Winifride's Church as a curate in 1950 and became the parish priest from 1953 until his untimely and tragic death when Maddie was aged only 10 in November 1959. Like a talisman around her neck, some of Father John's teachings would aid Maddie on her journey through stardom and all its excesses in the decades that lay ahead. They would also answer an often-heard question as to why she did not fall prey to the proliferation of sex and drugs that afflicted so many of her contemporaries.

Perhaps more traumatic for the very young Maddie, and quite possibly why Father John was such an influence on her life, was witnessing her father check himself into Bedlam Hospital for depression when she was only eight years old. Maddie remains certain it was over-thinking that created real problems for her father, alongside a possibly untreated depression borne out of hidden ghosts and dilemmas. Post-war Britain frowned upon mental illness; even today, it can sit uncomfortably in a society that prefers not to admit weakness of any kind, which is counter-productive in magnifying the solitude of the troubled mind. In 1957 and 1958, Maddie's father sought refuge from the world with others feeling as overwhelmed as himself by their lack of control over their thoughts. But it was in this institution that Bob found an inner peace. The many letters the family received from fellow patients, who wrote of how much solace Bob brought to them, reassured Maddie then and still gives her great comfort now. Bob benefited from the help he received in hospital, and was able to offer support to others in their own versions of hell. But the loss the young Maddie felt at his absence would take on a life-long presence in her psychology, with a longing to be looked after and protected against the tragedies that the world can create becoming a central need in her life. Indeed, Bob has always remained an important influence on her life.

> 'I have always been enormously influenced by the relationship I had with my father – that's not unusual for daughters and their dads, is it? What was perhaps different was that we could also fight like cats and dogs, with terrible arguments that could fester for days.'

It may have been this trauma, and watching her mother trying to cope, that helped to create a challenging only child. The ages of 4 to 11 were very trying school days for Maddie, representing a period of active engagement with the world around her and a yearning for something more. This started to gain some clarity with the music of the 1960s, when sharing a love for The Beatles and their music brought Maddie and her father closer together. 'Yeah, yeah, yeah! We both loved them and went crazy for them,' says Maddie, with a carefree abandon that suddenly lights up the cosy room where we have our chats about her life and career. Maddie and her father were undoubtedly kindred spirits. Under the slumbering issues they both felt, they enjoyed smiling and laughing together as only dads and daughters can do.

The Beatles first burst onto the music scene across Britain in the early 1960s. From their home town of Liverpool, their mix of folk and rock was a leading part of the counter-cultural music movement as they became one of the most prominent leaders in youth culture and fashion in the 1960s.

'Beetlemania' hit the country in 1962, when Maddie was an impressionable and happy 13-year-old discovering her own identity, looking at fashion and enjoying growing up. The music of The Beatles rang out across Kew Gardens as it did from the bedroom windows of tens of thousands of other young girls and boys, along with the jukeboxes of pubs and coffee bars. The youth-driven, groovy 'Swinging Sixties' had begun with perfect timing, just as the teenage Maddie Smith of Kew Gardens was emerging like a butterfly from its chrysalis phase, wanting to make her own mark in the changing, technicolor and liberated world. Before that, though, Maddie had to finish school.

## Chapter 2

# The Number 27 Bus to Freedom and the Road to Biba

'It was my father that noticed I had something from the age of 13, and he asked Fred [real name Lewis Morley – known by his friends as "Fred"] the photographer to take some shots of me. It was 1964, and that's where my interest in the magic of film began. I had no idea that was me. Only minutes before, Fred had just photographed Christine Keeler on the same Bentwood chair with her arms draped over the front.'

Madeline Smith

When Lesley Hornby began modelling with her androgynous appearance, coloured super-short skirts, big eyes and long eyelashes, she announced that a new age in fashion and culture had begun and that London was now going to be the new focal point of world style. The year was 1963; Lesley was only 14 and her professional name was 'Twiggy'.

In 1963, tens of thousands of 14-year-old girls also imagined themselves on a catwalk with Jean Shrimpton, maybe acting as an extra in the new film release *Summer Holiday* with Cliff Richard, while others persuaded pestered parents to allow them to wear one of Mary Quant's new dress designs or joined a march against nuclear weapons, such as that at Aldermaston in April that year.[1] On the roads, a new small car to rival BMC's Mini was released – the Hillman Imp. Dennis Law scored twice against Leicester City to win the FA Cup for Manchester United, Annabel's Nightclub opened at 44 Berkeley Square in London's Mayfair in June and the Secretary of State for War, John Profumo, resigned over his affair with showgirl Christine Keeler (presumably just after she had been photographed by 'Fred'). Signalling the end of an era in the face of so much change, Prime Minister Harold MacMillan resigned in October 1963, aged 69, but the major political event of that year was the assassination of American President John F. Kennedy on 22 November.

In the charts, The Beatles reached number 1 for the third time in 1963 with *I Want to Hold your Hand.* Thousands of girls wanted to hold anything they could get their hands on to do with The Beatles, hanging photographs and posters in their rooms of John, Paul, George and Ringo. In the new and expanding television schedules, the first ever episode of *Dr Who* was broadcast on 21 December. What a year 1963 was. The young, impressionable, ambitious, driven and bubbling Maddie Smith may have even noticed that the latest film in the James Bond series had just hit the screens. The suave and rugged Sean Connery played 007 in *From Russia with Love* – who could have thought that only ten years later, in 1973, Maddie Smith from Kew was going to be Roger Moore's first 'Bond girl' in *Live and Let Die*?

Maddie's father, Bob, had an eye for beauty and art. In the not-too-distant future, he would run his own art shop in Richmond, where he restored and bought and sold paintings. With the eye of someone who could appreciate true beauty, Bob had noticed something special about his emerging daughter's looks. He asked a friend named Lewis Morley, or 'Fred' – a well-known professional photographer – to take some trial photographs of Maddie just to see how her features translated onto film. His remarkable insight proved correct, the first professional images of Maddie showinng what the French refer to as '*gamine*' – beautiful boyish looks, similar to what we might call 'elvish'. Maddie had a thick fringe, with her hair swept back behind her ears, and her features were all in perfect proportion. Those very first images, which are still in Maddie's possession, are striking indeed, Lewis Morley having captured a rare moment in Maddie's youthful life. It would be Morley who would famously create images of not only Christine Keeler (before the Profumo scandal hit the headlines) but also Dudley Moore and Alan Bennett, who had been starring in *Beyond the Fringe* in 1961, both of whom Maddie would later meet and work with on new productions when her own career took off.[2]

Impatient for something, but not quite knowing what it was, the time was not yet right for Maddie Smith to emerge onto the scene. She was still at school, and things were not going well. When asked about her time at secondary school, Maddie reveals she had to face what we hope our children or grandchildren never will – what she refers to as a combination of depression, bullying, loneliness and illness.

The number 65 bus remains etched in Maddie's mind, and it was on the seats of this bright red double-decker that Maddie travelled to school for nearly seven years. There was nothing wrong with the now closed-down St Anne's Convent School in Ealing. A standard convent school of the time, with nuns for teachers, it provided a very good academic education for hundreds of girls. But even today it represents mostly very unhappy times for Maddie. Passing the Brentford FC football ground along what she recalls as the 'very ugly' Great West Road to get to the school, Maddie struggled through each year of her time there. It was not where she wanted to be any more, but she had earned a scholarship to a private school and this placed considerable pressure on a young person with a sense of responsibility to remain and see things through – especially so given that it been Father John who had suggested she take the entrance scholarship in the first place. It was not that Maddie did not have friends around her, but she was not aligned with the school ethos and found it hard to express any individuality.

### *Not Only Peter Cook*, 1965

Although Maddie could not have known it at the time, her first meeting with actor, comedian, writer and performer Peter Cook would not be the last. She was just 15 when she and a friend were given two tickets to attend a BBC recording studio to watch Cook and Dudley Moore rehearse and then perform an episode of their iconic series *Not Only… But Also*. This was fate at work, as the father of Maddie's pal just happened to work in PR at the BBC studios in White City.

> 'My friend and I sat entranced as privileged members of the audience in a drafty BBC studio. This was the first time that I had seen a star, or stars in this case, in action. The whole atmosphere filled me with excitement and I just wanted to experience live performance again. It was perhaps Peter Cook more than Dudley Moore that made me laugh out loud. I noticed for the first time just how important the pause was in comedy, and there were masses of those because Peter was just so funny.'

Inspired by what she had seen, possible salvation hove into view when Maddie experienced the thrill – a rare emotion for her in those days – of joining a local theatre group called The Questors. This small youth group gave Maddie an outlet of expression, a place to spill out emotion, pretend to be someone else and inhabit a space in which she felt safe and happy. She could have pursued her chosen path of acting with this group. She quickly learnt two speeches, which she can still recall to this day, and felt she truly belonged in this happy environment. 'I should have been Ophelia,' she says, with a tone of sadness and regret.

Ophelia is a model of obedience to her father, which Maddie certainly was too, and the character is also well loved, as is Maddie by fans around the world. Many similarities can be seen between Shakespeare's character and Maddie, but we would hope she would not suffer the same tragic end – although she did come close to Ophelia's madness.

The opportunities to act in small dramas was a lifeline for Maddie that, had it been encouraged and allowed to flourish, would almost certainly have avoided the catastrophe that was to follow. Peter Cook and the BBC studios had opened her imagination and the desire to perform, but disaster then struck a young emerging soul like a sword. It was Sister Philomena, one of the tutors at the convent school, who told a 15-year-old Maddie that she was not to continue with her involvement in The Questors – she was to focus solely on her O-Levels, which were due to be sat in1965. This rigid approach probably came with the best of intentions, but the result was to deny Maddie the outlet that she needed at school, a place to perform, to feel valued and to let her overactive imagination run riot. Perhaps of all the sadnesses that Maddie feels about her childhood, it was this refusal that seems to have hurt the most; it certainly caused the most damage, an almost terminal physical and emotional decline setting in – perhaps prophetically akin to Ophelia's madness.

> 'I have wondered about that moment all my life. Have you ever had something happen in your childhood that was so traumatic it has stayed with you all your life? Those of us who have will know that it never leaves you; it has a very strong power over your emotions for the rest of one's life. I had found what I wanted to do and what would make me happy, but I was now not allowed to do it. I have often thought that I should have just said "no, I am going to do it", but a Catholic convent school was based on rigid obedience and I was concerned how my parents would react. I just did not know how they would see this – was it admirable determination or abominable rebellion?'

Many of Maddie's friends had left her school at the age of 16, but, with a sense of responsibility still hanging over her and despite her feelings against Sister Philomena, Maddie stayed on. Months of sadness followed as she embarked on her A-Levels. Gradually overwhelmed by despair, having been robbed of the one thing she wanted to do, Maddie began to stop eating, suffering from anorexia. Medical science was increasingly using drugs for psychological distress, and a series of ghastly and powerful medications were duly prescribed, leaving Maddie's frail body and mind reeling. Severe weight loss left her in a skeletal state, impacting on her A-Level studies, and Maddie was removed from school and placed in a cottage hospital in Acton. It was a dreadful and serious experience.

> 'It was just awful. My studies were wrecked while my 16-year-old self recovered from weeks of triple doses of a lethal mood stabiliser called Largactil. I even grabbed my teddy and ran away from hospital to try to save my sanity. I was so confused and I made up my mind that this was not going to define who I was.'

Parallels with her loving father's own psychological distress are inevitable, but out of terror and despair grew some seeds of hope. Bob Smith's earlier efforts to capture that magical something that he saw in his daughter inspired Maddie to break away from the anchors of home and she did the best thing that she could. She looked for a job.

This was the age of the Saturday job as a step on the road to financial independence. New people, new faces and new horizons followed. Maddie made a whole new set of friends, now seeing herself in a positive way as she took on a series of different part-time weekend jobs. Gradually, as Maddie studied for her A-Levels, she also matured as a very striking 16-year-old. That doleful 'Maddie Smith look' began to take on a physical form in her face. Yet it was quite by chance – one of the many quirks of fate that Maddie was to experience – that one day on a trip into central London she visited a brand-new store in Kensington. Her life was about to change.

> 'I had had numerous Saturday jobs and one was working in Kempthorne's in Richmond, Surrey. It was a rejigged clothing store with a coffee bar and boutique, and my job was to work on woollies and jewellery. It was full of fun and I loved it – apart from anything else it gave me the confidence that I so badly needed. It was while I was there that a girl

> came in with huge black eyelashes and short black frock. I stared at her – "where did you get that dress" I asked. That's when I first heard of Biba, a new clothes store that had only just opened in what had been an old chemists on the Abingdon Road in Kensington. I made a mental note to take the bus and visit as soon as I could to spend my £1 per week wages – and I did exactly that a week later … I bought a very small dress, I was already very thin … it had lovely gentle pink and white stripes, [was] made of cotton and very, very short … Mini-skirts were already in by the time I was 15 and girls were, on the whole, very skinny – that was already the look, and Barbara Hulanicki designed clothes for thin people.'

In 1966, Maddie's dreams of freedom, fashion and expression had aligned exactly with someone else's dream: Polish-born fashion designer Barbara Hulanicki, who, after selling dresses by post, had seen her first Biba shop open at 87 Abingdon Road in Kensington in September 1964.[3] Hidden and working away in the shop was Anna Wintour, the future editor-in-chief of *Vogue* magazine, and the future actress Molly Parkin, who made hats for the store. Both were able to revel in and wear the brand-new designs from the Biba outlet. Maddi visited often and eventually asked if she could have a job at Biba as soon as she left school. On every future visit to this wonderful store, full of vibrancy and freedom, Maddie reminded the staff that she was coming. By the time Maddie left school, Biba had moved to a much larger and higher-profile store at 19–21 Kensington Church Street in 1966, and had begun to revolutionize the way people shopped.[4]

> 'I always took things literally and "As soon as I left school" to me meant the very next day, and the day after I left school in 1967 I could hardly wait and rushed to get on the number 27 bus and arrived at Biba and said, "Here I am – you offered me a job and I'm ready."'

Maddie was not the only person who saw the number 27 bus as a route to freedom in the 1960s. Actor Peter Cushing often used to take this route from Kew to work in Kensington, and Matt Munro was actually a bus driver on this very same route before he found fame as a singer.

For Maddie, working at Biba was a breath of fresh air and salvation rolled into one. As the shop's founder, Barbara Hulanicki, would say in 1970, 'It isn't just selling dresses, it's a whole way of life.' The vibrancy of the shop and the fashion styles allowed Maddie, at last, to express herself. Meeting people of a similar age to her finally began to liberate her own natural, very friendly nature, and this in turn lit up her eyes and drew people in to her natural beauty. Most of the customers were the same age as the staff – a deliberate store policy – and Barbara Hulanicki also wanted staff who could wear her clothes like models. A strange twist of fate was that the company that manufactured the Biba cosmetic range was based in Maddie's beloved East Grinstead.[5] Although Barbara had of course met Maddie in her store – and it was noticeable that there really was something special about the teenager's look that was exactly in keeping with the times – it would take a break in the relationship to enable Maddie to make a dramatic leap forward.

Bearing in mind that Maddie was only just 18, she had already begun to display what would become a singular feature of her future life – a fiercely independent spirit. She was not a groupie in any sense of the word, and remains to this day a lady of clear opinions and a strong set of core values which would help guard her in the loosening morals of the 1960s.

> 'Many of my friends were already going to pop concerts in and around London. Some were coming back into school telling stories and many were smoking and taking drugs – far worse and unrestrained than even today. They came back with some incredible stories of what they had seen and where they had been – it was all so new and unregulated in the 1960s. But this wasn't for me, and I kept myself apart from trouble. I don't know why, maybe it was my Christian upbringing. I am far from being a "goody goody" but this just didn't do it for me.'

Maddie agreed to have some publicity shots taken for a BBC documentary on fashion. Biba then selected her to meet John Cowan, an emerging and already well-known photographer, who was being filmed in his studio by a BBC film crew. Maddie was to be his model. It was at the time – and still is today – said of John Cowan that he

> 'epitomized the playful, graphically dynamic style of commercial photography practised in London during the period … he sparked an exciting period of high-octane image making for numerous magazines.'[6]

At the end of the filming, John spoke to Maddie and said, 'You have a great face – can my assistant take some shots of you?'

'So, on a sunny day that summer, I went back up to London and on my own (taking lots of risks which I was always prepared to do) to the studio where his assistant, Richard Dawkins, took these fantastic photographs - I think they were the best that were ever taken of me.'

## My First Films – *Escalation* and *The Mini Affair*, 1968

While those photographs were being developed, and typical of the exciting times when it seemed like opportunity could be around every corner, Maddie was walking to Biba for work one day when, quite out of the blue, she was gently tapped on the left arm. A young English guy who was walking the streets scouting for talent had spotted the gorgeous and trendily dressed Maddie Smith.

'He just asked if I wanted to be in a film and I said yes ... it was as simple as that ... and off I went to meet these rather fat Italian guys in a hotel in Sloane Square - anything could have happened really, but they were all absolutely fine. Lino Cappoliccio, a young Italian actor, who was already well known in Italy, was starring with Claudine Auger and looking to make a pseudo film, which was called *Escalation*, for an Italian audience.'

If you are ever lucky enough to sit and listen to Maddie Smith, and perhaps you will one day if she ever takes her book on the road, it can be incredible to hear the level of innocence with which she began her film career. Today, people can sense potential evil around every corner, that everyone is out to cheat theem – or worse. And yet here, in the mid-1960s and surrounded by one of the largest explosions in drug and pop culture ever witnessed in London, 18-year-old Maddie Smith just kept saying 'yes' to opportunity.

The film was well funded and supported by a strong cast, with the starring role taken by Lino Capolicchio opposite the already well-known Claudine Auger. Directed by Roberto Faenza, the plot of *Escalation* was a sharp-edged satire on the clash between free-spirited youth culture in London and the expectations of a merchant family within the capitalist establishment. Lino's character wants to party, enjoy life and live a hedonistic lifestyle, while his family want him back at any cost and eventually turn him into a ruthless businessman. Maddie recalls being part of the London scenes in the film.

> 'Lino was so nice – and preferred to stay with my grandmother in Kew rather than in a hotel. She loved him and fed him spaghetti for breakfast – well not everyone has the chance to have a handsome young Italian actor staying with them in Kew, do they? After the audition, they offered me £30 per day! The film was called *Escalation* – all I had to do was smile and sit on the back of Lino's bicycle with a sitar strapped to my back and my face painted white as they mimed the action in '60s London scenes. We zoomed around in little inserts in the film and had fun in nightclubs. I actually loved it, particularly when I had to dance in some type of weird psychedelic trance to 'This Wheel's on Fire' by The Byrds.'

A young and relatively unknown composer named Enrico Morricone wrote the soundtrack for the film, something which Maddie admits she has never seen.

The frightening speed with which Britain was changing was as much of a shock to the authorities and to parents as it was to the young people who were pushing the boundaries to find out exactly what the new rules were. Having started work at Biba in July 1967, Maddie was quickly 'encouraged' to leave.

> 'I had worked on the shop floor very happily for six weeks I think but I was not very good at looking for shoplifters, and one day I was found reading *The Brothers Karamazov* hidden away in the basement by the manager … oops!'[7]

For some, a six-week tenure as a shop assistant would have been the end of a very short career in the fashion world, but not for Maddie. Excitedly, she collected her photographs from John Cowan's studio in Holland Park and returned to see her friends in Biba, proudly showing off the oversized images. It was these that first fully captured what was going to become 'that Maddie Smith look' and it was plain for all to see that Maddie had a natural beauty on film.

Biba was a very lively place to shop, with music always booming across the shop floor – The Beach Boys and Simon and Garfunkel are just some that Maddie recalls – amazing smells of perfumes and cosmetics, gorgeously dressed shoppers and stunning girls, including a then-girlfriend of future Queen frontman Freddie Mercury, who became friends with Maddie.

> 'We were sort of gathered around at a counter with my friends and I was really quite thrilled with them, and it was the first time in my life that I saw my self-image really positively. Just at that moment, another one of those twists of fate occurred when one of the girls walked off to show Barbara an image - she happened to be in her office at that very moment. A minutes later, Barbara herself came out to say "hi" and, with one of my proofs in her hand, asked me in to come into the back office and cuttings room, and it was there that she immediately asked me if I would like to model for her first-ever properly photographed catalogue. She liked what she saw, and I was dead right for her designs and had the right body shape for her clothes, which is vital for a fashion or fitting model, and that was the start of my modelling career.'

Within a few days, a wide-eyed and beautiful Maddie Smith from Kew was again jumping on board the number 27 bus to freedom – but this time with a new level of excitement. With no previous training, she took to the role like a natural. Maddie was a 'fit-girl', which in the fashion and modelling business was the perfect body for the type of clothes that the designer wanted to make.

> 'Every Sunday I went to be fitted - Barbara made the clothes on me - and then a few weeks later when the collection was ready I went to the studio of Donald Silverstein and to his basement in Riding House Street, just off Portland Place near the BBC, and he would turn on thumping jazz music, in his black leather outfit, and start taking hundreds of black and white shots as I changed in and out of all these wonderful new designs which no one but Barbara and I had even seen. The photography was all done from the floor level looking up through my body and face, to grab the shadows of my face and eyes. Two full days of photography and I was paid £30 for each day - I couldn't believe it. It was simply a wonderfully exciting feeling.'[8]

Loving the atmosphere made the shots appear so natural, and the look and feel of the catalogue took shape around the petite size 6 model and the unique, innocent 'Maddie Smith look'.

The new Biba catalogue was quite revolutionary – clothing with a modern shape and innovative design – and both Donald Silverstein and Barbara Hulanicki were thrilled with the result. So was Maddie, who still treasures two surviving copies she has. The year was 1968 and the 18-year-old Maddie Smith was blossoming, with feelings of independence in that new world of the Swinging Sixties, some of the most popular emerging music being the pop and psychedelic rock of The Small Faces, Eric Burdon and The Animals, The Beach Boys, Cream and of course Pink Floyd. Waistcoats and the first flared trousers were beginning to appear on both men and women, and while the mini-skirt was still dominant, maxi-skirts were part of another new trend. The UK's high streets were full of young people and a mass of colour. Being seen out wearing your latest purchases while buying newspapers with headlines that the Rolling Stones had all been arrested in possession of drugs – now who would have guessed that? – was all part of the cascade of new social norms.

Maddie having left Biba in August 1967, her father decided that he should again step in and help his beautiful daughter further along the road to success. Bob managed to find Maddie a job in a nice little antique shop in Richmond upon Thames called Loco. After the fascinating and fantastic extremes of working in fashion and film in London, this short period gave Maddie time to settle and reflect – but not for long. Having recognized the up-and-coming actress Felicity Kendal ogling the beautiful objects in the shop window, Bob surprised Maddie by handing her a copy of *The Stage*, the premier magazine supporting the UK theatre industry.

> 'I scanned through pages and found a little advert that was looking for one more girl to join three others to make up a quartet of girls in a film that was going to be called *The Mini Mob* and was going to star Georgie Fame. I applied and got an audition – which was basically me being filmed just walking down a road and that was that … it wasn't until a few days later when my Mum and I were at home getting ready to leave to visit friends in Hindhead that the telephone rang and I was told that I had got the job! I was totally thrilled. It was going to be SO exciting!'

Maddie Smith can be very disarming – as well as charming. This comes from a lifetime of being a good person. The old saying goes that good things come to those who wait; well, Maddie had waited and now her time had come.

*The Mini-Mob* was a film well-funded by, amongst others, Douglas Vickers – chairman of Vickers Engineering – and had attracted a good cast of experienced and new performers who came together to make a romantic comedy about a pop star, an MP and a DJ kidnapped by four girls (cue Maddie as the tall Samantha) who wanted to marry them.

'I had the right look for the time … long straight hair, long false eyelashes, big lips and smouldering looks, and of course skinny – I had no breasts at that time and was the perfect '60s girl.'

Typically silly and fun, this 1968 film was directed by Robert Amram and starred Georgie Fame, Clive Dunn, Roy Kinnear, Clement Freud (the later TV chef) and the hugely experienced Irene Handl.[9] Georgie Fame was already an established pop star. This was an early venture into film for a 25-year-old who had already had three British number one hits in the singles charts. It was also the first film score written by the Bee Gees. If you can find a rare copy of the main poster for the film, it pictures Georgie Fame in bed with a dishevelled Maddie on the floor, having just been kicked out of bed in typical Sixties misogynistic style.

'I learnt a lot from that film, especially from Clive Dunn, who was very kind and a real professional, and from an actress called Tottie Truman-Taylor. I started to learn about comic timing watching Clive and Tottie as [the] Butler and Maid in the film. I laughed my head off in rehearsals, they were so good and quick-witted.'

Fun though the film was to make, Maddie was almost forced off the shoot before filming began in September 1967.

Seemingly one of life's good guys, Rick Dane, whose real name was Eric Haydock, played the part of DJ Mike Maroon in the film. Rick had come to the UK from South Africa and had ambitions for a career on the stage or in film. By the time Rick arrived to make what was now retitled *The Mini-Affair*, he had already studied acting at the Webber Douglas Academy and performed with Vanessa Redgrave in *The World's Baby* at London's Royal Court Theatre. Rick had moved on to become a disc jockey with the famous Radio Caroline in 1966. He met Maddie before filming was due to start and discovered that she had neither an agent nor an Equity card – both of which were essential for any acting job. She would not be able to act without them. Rick contacted Maddie's father and told him that she needed to get this sorted.[10]

'My life changed gear. Rick grabbed me and ran me over to the office of Joan Gray in Mortimer Street. I can still remember the scene now as she sat in a pool of light in a

> dark basement. I quickly signed a contract without reading it and left with an Equity card, and that was it – I later discovered that the contract was for hand modelling only, but it's all a bit late now!'

Without the help of Eric, or Rick, Maddie would never have starred in this film and may never have gone on to enjoy the fame that she did. Sadly, Eric, one of life's good guys, passed away on 16 November 2002, having built up a loyal fanbase as a DJ on Radio Jackie North in the 1980s.

## Modelling with the Lucy Clayton Agency

There was no longer any Lucy Clayton when Maddie became associated with the business of that name. Founded in 1928 as a finishing school, the failing company was purchased for £2,000 in 1956 by Lesley Kark, who saw the post-war potential of a combined modelling agency and school. It would be Kark's wife, Evelyn Gordine, who would use the name 'Lucy Clayton' for the business.[11] During the 1960s, modelling had become a premium profession, and the Lucy Clayton agency was highly regarded as one of the, if not *the*, best modelling agency and finishing school in London. So naturally, that is where the 18-year-old ambitious size 6 Maddie Smith headed in September 1967 as soon as filming on *The Mini-Affair* had ended.

> 'I just took a chance and turned up on the first day and was told that I was too thin and to come back in a few months' time … I was very disappointed naturally but I was not going to give up, so the next day I took the bus back to New Bond Street, where their offices were, and tried again. This time I met someone else, who said I looked amazing and they signed me on as a model there and then!'[12]

Thus began an eighteen-month period of serious modelling work which would lead to a series of adventures and the further development of Maddie's career. Working at the Lucy Clayton agency in the 1960s was exciting, fresh and new. New Bond Steet was at the centre of the latest music, clubs, nightlife and coolness in 1960s London, in contrast to the 'downtown Dubai' that it has become today, with sanitized, hidden-from-view apartments and high-end retailers, and black-windowed Rolls Royces parked outside unnamed shops. The Clayton agency introduced Maddie to the fast-paced world of photo-shoots and fashion, which proved such a counterpoint to the quiet, suburban world of Kew Gardens.

While Maddie was now working as a full-time model, she was walking down the vibrant King's Road one sunny morning in 1968 when her life was drawn in a dramatically new direction.

## Chapter 3

# I was Just Walking Down the King's Road When it Happened Again…

'If you remember the '60s, you really weren't there'
Charlie Fleischer, actor and comedian

It was in the late 1970s that a little-known but very talented Mod revival band called Squire, who strangely enough went to the same school as the iconic Mod musician Paul Weller, came up with a high-quality little song called *Walking Down the King's Road*. Listen to it on YouTube and its lyrics might take your imagination to where this next chapter in the life of Maddie Smith is going.

'Walking down the King's Road with some friends of mine
The streets are crowded, it's a sign of the times
Walking down the Kings Road with some friends of mine
The shops are busy, they've got Saturday on their mind'

A mixture of early '70s punk balanced with a 1960s melody, the lyrics of *Walking Down the King's Road* are a perfect metaphor for a fine, hot sunny morning in Chelsea in 1968. In our mind's eye, what can we see? Bustling streets, young people everywhere in amazing outfits, full of fun and just hanging around together; cars and buses throng the street, which is dotted with thriving shops. Predictable 1950s drab overcoat fashions worn by the older pedestrians contrast with a vibrant mix of knee-high suede and leather boots, stylish purple, red or brown hunter hats, long hair, short choirboy haircuts and beehive hairstyles all mixed together with mini-skirts – lots of mini-skirts – mini-jackets and mini-coats. It is a vision of the old world evolving like a chrysalis into the new.

> 'In The Chelsea Drugstore with some friends of mine
> Saw Mr Jimmy still standing in line
> In the Chelsea Drugstore with some friends of mine
> Mini skirts, dolly birds and Radio Caroline'

A few years earlier, in 1968, the King's Road in London SW3 was seen as the hippest street in the world. This area of south-west London has always attracted individuals with creative and adventurous spirits, but in the 1960s it achieved a whole new status as *the* road to be seen on. Spookily enough for Maddie's story, the creator of 007, Ian Fleming, lived on Cheyne Walk in Chelsea, and, in his book and the film *Moonraker*, Commander James Bond lives in a comfortable flat in a square off the King's Road.[1]

Mary Quant had opened her Bazaar boutique in Kensington, while on the King's Road, Hollywood-style ice-cream bars attracted clusters of young, happy people. Motorbikes and scooters of all colours were parked on every corner for zooming around town (with no helmet of course). There were happy faces in blue velvet jackets and tight velvet trousers, and very thin guys and very thin girls in crazy-coloured jumpers with large red buttons listened to the very cool John Peel radio show – or even considered buying their own shop on the King's Road for a whopping £30,000. Frankie's Nightclub and Club Del Arethusa were just two of the many places to be seen at (if you could get in).[2] All around the side streets, coffee bars and discos, hairdressers and art studios sprang up, while the Chelsea Drugstore opened in 1968, replacing the old White Hart public house with amazing decor across its three floors where people could eat, drink, dance and shop – it was quite a place, open sixteen hours a day, as were a whole host of other groovy places now long closed down and forgotten. You could be walking past the Cosy Dining Room, the Francis Marsden Bookshop, Topper Shoes, Kardomah Coffee House and Dandie Fashions at number 161 King's Road, where you could browse alongside Jimi Hendrix and a young David Bowie looking for inspiring clothes.[3] One of the backers of Dandie Fashions had been a very young Tara Browne, heir to part of the Guinness fortune and already married with two children. Tara's death in a car crash while driving a Lotus Elan at the age of only 21 in December 1966 shocked both London and his native Ireland. Driving too fast near South Kensington, the tragedy proved it was not just drugs that could claim the lives of the young, spirited and carefree in the Swinging Sixties. Tara's death inspired the lyrics of the 1967 Beatles song *A Day in the Life* – members of the band had shopped for their clothes in Dandie Fashions too.

> 'You had to walk down the whole length of the King's Road to get the full experience, and this meant going right down to The World's End, where there were loads of small galleries and artists selling their stuff – it was brimming with places like The Chelsea Arts Club and a super clothes shop called Granny Takes A Trip which had a car poking through the front window … it was wild, great fun and everyone was smiling; just a great time to be young and alive.'

This, then, was the 'King of Roads' in the Swinging Sixties. And just as the number 27 bus had done its job for Maddie Smith in 1966, then it would be the King's Road that would take her on the next phase of her journey in 1968 and 1969.

Imagine the scene: only just 18, with long, mousy-coloured hair, big goggle eyes and black eyelashes, knee-high white boots and a short skirt, Maddie Smith was walking down the King's Road one Friday afternoon in January 1968. Under one arm was a large folder – her portfolio of test photographs to date – and in her hand she held a list of photographers to try to find and visit that day.

> 'I was with one of the largest modelling agencies in the country but even they expected you to go out and find your own work. The idea was you popped your head into the photography studio, smiled and hoped that they would agree to take some free test shots and, even better, offer you some modelling work.'

In 1963, Burt Bacharach and Hal David wrote a lovely melodic song for Dionne Warwick called *Walk On By* and it became a worldwide hit, not least because it resonated with the new-age social pastime of walking along the high street of your local town or city.[4] With her mind seemingly in the clouds – which was part of the Maddie Smith look – Maddie failed to notice a tall, unshaven man with shoulder-length tousled hair whose head turned towards her as she passed by. This was Donald Cammell, and out of nowhere came another one of those sudden taps on the shoulder that were to be a feature of her life. It was as if men thought she was just too beautiful to allow her to 'walk on by' without taking a chance to say something.[5]

Spinning around, Maddie set eyes on this tall, elegant man. But this time it was not a young English lad scouting for talent; instead, this was Maddie's first meeting with someone who was already *en route* to becoming one of the absolute icons of '60s and '70s Chelsea style. Dressed in a scruffy, wide-lapelled beige jacket, with collar up, dishevelled hair, long coloured scarf and equally long, lugubrious and lined face, Donald had a captivatingly wide and welcoming smile.

> 'Donald was very good at picking up girls, and he had spotted that I had a portfolio of photos under my arm and asked if he could introduce me to Michael Cooper, who was a photographer he knew. I didn't know at that moment who I was speaking to or who the photographer was, but I soon found out.'

If you were writing a novel, it would be hard to persuade your readers that, out of the thousands of people on one street at one time, your heroine, looking for a sponsor in the fashion industry and a famous photographer, should, quite by chance in a million-to-one moment pass by both of them at the same time. It was even more incredible that she didn't even see them. But this was another example of the Maddie Smith look doing its thing. Even on a bustling London street full of beautiful men and women, all in amazing clothes and giving off vibes that they wanted to be seen, it was a young vacant-looking 18-year-old girl with her mind elsewhere – not really caring whether she was seen or not – that stood out. Maddie Smith caught the eye like a yellow English rose in a field of red poppies, impossible to miss; a once-in-a-lifetime opportunity to say 'hello' to a stunning young lady. Her look of naivety and innocence was all part of Maddie's chemistry, and, with his creative artist's eye, Donald Cammell had noticed it straight away, stopped dead in the street and just had to talk to her. But who was Donald Cammell?

Born on 17 January 1934, Donald Seton Cammell described his own upbringing as being one 'filled with magicians, metaphysicians, spiritualists and demons' – in other words, a quite extraordinary childhood. Instinctively, one senses that these 'demons' were always going to be a part of, and fuel, his very complicated and creative life. Donald was a precociously gifted artist. Gaining a scholarship to the Royal Academy at the age of 16, he tried to stick to painting but moved on to screenwriting and film directing. When Maddie met him by chance on the King's Road, he had just returned from a hedonistic period in Paris. Amongst his many Parisien acquaintances had been 1960s and 1970s 'It Girl' Anita Pallenberg, a stunning Italian/German film actress and model who was already known to be the 'muse of the Rolling Stones'.[6] It was through Anita that Donald had met the Rolling Stones and formed a good friendship, no doubt based heavily on their love of psychedelic drugs and a hedonistic lifestyle.

Pallenberg had recently been the partner of the founder of the Stones, Brian Jones.[7] Brian would become one of the '27' – a collection of stars such as Jimi Hendrix, Janis Joplin and Jim Morrison who would all die at the age of 27 – when he was found floating in his swimming pool in 1969 at Cotchford Farm in Hartfield, East Sussex – curiously, the same small village where Maddie had been born twenty years earlier. He was another casualty of the Sixties.

Now in London and in a new relationship with Keith Richards, with whom she would have three children, Pallenberg was a well-known celebrity within the King's Road and Chelsea set; by 1968, so too was Donald Cammell. Everyone knew Donald: he was at every party, living long days, long alcohol- and drug-filled nights, partaking in sexual experimentation, all of which became etched into his face. Donald was everything Maddie was not, but she was fascinated by him and the world in which he lived. At the time Maddie met Donald, he was deep into writing a screenplay for what would become his most famous film – *Performance*, starring Mick Jagger – which would ultimately be listed as the forty-eighth greatest British film of the twentieth century by the British Film Institute.

The relationship that now developed between Maddie and Donald was an interesting one, where the experienced and drug-fuelled Donald was fascinated by the naivety and innocence of Maddie. It was possibly his artistic appreciation of her beauty that prevented their friendship developing into anything more abusive. Donald and Maddie would eventually drift apart, long before the passionate voyeur Donald Cammell shot himself in the head and infamously asked for a mirror so that he could watch himself die – a dreadful process that would take forty-five minutes.[8]

Within a few days of their first chance meeting, Maddie would get together with Donald again, this time to meet with photographer Michael Cooper, lauded for his work with many of the top rock and pop acts of the era. With her huge, wide-open blue eyes of incredulity, Maddie could not believe her luck.[9]

> 'I had no idea at the time who he was but Michael Cooper was a close friend of the Rolling Stones – in fact he lived with Keith Richards in Chelsea. Michael had just completed his latest work taking the photographs for perhaps the most famous record album in history – *Sgt Pepper's Lonely Hearts Club Band* – and here was little me, I was still not quite eight stone, having my next set of test photographs taken by lovely Michael and all thanks to Donald, whose memory I treasure.'

Cooper was at the epicentre of the rock and roll culture of the 1960s, and for a decade or so was a companion to the Rolling Stones in a way that would never happen today. His pictures taken at airports, in the back of limousines and in recording studios – and outside courts – created an invaluable record of an era. It would be Michael who had privileged access not only to the lives of the Rolling Stones but also that of the Beatles, the corridors of *Vogue* and even the Guinness clan in Ireland. But he would also become another casualty of the '60s; a drug addict and suffering from depression, he would commit suicide aged 31 in 1973.

However, before that session took place – in fact the very next day after meeting Donald Cammell in the King's Road – Maddie was on her way to celebrated film director Roman Polanski's wedding. Not many 18-year-old girls from Kew could have said that.

> 'Donald had asked me if I would like to meet a photographer friend of his – and after I had immediately and excitedly said 'YES', he asked what I was doing the next day … I probably mumbled that not much was happening – although no doubt I would have been back on the King's Road as Saturday was absolutely the best day to be there. He asked if I would like to go with him to a wedding reception and just dropped in the names Roman Polanski and Sharon Tate. I maybe thought about it for less than a millisecond and said 'YES' – well who wouldn't!?'

Back in Kew, Maddie's mum, Ursula, was getting quite used to picking up the telephone for Maddie and taking down her messages, and having conversations with all sorts of agents, photographers and actors, and now it was Donald Cammell's turn.

> 'My Mum thought that he had the most beautiful, deep, booming voice and loved speaking to him when he called – usually just to make arrangements with me about where and when to meet. On the Saturday, I put on one of my favourite dresses ever. I can still remember it as it was below the knee in black crepe with a white lace collar and I wore a pink rose on the shoulder – very understated, not at all like a Biba dress and very lovely. We met near Sloane Square Station just after lunch and then went over to the Playboy Club by taxi, which is where the reception was being held from about 4pm onwards. I remember that sharing the cab with us was [actor] James Fox. He was so beautifully handsome but he looked so ill – mind you anyone close to Donald Cammell was flirting with danger. Donald was very dangerous in those days and they spent a lot of time together working on *Performance*.'

The suavely dressed Polanski was a handsome 35-year-old movie director whose breakthrough film, *Knife in The Water*, had been nominated for an Academy Award in 1963. Other films had quickly followed, such as *Repulsion* in 1965 and *Cul-de-sac* in 1966, both of which displayed his interest in psychological horror..It would be his 1967 film *The Fearless Vampire Killers/ Dance of the Vampires* that would see him work with Sharon Tate and, in a whirlwind romance, they were married on 20 January 1968.[10]

> 'The Playboy Club had only just opened in 1966 and was really a top venue – I was so thrilled to be invited. There were famous faces everywhere. I didn't get to talk to Roman or Sharon at all, she was just flitting around everywhere, but Michael Caine was there, as was Warren Beatty who was in London with Faye Dunaway promoting his latest film *Bonny & Clyde*. In fact Warren Beatty came up to speak to me and we chatted away for quite a while … he said I was the most beautiful girl he had ever met – but I expect he said that to everyone. Warren pressed his address into my hand and said he would love to meet me again and could I come for afternoon tea?'[11]

Maddie's eyes were pooping out of her head. Not only had she just been to Roman Polanski's wedding, but she had now been invited to meet Warren Beatty. Arriving at the door, Maddie described the scene as she went in.

> 'I made my way to South Audley Street – Warren was staying there at a friends' house I think and that was quite an American quarter in those days – left over from the war and being near to the American Embassy at that time. A nice man met me at the door and went 'Oooooh, they never come to visit me!'. As I entered a bedroom, I saw Warren who, to my amazement, was not wearing any clothes and was on the bed I think talking to Julie Christie on the telephone … I could not see the tea or cucumber sandwiches anywhere but I could see that Warren was physically very excited. This was the first time I had even seen a naked man and it was Warren Beatty the Hollywood star. Not only was he naked but his manhood was fully ready for action. Warren had a lot to brag about I can tell you, but I didn't know what to do, I was far too young, far too naive and I just flushed red with embarrassment and retreated back to the doorway, spuffled something about not having the time to stay and ran off. Maybe Warren carried on with his telephone call but I never heard from him again.'

Not many people turned down an invitation to try out Warren Beatty's mattress – indeed, many accepted willingly – but Maddie was not that sort of girl, as she would have to demonstrate endlessly throughout her career. She recalls the 1960s and 1970s being an especially sexually liberated era.

> 'I often get asked how I managed to survive with my honour intact, and it was hard. It was almost acceptable to be propositioned, and especially if you were an attractive girl let alone a model. I just enjoyed being with people but I didn't want all the excesses that came with it. I had to live with myself and I had a strong set of personal values that had been built over many years as a child – but I am not saying I am a goody-two-shoes at all, because I'm not, but the levels of drug taking and sexual excess were staggering looking back now.'

Along with freely available drugs, the contraceptive pill had become available in 1961 and, despite the risks associated with it, promiscuity expanded exponentially.

> 'It's hard to appreciate just what a difference the availability of the contraceptive pill made to the 1960s and 1970s. In an age where sex was now no longer a taboo subject and swept under the carpet, younger generations just let go and expected to be able to experiment from the earliest opportunity. Unwanted pregnancies sky-rocketed. Men expected women to be even freer with their bodies, but I swam in the opposite direction – much to my cost. I can recall dozens of times when I was propositioned and expected to conform, but I didn't, and I refused to take the pill as I had been warned

about the awful side effects that were possible. Sadly, these encounters could end up very acrimonious or worse, but I never changed.'

In February 1968, Maddie received some good news: one of the photographs that had been taken by Michael Cooper had been published in *The Times* as part of a fashion article written by Prudence Glynn.[12] Prudence, otherwise known as Lady Windlesham, became the first fashion editor for *The Times* in 1966, the start of a fifteen-year period covering the huge changes happening in the UK fashion industry as society moved from the formality of 1950s style into the pop and rock culture of the 1960s and beyond. Noted for her sometimes uncompromising honesty, it was Prudence Glynn who accompanied the image of Maddie Smith with the comment 'Watch this Space – this girl is going places' – and she was right.

Part Two

# From Modelling to Film and Television, 1968–1972

## Chapter 4

# With Ava Gardner in Tam-Lin, 1969

'1968 was a manic and magic year for me … I loved it all but I didn't know what I was doing from one day to the next – but then that was true of so many years!'

Madeline Smith on 1968

Having started the year with an invitation to Roman Polanski's wedding reception, one could be forgiven for thinking that nothing in1968 could top that moment – but you would be wrong. Having met Maddie, Donald Cammell wanted her around a lot more – perhaps as some sort of pseudo-sexual muse, or possibly he loved her naivety and innocence as well as having an artist's eye for beauty. Whatever his reasoning, Donald wanted to keep the friendship alive. Despite all his other projects, especially the all-consuming work on his screenplay for the new film with Mick Jagger, Donald saw the infinite beauty that Maddie exuded from every smile and coy glance. Mick and Donald were very close at that time, so it was inevitable that Maddie would one day meet the famous rock and pop icon.[1] But along with Donald's free creative style came many excesses, and the world of late 1960s and early 1970s London was a perfect incubator for any extreme of behaviour that could be imagined.

'I met with Donald quite a lot. He would often call me from his home in Mulberry Walk near the Chelsea Arts Club, and my mother would often answer the phone and, after the usual comment about what a beautiful voice he had, I would eventually be passed the 'phone. Donald was always inviting me out … he was a very nice man … He wanted to get me embroiled into all kinds of things and to meet new people at parties or events and loved having me around.'

Inevitably, Maddie would be exposed to more than just Warren Beatty's 'Oscar' and his particular approach to seduction, and she would often be asked, through conversation, if she wanted to join in some sexual extravaganza or other.

'Donald was into all sorts of interesting scenarios - groups, androgenous sex and so on - all of which I declined. Instead, I used to run back along the King's Road to the safety of Sloane Square Station and home to Kew ... I liked Donald very much, he was kind and never anything but nice to me, but I was still so young and easily shocked and it all came at me so fast. Donald was always incredibly busy and stressed. I remember I was able to sit in on some of his film-script meetings. Drugs were writ large with all the creative types, artists at that time, models, directors, actors, writers - you couldn't get away from it ... they were all high as kites with drugs as easily available as sweets.'

Anyone close to Donald Cammell at this time in his life, and against the background of the late 1960s world in which he operated, could not avoid meeting some of the era's greatest stars. One day in the spring of 1968, the telephone rang again in the Smith household in Kew. This time Donald was going to meet Mick Jagger and his girlfriend, Marianne Faithful, for dinner at the exclusive Cheney Walk where Mick was living in a beautiful house.[2] At dinner, it was just the four of them chilling. The air was thick with cigarette and marijuana smoke, LPs spun around on the state-of-the-art audio system, and they reclined on huge cushions and funky sofas.

'Mick was just another lovely man, kind and polite, and he spent a long time chatting to Donald about the film and the part he was going to play. Meanwhile, Mick's girlfriend at the time was Marianne Faithful and I was left trying to chat with someone who was clearly very depressed - she was so pretty but maybe it was her drug use that caused her to continually talk about death all evening.'

Marianne Faithful, like so many of the new young singers, models and actresses of the period, had shot to fame. Going from obscurity to stardom between 1964 and 1968, Marianne was another beautiful and impressionable girl who had fallen in with the Rolling Stones, becoming close to Anita Pallenberg before starting her well-publicized relationship with Mick Jagger in 1966. It would last until 1970.

Like Maddie, Marianne had endured a troubled childhood, with parental divorce, a severe illness and a love for a local drama group before her voice was 'discovered' by Andrew Loog Oldham – who just happened to also be the manager of the Rolling Stones![3] Maddie would have been unaware that Marianne was another of the muses within the coterie of the Rolling

Stones; neither would she have known that Marianne was already a heavy smoker of marijuana, was taking cocaine to excess and had recently left her husband to go and live with Mick Jagger. Marianne had also given birth to a daughter that she had with Jagger. The baby was still-born as Marianne returned from Jagger's country house in Ireland, and it may have been this that was playing on her mind all evening as the now 19-year-old Maddie Smith tried, in vain, to make conversation with her.

Maddie would only meet Mick Jagger once more in her life.

> 'One day sometime later I was walking down (guess where) the King's Road and so was Mick ... he recognized me and picked me up and spun me around on the pavement, and we laughed and chatted, but I never saw him again.'

This fleeting reunion reminds us just how momentary relationships can often be, especially so amongst those in the spotlight. Endless new faces appear and disappear with such regularity that it is impossible to maintain a stable balance of contacts unless one reduces the number to just a small group – and Maddie Smith was now a member of some of those elite groups. If we add in the daily intake of hallucinogenic drugs such as LSD, the longer-term effects of which were unknown at the time, and the easily available and regular taking of cocaine, then it is unsurprising that faces came and went so quickly, in what was mostly a drug-fuelled haze. For many, it was impossible to know who they had recently met, let alone if they would meet them again.

For Maddie, the rest of 1968 was largely taken up with travel and modelling work, plus relationships too fleeting to ever have the chance of developing into long-lasting friendships, but that was part of city life, and certainly part of the chaotic world of London's streets in the 1960s.

## *The Killing of Sister George*

It would be another telephone call at home in Kew that brought the news of an audition to play a small part in a new film being recorded that year. Beryl Reid, Susannah York, Sam Kydd and Hugh Paddick would be part of the superb cast in a film called *The Killing of Sister George*, and Maddie was asked to meet with its director, Robert Aldrich, in a club on the King's Road.

*The Killing of Sister George* had been written by Frank Marcus and was published in book form in 1965. It was, at the time, a ground-breaking painful black comedy based on the breakdown of a long-term lesbian relationship between a younger woman and her older partner. Often seen as a cult film, it can be uncomfortable watching and has a macabre element in the lead role of an actress famous for playing nurse Sister George, beautifully played by Beryl Reid, a precociously talented actress herself. When Maddie arrived on the King's Road on this occasion, she ventured into a whole new world of surprise and sexual freedom.

> 'By the time I was eighteen, I thought I knew most places on the King's Road – after all, I had walked it enough times and been out and about so much. But this was new. Robert Aldrich was already a very famous American director and had only recently, in 1967, completed filming *The Dirty Dozen* with Lee Marvin. When I arrived, it was lunchtime and yet, as I walked in, the club was in full swing – I had never seen a club so busy, with women kissing each other in the foyer and down the stairs. It was a club just for lesbians, but I had never knowingly met a lesbian and the whole thing knocked my senses. In a way it was lovely to see so much emotion between women going on, but I was scared of what might be happening downstairs so I just sat at the top [of the stairs]. It was the strangest audition ever really because I saw Robert Aldrich appear at the bottom and he just smiled and went away. He had seen me and that was all he had needed because after I had left, I heard from Joan that I had got the part.'

Although Maddie would play only a small role at the start of the film, dressed as one of two nuns who help a very drunk 'Sister George' into a taxi driven by Sam Kydd, she was directed by Robert Aldrich, which in itself was a moment to remember.

> 'Beryl Reid was brilliant – powerful and persuasive – she really was a fine actress and I found her enchanting even though I was only on set for a few days. We rehearsed our scene a few times, filmed it and that was that. But I had been a small part of an iconic film and I was only aged 18.'

The movie had to be cut in many places to ease the sensibilities of the British film censor, but eventually passed for cinemas in 1967 and was classified as an 'X'-rated film.

There is one final piece to add to this story. On her way home after filming her scene, Maddie slumped down onto a seat on an underground train. She scanned the carriage, to note any persons of interest, and it was with a sudden sense of shock that she saw a nun sitting opposite her. Having been dressed as a nun all day, this produced a smile on Maddie's face that quickly disappeared when she noticed that this was no ordinary nun – it was Sister Philomena, she of the tortured school days and her refusal to allow Maddie to join the little drama group, The Questors. As both teacher and nun, her attitude towards Maddie had made her feel insignificant and unworthy. A few moments passed. Maddie could have chosen to ignore her, or even to make a small riposte on how she had made her feel at school. Instead, Maddie selected the deferential and submissive role that she had been taught for so long. With her heart pounding – to such a degree that she can still feel it over forty years later – Maddie simply said, with a gentle sense of dry irony, 'Hello Sister, I've been a nun all day today', and smiled, expecting something similar in return. It seemed a nice way to hopefully open a conversation, but predictably, Sister Philomena did not recognize Maddie or even attempt to converse with who she no doubt thought was a stranger. That would be the last Maddie would see of her – but was certainly not the last time she would think of her. Sister Philomena is part of Maddie's life, a reminder of troubled and painful times and a weight on her soul. But talking about her seemed to help, and we were both pleased to discuss what was an extraordinary experience.

Far more positively, the Lucy Clayton Modelling Agency had been very busy, developing a business partnership with a German fashion magazine in Hamburg. Looking at all the models the agency could offer, it was Maddie Smith whom they liked the most, possessing that certain something that they felt would appeal to a German audience. The modelling career that had started so recently would now run for eighteen months, into the middle of 1969.

> 'I started to fly from London to Hamburg quite a lot for modelling shoots and I really felt like I was making it into the big time. The magazine was called *Brigitta* and their photographer, a guy called Glundach, loved my look and I felt excited with the shoots.'

Although now totally overlooked as part of Maddie's career, her modelling work in Germany was impressive and of the highest quality. Not only did *Brigitta* regularly enjoy featuring Maddie in articles and fashion pieces, but she was also often interviewed for random editorials on life in London. In one particular piece in *Brigitta*, bearing the title '*Ich will berhumt werden is das schlimm?*' ('I want to be famous, is that wrong?'), Maddie revealed that early on in her modelling career she had ambitions to be more than just a pretty face and a model whose looks would inevitably fade. The modelling jobs in Germany dominated a large part of 1969, but one incident reveals that the adrenaline and excitement of being a successful model ran alongside a sensitive and very young personality

> 'It was after a trip to Berlin to do a modelling session at the Olympic Stadium, that I lost my teddy bear "Meow". I was en route to meet Klaus-Jurgen Simon, who was a male model from Hamburg that I began to develop a real friendship with, and, somewhere in transit, I lost my favourite childhood toy. "Meow" went everywhere and spent every night with me ... I was really upset ... it was like a talisman and had lots of comforting memories for me. When I got to Hamburg, the wonderful Klaus gave me a new teddy, which I named "Klauschen", or "Little Klaus", and it's still with me today and everywhere I go. I would love to know what happened to "Big Klaus" - he was very sweet'.

The mind boggles what Warren Beatty might have had to say if 'Meow' had joined him in bed along with Maddie.

In all sorts of ways, 1969 was a year of change – both for Maddie and for the world. It was the year the first ever Boeing 747 'jumbo jet' took to the air, that John Lennon and Yoko Ono got married, and in July 1969, while Maddie was modelling in Germany, Neil Armstrong took mankind's first steps on the surface of the Moon. Shortly after the latter monumental event, the world was horrified when, on 9 August, members of the 'Manson Family' invaded the home of Roman Polanski and murdered his pregnant wife, the lovely Sharon Tate. Six days later, on Max Yasgur's dairy farm in Bethel, New York, the Woodstock Music Festival began, signalling that the 1960s counter-culture was about to pass the baton of change and revolution to the new generations of the 1970s. Maddie was seeing less of Donald, as he immersed himself in the final preparation stages before filming of *Performance* and she spent time away in Europe every month.

Following in Donald's footsteps, Maddie flew to Paris, where she was booked for a week-long photo shoot. The trip began badly but ended amazingly, in typical Maddie Smith style – it would all be OK in the end, she just didn't know how or why, it was just a 'Maddie Smith thing' where she muddled through, smiling, and the universe seemed to look after her.

It was a week of industrial protests in France. Parisian workers enjoyed a good disruptive strike in the Sixties and Seventies, as if they were trying not to forget their age-old skills of bringing down governments. Maddie had her purse stolen by an 'unofficial' cab driver, as the 'official' taxi drivers were on strike. Left with no money, but still having her return flight ticket, Maddie found her way to her little boarding house and burst into tears in front of a not bad looking male receptionist: 'In fact he was quite handsome, I seem to remember,' says Maddie, insisting that the tears were heartfelt and spontaneous, not simply a well-timed exercise in eliciting pity from a handsome stranger. One of Maddie's secret weapons is the ability to immediately become a different persona in a situation where she has a desire to make something happen. I have seen her gently swoon in the sunshine where there are no chairs available outside coffee shops, then witnessed countless customers deftly offer up their own chair and table to a grateful Maddie. I have also seen traffic wardens, trained in the best Gestapo techniques, allow us to park not only where there is a parking restriction but where there is actually no parking space at all. These skills are a gift that keeps on giving, enabling Maddie to survive and indeed thrive in a world where there no longer seems to be any give and take.

It comes as no surprise to learn that Daniel Lugassy, a trainee psychiatrist who worked in this small Parisian boarding house part-time to raise money for his studies, was completely bowled over by Maddie's tears. Neither Maddie nor Daniel could believe their luck – she had found her White Knight, and he had found a top English model. What could be better? Young and carefree, Daniel and Maddie enjoyed the rest of the week together on the South Bank, meeting French student friends of Daniel, chatting (Maddie had studied French at school right through to A-level) and just kicking back and enjoying life. Daniel apparently proved a perfect gentleman, sleeping on the floor of his flat so Maddie always had a bed for the night. Once again, it was part of the charmed life that seemed to accompany the righteous soul of Maddie Smith that everything worked out well in the end.

At the end of the week and in the best traditions of holiday romances, Daniel and Maddie said their goodbyes, never to meet again. But further disaster was ahead, Maddie arriving at the airport only to find that, true to form, it was now the French air traffic controllers who were on strike – in sympathy with their colleagues who were on strike in the USA. No flights were landing or leaving and Maddie had to leave the airport, along with everyone else, so she was once more on the street with no money, nowhere to stay and no Daniel either. Once more Maddie just burst into tears, and again it worked for her.

> 'A super tall gentleman walked over and asked what was wrong. He was an Algerian vet who lived in Paris and was travelling to London. I was amazed that he invited me back to his apartment, where he promised to sleep on the floor, which he did, and take me to the airport again at 3am as he knew that an African Airways flight would be landing and leaving for London with or without the help of French traffic control – it was a different world then and I'm amazed I was so trusting. Sure enough that's exactly what happened. I was able to use my ticket and we managed to get back to Heathrow that morning. He was amazing, one of the many wonderful people I have met in my life. A few days later he did call me at home and Mum answered the telephone, but I just didn't know what to say and I regret to this day that I didn't speak to him … I was just too immature to deal with older men and I had met so many already and always felt like running away.'

Back in London, during the spring of 1969, Donald Cammell was intensely involved in filming *Performance* with Mick Jagger and James Fox. On locations across London, this 'eye-popping melange of magic mushrooms, homoerotic gangsterism, rock decadence and gender fluidity' was coming together in a far more violent and shocking way than Warner Brothers had imagined possible.[4] As Donald and his film crew rocked up to the Fulham Road, Notting Hill, Mount Street in Mayfair and Wandsworth, so Maddie was at home in Kew when her agent, Joan Gray, called to speak to her. Joan had been aware that Maddie harboured a strong desire to break away from modelling and to move into acting.

Maddie had already experienced the thrill of making a film and she wanted more. In mid-1969, Maddie had been asked to play a small part in a low-budget short movie called *Come Back Peter*, which was written, directed and produced by Donovan Winter, a creative talent looking for his big break; sadly, this would not be it. The film was another attempt to capture the mood, feel and smell of the Swinging Sixties, but very few films managed to get anywhere near that. However, the experience merely encouraged Maddie to look for other roles, and then she heard from Joan.

> 'I was getting bored with modelling and was actually doing some catalogue jobs for a while which was really dull. When the call came, Joan said "Do you still want to play at being an actress?" Naturally I said yes and did not really care what the job was; I just wanted to give something a go. It could have been anything - even a local "am dram" would have been great, but I could not believe my luck. A film company was casting for a new film to be called *The Ballad of Tam-Lin*.'

It was Roddy McDowall who wanted to direct this new film, which was originally intended to be called *The Devil's Widow*. In keeping with the wave of interest for horror movies, this was to be a film that would try to weave together the renewed success of folk-music – such as that of Fairport Convention, whose latest album, *Liege and Leaf*, had just hit the charts – with a search for traditional folk tales and witchcraft. The film's makers aimed to feed the desire for authenticity in what was now a world of superficiality – a backlash, if you like, against the counter-culture of the late 1960s.[5]

Tam-Lin was a centuries-old story that had been translated by Robert Burns in 1796 and, according to Wikipedia, was 'steeped in the Celtic night of Samain, or our adopted Halloween or All Saints Day. The night when bonfires are lit to renew life in the pre-winter earth, when all-natural law is suspended and ghosts and demons are abroad. The fairies' myths in the Scottish borderlands likened Elves to humans in their physical size but gave them a compulsion to steal new born children and men.' This was to be the premise of a film that would be funded by Alan Ladd Jr and Stanley Mann, and would field established Hollywood stars like Ava Gardner as Michaela Cazaret and the lovely, elegant Richard Wattis as Elroy.[6] The film also aimed to headline some new talent, such as Ian McShane as Tom Lynn, Stephanie Beacham and, after a successful audition, a very young Maddie Smith, who was given a few lines in the part of Sue.[7] It was a film as far removed from what Donald Cammell was making in London, both in location and composition, as one could imagine.

> 'I was thrilled. Just think, little me to be playing in the same film as Ava Gardner. She was lovely and really kind but a true Hollywood star; you could feel that each time she appeared on set. I adored her. Someone else who had a small part in the film was Joanna Lumley, who was, like me, trying to break through into films and acting. Filming took place in Scotland, in Peeblesshire, and I remember it really well … lots of rolling mountains and green landscapes and we all stayed in a beautiful hotel called the Peebles Hydro which was also a very popular hotel for golfers. Our filming mostly took place at Traquair.'

Maddie was right: the Peebles Hydro Hotel was a perfect and very grand place to stay for those wishing to play golf at the renowned Peebles Golf Club and to enjoy all the baths and spa facilities of what had been – and still was – a health-inspired venue.

Traquair House had been chosen as the main location. Seven miles south of Peebles, the huge fifteenth-century baronial-style walls and high turrets gave the splendid gothic feel that Roddy McDowall wanted to be the backdrop to Ava Gardner's mysterious role. Filming began, as Bryan Adams would one day sing, in the summer of 1969.[8] Maddie Smith's memory is quite astounding, and she is able to recall almost every detail of her life, including her time filming *The Ballad of Tam-Lin*:

> 'She [*Ava Gardner*] hid herself in her room a lot and was rarely seen on set before midday. Joanna [*Lumley*] had only one line in the film so had lots of free time and would go and knock on Ava's room and say "Come on Big A!" I think Ava was actually very shy. She had achieved so much, we were in awe of working with her; she had made and starred in so many films – a real Hollywood superstar … Ava was really kind though and, after the film, we all kept in touch and she invited us all to her 50th birthday party in her flat in London.'

That birthday party would take place on Christmas Eve 1972, and it's easy to see that Maddie cherishes many happy memories of being a part of this film – a time and a place where everyone just got along, the whole experience being a positive one.

> 'I loved Ian McShane too. He was very gentle. Everyone in the film was lovely. The cameras in those days were huge and I remember an equally huge, handsome man called Kip Gowans. He was the 1st Assistant Director. He was lovely too and helped a lot to get everyone feeling that they were making a super film. Kip Gowans was married to Lee Remick, and I remember that she was in the UK at that time and came up to Peebles to visit her husband on set.'[9, 10]

Although Maddie was unaware at the time, Gowans and Remick had only met by chance on a film set the previous year; after a lightning divorce, Gowans had married Remick shortly before filming of *Tam-Lin* began, hence the desire for them to be together on set in Scotland. Also in the cast – in the 'bad' coven, compared to the 'good' of Maddie – was Linda Marlowe, ex-wife of actor William/'Bill' Marlowe. Already well-established at the time, Linda continues to perform her one-woman shows even to this day, and is still considered a very dear and loving friend by Maddie.

Lee Remick, a rising star herself in 1969, was not the only Hollywood A-lister to visit the set.

> 'Roddy McDowall, who would later go on to star in the *Planet of the Apes* films, told us that Lauren Bacall was coming to say hello. Can you believe it? Ava Gardner, Lee Remick and Lauren Bacall all coming along to watch the film that little me was a part of. It was like a dream.'

Although 'head in the clouds Maddie' had lots of time to watch how the film was being made, she did not know that the star of five James Bond films already, Sean Connery, was also staying at the Peebles Hydro at the same time as all the cast of *Tam-Lin*. Aware that he was in line for one more 007 role in *Diamonds Are Forever*, which would start filming in 1970 for release in 1971, Connery was taking a break and playing golf with friends at the Peebles Golf Club. Having already made *Dr No* (1962), *From Russia With Love* (1963), *Goldfinger* (1964), *Thunderball* (1965) and *You Only Live Twice* (1967), having Connery in the hotel along with all these other stars made it a very rare and surreal moment in time as they mixed together in the restaurant and the bar in the evenings.[11] Clearly, Maddie Smith and James Bond had something of a connection – after all, it would only be three years later when she would be playing a Bond girl herself. However, the current

Bond, Connery, decided one night to pre-empt events by following Maddie upstairs and actually into her room.

> 'I knew he was walking behind me because I had seen him leave his seat at the bar when I decided to go to bed. I had that copy of *The Brothers Karamazov* in my hand – the same copy from Biba all that time ago – and I still had not read it! As I walked along this lovely thick plush carpet he came up beside me and asked if he could run me a bath and read some of the book with me … I just didn't know what to say … I'm sure many girls in a similar position would have said yes, but I just spluttered … this was Sean Connery after all … but he wasn't really my type and I said I didn't think that was a good idea and rushed to my room, where he followed me and I had to be really firm to get him out again.'

It's not often that you see James Bond turned down, so this was something of a first. Perhaps Sean Connery had become confused between fiction and reality, and he could be forgiven for being carried away with his celebrity status. However, a few days later when Maddie was out walking in the grounds, Sean Connery walked towards her – and went straight past without even saying a word.

As a footnote to this story of *Tam-Lin*, Maddie would see Ava Gardner once again after the invitation to her birthday party. Ava was very friendly with Charles Gray; in fact, they were often seen together, Gray acting as her 'walker'. He would star opposite Sean Connery as arch villain Ernst Stavro Blofeld in *Diamonds Are Forever* in 1971, and became one of Gardner's most trusted gay friends. After a life of alcohol and arguments with husbands such as Frank Sinatra, Gardner chose London as her last, anonymous refuge in what became known as 'Fortress Gardner', her small second-floor apartment at 34 Ennismore Gardens, with iron grilles over every window.[12] With a wry smile on her face, Maddie recalled the last time she bumped into the Hollywood legend.

> 'I used to attend a fitness class in Knightsbridge in the 1970s. It was called "Grannies with Beautiful Bodies" and one day I looked across and there was Ava Gardner. Dressed in a grey tracksuit, she looked over and recognised me and we just smiled at each other.'

### *But Also Dudley Moore*, 1969

After filming *Tam-Lin*, Maddie returned to London and started to wonder what to do next. There was still time for 1969 to hold something more for her, and she was keen to fill every day – just as she still is now. She could of course have returned to modelling, but ideally it was either theatre, film or television work that she now wanted. The gods must have been listening, because it was not long before Maddie was again contacted by agent Joan Grey about an audition for a part in a stage production called *Play It Again, Sam*, starring Dudley Moore, who had gained the rights to perform the new Woody Allen play that had just run for a year on Broadway. The play was due to open in September 1969 at the Globe Theatre in London's West End.[13]

Maddie went along for the audition and got the part. Rehearsals began almost immediately in June 1969, Maddie joining Dudley Moore on stage.

> 'It was a very slight piece but, given that he was the lead, it opened in the West End without a tour. By now, Dud was box office magic and, as an actress in the 1960s, it was my destiny to portray every man's dream dolly - including [in] *Play It Again, Sam*. Very little acting would have been required for my tiny part in the play, but the thrill of having the chance to spend each night for a year in the company of Dudley Moore was overwhelming.'[14]

However, disaster then struck for Maddie – the first but not the last painful lesson that she would have to learn in her chosen profession. The producers of *Tam-Lin* had included a clause in her contract that tied her to them for twelve months, and she was not allowed to take on any other work in that period:

> 'I can't remember if I had been paid for a year or if they paid me a small amount each month but I was held by them on standby in case they wanted me to play a role in another film. I think it was standard stuff but I had never dreamed that this sort of thing happened - Joan was not very good at telling me these things. Again, I was just so young and learning the business so I had to sadly tell Dudley and the lovely Terence Edmund, who also had a part in the stage play. Dudley was great about it; we got along so well and it was such a shame because I thought that this was my chance to get on the West End stage and it might never come again. It was all so abrupt but I learned then to always read my contracts.'

Despite the disappointment of not being able to take part in *Play It Again, Sam*, 1969 had still been an amazing year for Maddie Smith. She had broken away from modelling and was now starting to put on a little weight, which was ideal for her move towards film, stage and television.

> 'It was also not the last time I met with Dud. He had secured my home telephone number and, occasionally, he called to arrange to meet and have dinner. I have to admit that on one awkward occasion, he did try to get "amorous" with me in his studio flat in London. It wasn't a success. He was unable to share anything of himself, except to talk in deadly earnest, endlessly, and with absolutely no humour at all, which came as a complete surprise to me and we didn't quite click. But he did, however, say that he loved my company and when he left to work in the States, he asked my permission to contact me again. This he never did.'[15]

Pictures of Maddie from this period show her with a rounder face but still retaining that sublimne look of naivety and innocence that had first marked her out as a truly individual soul and personality – something her father had probably been the first to notice. Maddie's hair was now summer-blonde and long, giving her quite a carefree look in contrast to the carefully coiffured and practiced smiles of her modelling work.

But the year was still not over, and two further events happened almost simultaneously in the autumn of 1969 that would dramatically change the direction her young life was about to take.

### *Cribbins*

An already well-established comedy actor was casting around for a group of talented individuals to join him in filming a new TV show that had been commissioned by Thames Television. That actor was the lovely, beloved and very talented Bernard Cribbins.[16]

By the end of the 1960s, Thames TV was still a relatively new franchise-holding region of the ITV network, which served London and the Home Counties and began broadcasting on 30 July 1968 (its last broadcast was on the night of 31 December 1992). Formed out of a complicated merger between ABC and Rediffusion (two of the earlier independent TV companies), the aim of Thames TV was to broadcast Monday to Friday and then hand over to

London Weekend Television at 7.00 pm on a Friday night. With refurbished studios at Teddington, where experiments with colour television had been taking place for some years, Thames Television carried on producing exciting programmes such as *Callan*, *Opportunity Knocks* and *Do Not Adjust Your Set* while at the same time scouring the country for new, up-and-coming talent to attract television audiences.[17]

This was Cribbins' first television comedy series of his own; he would write and star in every sketch, with as many as eighteen short comedy sketches in every thirty-minute episode. Again, it was Joan Grey who arranged for the audition, putting Maddie forward as a new talent worth watching who had already played in a number of films and had a successful modelling career behind her. Maddie was duly given a part.

For Maddie, this was a totally new adventure. She loved the allure of the script-reading, meeting and working with a host of well-known comedy actors and the whole television production process. The pace of the sketches was lively, almost like a university revue, and there were quickies as well as musical numbers to provide variety and pacing, where Cribbins 'romped through a gallery of outrageous comedy characters'.[18]

> 'I remember that rehearsals took place in the boat club in Teddington and we overlooked the Thames – it was amazing and I took to it like a duck to water! I would appear in many sketches in the first series and loved every moment of it. The content was designed for TV audiences in the early evening around 6.30 pm so it was all very mild stuff, but also very quirky at times and always funny. The kind and lovely Bob Todd was often there – he was already well-known but would also become a stable part of Thames TV. We would see him in all sorts of programmes but of course he was especially well-known for his side-kick roles with Benny Hill – another Thames TV creation.'[19]

The first series of *Cribbins* was launched on 18 November 1969, an auspicious date as this was the very week that ITV transmitted in colour for the first time. The sale of colour TV sets boomed across the nation, with Maddie's face being one of the first to be consistently seen in the vibrant new format. Maddie worked alongside established comedy stars but also some new talent, including Sheila Steafel and the now largely forgotten but wonderful Carmel McSharry, whom Maddie remembers well.

> 'Carmel was just adorable – so funny and so calm; it was as if it were all real life and not a sketch show. I know Carmel is forgotten now but at the time she was everywhere and played parts in *The Liver Birds*, *Casualty* and of course *Z-Cars*. Her eyes could light up a room, the set or a sketch – I loved her very much.'[20]

If you take the time to look up *Cribbins* on an online channel such as YouTube, you can see Maddie Smith as she appeared in 1969: demure, but with a spark of defiance (still evident today); a hopelessly trusting face with a desire for understanding (also still evident today); and a small frame – the body of a nymph (still there today too). Maddie Smith retains the energy, love for life and innocence that she has always had, all her endearing qualities remain, and it is just the natural gaining process of age which we all face that has moved forward since those heady days of 1969. It is the world that has changed around her, but she could still easily step into the parts that she played over fifty years ago.[21]

# Chapter 5

# 1970: What a Year – The Vampire Lovers, Mr Forbush and Paul Eddington

'Run Alice! Run as fast as you can away from here!'

Paul Paxton to Alice Hargood in *Taste the Blood of Dracula*, 1970

## *Taste the Blood of Dracula*, 1969

Luck, or what others call fate, plays a large part in all our lives, and before the end of 1969, Maddie had yet another stroke of luck – or fate intervened – which would introduce her to the world of the horror film. It was while Maddie was recording her parts in *Cribbins* in September and October 1969 that she received another call from Joan, who asked if she could pop along to meet a casting director for Hammer Films.

Hammer Films had begun in 1934, and its rustic film studios in Bray, Berkshire, would go on to enjoy global fame from the mid-1950s through to the mid-1970s, creating classic and world-renowned horror characters such as Baron Frankenstein, Count Dracula and The Mummy.[1] Hammer Film Productions, a new part of the company, was founded in 1949 and moved to new offices at 113–117 Wardour Street in London, which in turn became known as 'Hammer House'. New offices coincided with new technology, the arrival of vivid colour film giving horror movies a whole new dimension in blood and gothic fashion. Through their distribution partnerships with Warner Brothers, United Artists and Universal Pictures, the Hammer House brand became a household name.

Maddie recalls that her first contact with Hammer House came about as the result of her agent Joan, working away promoting Maddie as a new and rising young film star and managing to open the door to an interview with a female casting director named Aida Young. This was meant to be a 'go see' meeting, to see what developed, but turned into something of an audition. The result was an immediate small role in *Taste the Blood of Dracula* starring Christopher Lee. Filming began straight away and was over before the end of 1969.[2]

*Taste the Blood of Dracula* was the fifth in the Hammer *Dracula* series and featured a range of well-known character actors, which was one of the strengths of Hammer. This always impressed Maddie.

> 'Most character actors were in the theatre and radio and readily accepted short parts, and you were very quickly in and out and on to the next job. I so wish I could have sustained my promise of being a character actress. The ability of these people to just step into someone else's shoes and become that person was incredible, and still is. The British film industry back then was littered with these talented actors, who could transform into someone else right in front of you.'

Hammer was already a major employer of character actors, such as Peter Sallis, who played Samuel Paxton in the film and was already a well-known and experienced stage and television performer. The film also featured Roy Kinnear, who played Weller, a travelling salesman who witnesses the death of Count Dracula and collects his cloak and ring to sell on to three so-called 'respectable' gentlemen.[3,4]

Christopher Lee was already a household name in the world of the horror film, and was always in great demand. However, during filming, Maddie never actually met Lee; there seemed to be something going on behind the scenes between him and the Hammer management.

> 'I suppose he was so busy that he just arrived and played all his scenes and then left for another project. I never actually met him, but on screen, I found his acting brilliant and terrifying.'

Directed by the Hungarian Peter Sasdy, and with the imaginative tagline 'Drink a pint of blood a day', filming took place between 27 October and Christmas Day 1969, mostly at the chilly Elstree Studios, but also at Highgate Cemetery in north London and St Andrew's Church in Totteridge. What Maddie did not know at the time was that Lee had tried to avoid playing any part in the film. He'd had enough of playing Dracula – having already played him in four films – and did not want to play the role again. It was only because Warner Brothers in Hollywood said they would refuse to release the film if he was not in it, that Hammer persuaded Lee to come on set at all. This threat, plus Lee's agent managing to get a better financial deal for him, persuaded Lee to rise from the grave once more and do the film.[5]

'By this time, I had discovered just how successful Hammer films were in the United States, and how well known I was,' the legendary actor said in Marcus Hearn and Alan Barnes' book *The Hammer Story*. 'I told my agent to tell Hammer if they really didn't have any money then they could pay me a percentage of the American distributer's gross.'[6]

Maddie played a small part as Dolly, a naïve young prostitute in little white embroidered pyjamas, appearing with Geoffrey Keen as William Hargood, one of three so-called 'respectable' gentlemen who entered a bordello.[7] During the filming, Keen – another very well-established star who usually played solid, British establishment figures in films such as *Sink The Bismarck* (1960) and *The Third Man* (1949) – found himself with tiny 7-stone Maddie riding on his back in a sexual orgy as part of their scene together. Many years later, John Carson, another popular British character actor, would relate to Maddie how Geoffrey 'had moaned continually about how heavy I was on his back – when I only weighed all of seven stone!' One of the other stars in the film was Ralph Bates, who played another of the gentlemen, Lord Courtley. Maddie supports the view that Bates was being groomed by Hammer to take over from Christopher Lee as a future Dracula.

> 'This was Ralph's first film for Hammer. Ralph was an actor who passed before his time and before he could fully achieve his potential, which was considerable. His premature loss was a tragedy for us all and for his lovely wife, Virginia Wetherell.'[8]

Released in 1970, her small role was enough for Hammer to see that, in Maddie Smith, they had the almost perfect female innocent victim to be devoured by evil spirits and those intent on carnal pleasures and blood. Before the end of filming in Elstree, a new script found its way to her door in Kew. Maddie was about to be cast in what would become one of the defining roles of her career to date, being offered a lead part in the next major Hammer production, *The Vampire Lovers*.

## 'You must die! Everyone must die!' – *The Vampire Lovers*, 1970

*The Vampire Lovers* was based on the story *Carmilla* by Sheridan Le Fanu, a nineteenth-century Irish writer of Gothic literature.[9] Le Fanu is still regarded as one of the leading ghost story writers of the Victorian era, his talent being described by author E.F. Benson as follows: '[Le Fanu's] best work is of the first rank, while as a "flesh-creeper" he is unrivalled. No one else has so sure a touch in mixing the mysterious atmosphere in which horror darkly breeds.'[10]

It is not uncommon for the Hammer film genre to be somewhat ridiculed for its storylines and carefree use of red wine and blood. However, to the purist and the film critic, some of the movies produced by Hammer and its directors were of very fine quality, capturing perfectly the tone and emotional stress of the ghost story – and *The Vampire Lovers* definitely falls into this high-quality category. The Gothic tension of the film, even today, lends itself to the smell and feel of a Victorian manor house, complete with dust, musty air, thick-pile carpets and the faint whiff of over-imbibed laudanum in the air.

Taking on this particular story was a serious matter, and it needed a good director. Step forward 53-year-old English film-maker Roy Ward Baker.[11] Having worked his way up from the studio floor, Baker had a spell of three years in Hollywood and directed two of the greatest A-list stars of the period, Marilyn Monroe in *Don't Bother to Knock* (1952) and Robert Ryan in *Inferno* (1953). Upon his return to England, Roy Baker directed the iconic *A Night to Remember* (1958), with Kenneth Moore starring as the first officer on the doomed RMS *Titanic*. He went to direct a miscellany of famous and successful TV shows, such as *The Avengers*, *The Saint*, *Randall and Hopkirk (Deceased)* and *The Champions*. In Roy Baker, therefore, Hammer had selected one of the best directors around at the time, underlining the seriousness with which they treated the planning and funding of this film. Thinking the film over during the Christmas holidays, it was one of the producers, Michael Stiles, who telephoned Maddie at home. As ever, her mother picked up the phone and enjoyed a chat with Roy before handing the receiver over to Maddie.

> 'He wanted to know a little more about my "assets". He wasn't being funny or anything, in fact he was evidently embarrassed to ask this question as Michael was a complete gentleman, but he was up against the requirements of his producers. Clearly, he was worried that I was not voluptuous enough to play one of the three lead victims in a sexually charged horror film – which is exactly how the book treats the subject. I had the looks but my body was still developing ... feeling the part might be slipping away from me, I assured him that I would have the best assets in town by the time it came to filming! My dad was sitting in the kitchen drinking tea with Mum while I was having this conversation about the size of my breasts so, as you can imagine, it was very awkward to say the least. Anyway, I told the producer that I was determined to eat as much muesli yoghurt and drink as much full cream milk as I could stand over the next few weeks (it was great!), and my local dairy Hornby & Clarke, in Kew, could not believe their luck. By the time filming began at Elstree studies, my "assets" were very visible through clothes that had been especially cut to a Regency design.'

Although the local dairy may have found it hard to believe how much milk and yoghurt the Smith family were suddenly consuming in early 1970, it was down to them that, over the next few years, Maddie Smith would become a nationally recognized symbol of sexual allure.

Further underlining the fact that Maddie had really scored a bull's eye with being cast as a central figure in this film was the cast that was assembled around her. Fresh from her successful role as British spy Heidi Schmidt in *Where Eagles Dare* (1968) was Ingoushka Petrov. Better known as Ingrid Pitt, this Polish-born survivor of the Holocaust had, like Maddie, also enjoyed a lucky break when she had been cast opposite Richard Burton and Clint Eastwood (although it had nearly been Lee Marvin) in this Second World War adventure film from the book of the same name by Alastair MacLean.[12] Born in Warsaw to a Jewish mother and a Russian father, Pitt had found the making of *Where Eagles Dare* pretty uncomfortable, given that she had spent part of her childhood in the Stutthof concentration camp in Sztutowo in the city of what was then Danzig (now Gdansk). Pitt was curvaceous, with a strong sexual presence that was unmistakable, and she was experienced enough to know that Maddie was neither of those things – that would be part of the central magic of the film, which had been cast brilliantly.

The emotional, physical and sexual tension between 32-year-old Ingrid, who played the leading role of Carmilla/Mircalla, and 20-year-old Maddie, whose character was Emma Morton, was deliberate. This would be Hammer's effort to push the new boundaries of the permissive society of the early 1970s, with themes of both nudity and lesbian relationships. Ingrid was very much a woman of the world, had been married to an American major in Berlin almost ten years earlier, had already lived in California and reportedly had a fling with Burton on the set of *Where Eagles Dare*. Maddie, meanwhile, had yet to experience any sort of sexual encounter – apart from being given a preview of Warren Beatty's not-so-secret weapon. The counterpoint that was central to the film was the physical difference between the highly sexual and lustful Ingrid and the naïve, innocent Maddie.

> 'Actually, I had no idea what a lesbian was. I had read the script and there was no mention of any nudity – in those days you didn't have to explain everything in the contract as you do now – it was quite a fast learning experience, I can tell you.'

Also starring in the film was Peter Cushing, already a significant name in the film industry on both sides of the Atlantic and well on his way to making the 100 films that would mark his career.[13] It was in the late 1950s that Cushing had stumbled across the Hammer production company by accident and registered an interest. Once Hammer co-founder James Carreras heard of Cushing's interest, he was elated. Carreras had been trying to court Cushing for some time and was anxious to give him the role of Baron Frankenstein in 1957's *The Curse of Frankenstein* – the first of twenty-two films that Cushing would make for Hammer.[14] But Cushing was not the only big name that Hammer attracted to this risqué new film with its tiny £165,000 budget. Also cast as Maddie's father was George Cole, later of Arthur Daley/*Minder* fame, but in 1970 already an established actor since his first outing in *Cottage to Let* (1941).[15] Cole had played Flash Harry in all four of the St Trinian's films, as well as appearing alongside Sir Laurence Olivier in *Henry V* (1944) and starring in *The Green Man* (1956), and was a talented and professional actor, which belied his casual and natural image on film. Another aspiring actress was Kate O'Mara, whose recent TV appearances in *Z Cars* and *The Avengers* had caught the eye of both directors and producers. She would go on to build her own vibrant career with her devilish and piercing blue eyes.[16]

Cast and a substantial crew assembled from 19 January 1970 across three locations – Wall Hall in Hertfordshire, Moor Park Golf Club near Batchworth and Elstree for the studio scenes. Shooting would continue until 4 March, with a release date scheduled for 13 September that year. Maddie was a little nervous of being required to ride in some scenes.

> 'I had no idea which end of the horse was which, in fact I had never ridden but I was determined to do all I could to make this film work for me. I did not want the embarrassment of having to say I couldn't, so I just arranged my own riding lessons in Richmond Park in early January and by the time I arrived on location I looked as if I had been riding side-saddle forever.'

During filming, Michael Styles and Harry Fine arrived from American International Films at the invitation of Hammer and James Carreras in order to 'spice things up'. The film industry needed to combat the growing challenge of television and, without warning, Maddie was told that she 'HAD' to take her negligee off in her sexual lesbian scene with the smouldering Ingrid Pitt.

> 'He [*Styles*] told me to moan and groan in an erotic way and take my negligee off and reveal my body or people would be "falling asleep in the aisles", and that it would only be the Japanese market that would see me nude anyway. When you are as innocent as I was, you believe anything that someone as important as him told you, so I just went along with what they told me to do. This is one of the drawbacks of a very strict convent school upbringing – you were trained to do as you were told without question, and I had been well trained. But I was not the only one feeling uncomfortable on set. The director, Roy Ward Baker, hated having both Styles and Fine anywhere near the filming and, at one point, just marched them out of the studio. Roy was brilliant; he guided me and suggested that, in a second scene where I lay on the bed and Ingrid comes to me disguised as a cat to "ruffle" me, to imagine that I was asleep and was having a bad dream – which I was! It was my genuine innocence that was the very reason I had been cast for this part, and it was my innocence that they had to exploit for the film … Naturally, the film was not just shown in Japan!'

Both the lustful Pitt and virginal Maddie would be elevated to cult figure status by this film, and it has remained high on the list of any vampire or horror film fan as one of the most ethereal and well-made of the films of that period. *Time Out* referred to it as having 'a dreamy beauty'.[17] A.H. Weiller, writing in *The New York Times*, often the most critical reviewer of all, commented in 1971:

> '*The Vampire Lovers*, praise be, does manage to be a departure from a hackneyed, bloody norm. It is also professionally directed, opulently staged and sexy to boot … Ingrid Pitt is a vampire to delight and red-blooded Peeping Tom, despite her German-accented English. Sure, she also entices and destroys a couple of guys, but only because they're in her way en route to those gorgeous girls. Miss Pitt specifically, is a luscious brunette, who is exposed in a nude scene and who prowls about the rest of the time in a diaphanous shift that leaves little to the imagination. And her willing victims – Pippa Steel, Madeleine [*sic*] Smith and Kate O'Mara as Miss Smith's governess – are just as nobly endowed.'[18]

In an era so different to our own, when the sexualization of women was still in its heyday, Hornby & Clarke Dairies of Kew had done their job well.

### *Mr Forbush and the Penguins*, 1970

In what could be described a shift from the sublime to the ridiculous, Maddie recalls that she was very quickly offered another role, and for a short time it looked as if her film career was taking off. Hardly had the Elstree set of *The Vampire Lovers* been shut down when that for another movie was almost complete. There is a marvellous 1970 black and white image of Maddie and two friends standing under a signpost cleverly manufactured by the carpenter on site, which pointed one way to 'Vampires' and the other way to 'Penguins' – perhaps to avoid confusion.

> 'When I say I was next offered … it was in fact almost immediately that we finished filming *Vampire Lovers* that I was asked to play quite a nice part in a strange film about a man and his penguins starring the wonderful Shakespearean actress, Susan Fleetwood, and lovely John Hurt. Susan was another very talented actress that was sadly taken from us all prematurely – she was just a lovely, kind person.'[19]

The film was to be directed by Arne Suksdorff and Roy Boulting, and was designed to be a 1971 British comedy-drama based on the 1965 novel *Forbush and the Penguins* by Graham Billing, who had worked for the New Zealand Antarctic Division and written the book as he observed how penguins interact with humans. Interestingly, this was the first of what was meant to be a slate of fifteen films agreed in a collaborative relationship between EMI Films and British Lion Films, to be overseen by established and popular screen actor Bryan Forbes.[20] For Maddie Smith, this film should have been a stepping stone into more substantial film roles, and she looked forward to expanding and challenging herself. It thus came as quite a shock, and still causes ripples even today, when all the work and the entire cast were rejected.

One of the challenges of a film like this was, and is, the cost and quality of location filming. The main star of the film was emerging actor John Hurt.

> 'In the November of 1969 and while I was filming *The Vampire Lovers*, John and fifteen crew plus producer Henry Trettin and the director Al Viola had travelled to Antarctica and spent eight weeks filming with the penguins. On their return, we all assembled at Elstree Studios and started filming in the studios … I had learnt all my lines and it was all going so well … we also filmed in Ealing Technical College and I had some lovely pictures taken of me by the studio photographer.'

It came as shock to Brian Forbes that the footage taken in Antarctica did not cut at all well into the studio scenes. Given the huge financial outlay that had already been made, the spring of 1970 would reveal some significant problems for Forbes, and, as Maddie and the rest of the cast completed their scenes in Elstree, the Boulting brothers – twins Roy and fellow director John – insisted that director Al Viola be sacked along with the entire cast and that Roy Boulting's wife be cast in the leading role – this was Hayley Mills, daughter of Sir John Mills. Forbes writes that he had to work for an 'entire evening' trying to persuade John Hurt not to quit. Hurt was very angry that the director and the whole cast with the exception of himself were being let go, and it was left to Forbes to inform the original cast that it was all over for them.[21] Filming began again with a new cast. A finished product was released, but the whole project lost a great deal of money. Maddie had learnt another painful lesson – that in the film business, at the end of the day and with all the talk of creative wonder, it is only partly about the quality but mostly about the money.

## Paul Eddington and *Blue Comedy* – the start of a lifelong friendship, March 1970

While Maddie was filming for *The Vampire Lovers* and learning her lines for *Mr Forbush*, yet another little gem came her way. Once more, it was thanks to her agent that Maddie was invited to audition for her first stage play. Her life was becoming packed – just as she liked it to be. At last, Maddie felt energized. It was a tremendously exciting opportunity, one where Maddie felt she could at last connect with her first love – the stage.

> 'So far it had all just been a whirl of films and television. I just kept saying "yes" and doing everything that I was offered. Looking back, I was so lucky and met some tremendously talented and lovely people, but it was the stage where I wanted to be. I turned up for an audition for a pair of plays under the central title of *Blue Comedy* and went back stage to wander around and wait to be called. For anyone who has never been in the back stage area of a major theatre, it is a magical place - atmospheric and ethereal, where the ghosts of past plays and players are everywhere, as are their smells - an intoxicating mixture of varnish from the sets in storage, make-up, wax, wood, old clothes in storage and fear. Nothing else smells like it anywhere in the world. For some of us, it is a drug and it is why even successful and well-established film stars want to return to the theatre and put themselves through the torment and terror of another first night or a run on the West End or on Broadway. Those smells are a heady drug for an actor.'

Set to open in six weeks' time in May 1970, *Blue Comedy* included *Hank's Night* as one half of a double-bill and was backed by London theatre impresario Donald Albery. Casting for the plays had been difficult. The casting director, the respected and experienced Anne Rawsthorne, was looking for the perfect foil for the star of the production – Paul Eddington – and so far they had not been able to find the perfect face or personality.[22] Paul Eddington would become a well-known figure for his portrayal of Jim Hacker in *Yes Minister*, but that would not come along for another ten years, in 1980. By the time *Hank's Night* came along in early1970, Paul was still carving out an acting career in any way he could.[23] A series of small roles in *The Avengers* (1963), *The Prisoner* (1967) and *The Champions* (1969) marked his television career to date, and he had played a role in *A Severed Head*, a play adapted from an Iris Murdoch book, for Donald Albery in 1964, so a return to the stage for the now 43-year-old Eddington was natural. Although not yet a household name, this new opportunity would be the start of a lifelong and affectionate relationship with Maddie., who was thrilled to be cast opposite Paul.

> 'I have met some wonderful people in my life but Paul was special. He was as you might know a lifelong pacifist, and his calm exterior belied a very strong personality – nothing like the dithering Jim Hacker of later years – that was just a reflection of what a superb character actor he was.
>
> 'We began rehearsals at the YMCA in Great Russell Street in London in the March of 1970, with the opening night scheduled for May 1970 in Guildford at the Yvonne Arnaud Theatre, which was a tried and tested place to try out new material to a knowing audience prior to hopefully moving to the West End. Paul was marvellous – his comic timing was second to none and he knew exactly how long to pause or to pre-empt my lines and bring me along seamlessly.'

Maddie and Paul had completed rehearsals for both plays in *Blue Comedy* by April 1970 and a strong friendship had developed. They were both morally self-regulating personalities and could feel a mutuality of values, and there was no doubt that Maddie invested in Paul emotionally.

Maddie had come a long way since needing to be pushed onto the stage for her audition by Anne Rawsthorne, but confidence now took over.

> 'I have never been happier than I was in those little plays – Paul was outstanding and both plays were very funny. They ran for a few weeks and were meant to come to the West End but Donald [*Albery*] decided against it which was a great shame, and Paul was very disappointed. He had commented to me that he "didn't do it for the country air!" Paul had just had some leading parts at the Bristol Old Vic and although not a major star yet, was one of the best things that ever happened to me. He became a family friend. His acting was stunning; the discipline and the timing of his comedy was amazing – I was agape and was so thrilled to be in a wonderful play with an actor of Paul's ability. It was just another world.'

Paul Eddington's Quaker background gave him firm views about right and wrong, and he was not afraid to voice his opinions. It was through Paul that Maddie would later meet with both Alan Bennett and Jonathan Miller, who were two of her idols.

Also involved in the play was the director, Charles Marowitz, whom Maddie grew to greatly admire.[24]

'He was a bearded very nice man; a sort of Edward Lear type of character and he loved experimenting with theatre. Marowitz had his own experimental theatre called The Open Space in Tottenham Court Road (now demolished) and actors would flock to work for him. Marowitz wrote his own plays and worked with Peter Brook at the Royal Shakespeare Company, and I learnt a huge amount from his clever direction in rehearsals – don't forget, I had no formal training – every day. I was elated and on super-charged adrenaline to have the chance that others would have dreamt of – I love to work. Marowitz liked me very much and was very eccentric. At the end of one of the two plays he asked that I jump up and down on a pouffe and take off and throw my bra into the flies [flies refers to the rigging system in theatres used to lower and raise scenery, lighting and curtains] as I had to shout "let's have an orgy!" Paul was visibly shocked at the idea and quietly said to me "NO – he is just exploiting you … don't do it." It was Paul who gave me the protection I had not had on the set of *Vampire Lovers* and Marowitz respected my decision.'

Despite their enjoyment and all their hard work, Albery decided that this play would not make it to the West End, and it ended after a ten-week run – but not until Albery had taken Maddie to tea at the Dorchester and shown her some obvious but unexpected affection.[25] Albery had been married in 1934 to Rubina Macgilchrist, and then in 1946 to Cicely Boys; he would marry for a third time to Nobuko Morris in 1974, and it seems possible that Maddie may have been in the running in 1970 before Nobuko came on the scene.

The closeness of Maddie's relationship with Paul was underlined when, only weeks later, she would paradoxically play Paul's daughter in an episode of a television series called *Hine* about gun running, produced by Wilfred Greatorix. Paul and Maddie would remain close friends for the rest of his life; Paul would often drop by the house in Kew or into her father Bob's new art shop in Richmond. Maddie remembers precisely when she last met Paul Eddington – it was in 1992, when he was invited to Bob's 70th birthday party. It was a jolly occasion, but to Maddie, Paul looked quite ill. He eventually just stopped coming to visit, and passed away three years later in 1995.

'Paul died of cancer in 1995, aged only 68. I recently learnt, while on a visit to the tiny Quaker church in Sudbury, Suffolk, that the dying man used to pray alone on a Sunday. He would enter and leave in silence. Paul will never be forgotten. Immortalised on our television screens, he will outlive us all.' (from Maddie's tribute in *The Oldie*, March 2025)

## *His and Hers* with Tim Brooke-Taylor, Spring 1970

Despite not getting picked up for a run in the West End, *Blue Comedy* had done Maddie a lot of good. Not only had she made some new and lasting friendships, but she had also worked under the direction of a talented director in Charles Marowitz, honing her stagecraft and timing so that she felt far more comfortable with her own abilities, although the ten-week run of shows had been pretty exhausting as well as exhilarating. Improving her skills and confidence was not all that *Blue Comedy* did for Maddie. Sitting in the audience during one evening performance was a lady named Maureen Riscoe.[26] At one time, Maureen had harboured a desire to be a film actress herself, and even appeared in two films in the 1940s before moving into casting. She was currently on the lookout for actors for a new series that was being planned by Yorkshire Television for early evening pre-watershed family viewing. Maureen must have been pretty sure she had seen who she wanted to play opposite another young and upcoming actor named Tim Brooke-Taylor, because after the show she contacted Maddie and offered her the part without the need to audition.[27]

Maddie's face was becoming even more well known by British television audiences, and she would star in the first six of the twenty episodes of *His and Hers*. The central concept of male/female role reversal – where the newly liberated City accountant wife, played by Sue Lloyd, went out to work while the freelance writer house-husband, portrayed by Ronald Lewis, got a shot at housework – was a novel one, redolent of the changing values and social concepts that came with that decade. In a pairing that echoes *The Good Life* of a few years later, Maddie and Tim Brooke-Taylor played the traditional couple – the Burgesses – stuck in their predestined roles, displaying confusion and scoffing at their neighbours' role reversal:

> 'I remember that the rehearsals prior to filming on set were held in St Paul's Church Hall in Hammersmith - where I ate cheesecake almost every day until I was almost sick - and the sessions lasted all day. Tim BT was as lovely as you expect him to be - a really soft, gentle and funny man. Sue Lloyd was so gentle and calm and striking as well. Sue was very refined and had been at ballet school before moving into theatre I think, and told me she had once danced as part of Lionel Blair's group of dancers. She'd

> already played opposite Michael Caine in *The Ipcress File* and been in a lot of 1960s TV series … I loved her very much.'[28]

Someone else whom Maddie loved very much was her cat, Tigger.

> 'Tigger was my beautiful semi-Persian black cat with long black fur. Tigger had been my companion for years and had never gone further than our front wall on the main Mortlake Road – I loved him to pieces. I came home from rehearsing an episode of His and Hers to find he was gone – it destroyed me – it was like losing a lover and I have never got over it. My dad had obviously found him unwell and out of kindness took him away to be put down. We never spoke about it again but I wept my way through rehearsals all the next day. As an only child, which isn't always great, you can come to rely on certain things and I sometimes think that, to me, Tigger was in some ways the little brother I always wanted but never had.'

Always present at rehearsals for *His and Hers* was Welshman Ronald Lewis, who was perhaps a strange pick for a role in a comedy such as this.[29] Although a well-known face on film, Lewis had been through a chequered career. He had starred in numerous films during the 1950s and 1960s, and *Variety* once wrote: 'he [Lewis] scores as the native male charmer, using his handsome mien, flashing teeth and an attractive broken accent to spout his oddly-constructed sentences.'[30]

The potential that Lewis clearly had to become a truly famous star was never realized, partly due to his dependency on alcohol, which had led to various brushes with the police and pushed him towards television and away from film roles. Maddie recalls being somewhat perplexed by Lewis.

> '[*He had*] a sort of dark shadowy sense. He was quiet, handsome and very professional with a lovely smile, very easy to be with and to laugh, but there was also something of the storm clouds hanging over him which I could not quite understand.'

Indeed, a tortuous future lay ahead for Lewis, including bankruptcy and alcoholism, and this handsome, funny and talented actor eventually took his own life in 1982.

After recordings were complete, the first episode aired on Tuesday, 23 June 1970 at 8.30 pm on ITV. Although Maddie felt then that her part was vapid and underdeveloped, she still thoroughly enjoyed her time with this team of actors. Her role was later dropped, along with that of Tim Brooke-Taylor, and there would only be one more series filmed.

In the summer of 1970, something of an epiphany occurred for Maddie – not in a religious sense, but in the realization that her natural voice, as far as acting was concerned, was terrible. The first clue that there might be a problem came with *The Vampire Lovers,* where viewing audiences over the years may not have realized that her speaking parts had been dubbed.

> 'By mid-1970 I was changed. I was becoming not only more mature but also a better actor, and it was about this time that I received a telephone call asking if I would like to go to dinner with Dudley Moore's agent. We had met in the auditions for *Play It Again, Sam* and he had never forgotten me. During dinner, and after a drink or five, he really let his guard down and asked why I used such a squeaky high-pitched voice – as if I was putting it on. He sort of scolded me and told me I needed to stop it if I was going to get anywhere. This really upset me – but he was quite right and no-one had ever told me as straight as that before.'

Bruised by that encounter, Maddie decided she must try to deal with this by using the remaining weeks and months of 1970 to enrol in acting classes. So many of her fellow actors had studied at RADA that Maddie felt it was time she accumulated some professional training of her own. Life had not allowed Maddie the opportunity to go to drama school, and she recognized that this was important. To her credit, it is worth reminding ourselves how far the young Maddie Smith had come in such a short space of time – it had only been just over five years previously that she had turned up to work straight from school at Biba, aged just 16. Since then she had gone from a famous model working all over the UK and Europe, on to numerous television shows and already four films, and all this with no formal training of any kind. Maddie recalls loving her time learning the basics of acting.

> 'I enrolled into acting classes at the City Lit in Holborn, which was one of the largest adult education centres in the city. My Saturdays became focussed every week on a three-hour session led by tutors from RADA, who were amazing, and I studied acting along with voice work and improvisation. I absolutely adored it. Sure enough, they said my voice was far too high and, over time, the tone came down. One of the teachers once

> asked why I did not enrol full-time at RADA, and I wished then and always have done that I could have had the courage to try, but I still did not have the confidence then and probably would not have now, to try for a full-time place at RADA for fear of rejection. I admit to being quite a conundrum – I come across as very confident but underneath I have always been incredibly shy and insecure.'

It was while Maddie was studying at City Lit (formerly known as the City Literary Institute, founded in 1918) that she met a young man named Rowan Dore. They were in classes together, and Rowan was 'lusting' to become an actor.[31]

> 'Rowan relished every session just as I did. I really enjoyed meeting him each week and we used to go off for lunch in the park and a drink in the evenings. It was just a lovely innocent time.'

Not for the first time, Maddie's narrow emotional radar had not picked up how her charm, outgoing personality and amazing beauty had claimed yet another victim. Rowan had hoped for and harboured a desire for a relationship with Maddie that never seemed to blossom.

> 'One day a parcel arrived at home and I opened it to find a record in there – it was the very romantic *Where Do You Go To My Lovely* by Peter Sarstedt, which had been number 1 in the charts a couple of years before. Along with the record, there was a letter from Rowan where I realized that he had fancied me from the moment we had first met – but now felt somehow jilted. I really had had no idea and missed any romantic signs completely. I have never forgotten it ... so very sad how these things can happen quite accidentally. I heard many years later that Rowan had become a very popular and talented journalist and then sadly succumbed to depression. But I still have very fond memories of those sunny days in 1970 with the kind and sweet Rowan.'

As happened to so many creative people whom Maddie met on her journey through life, the well-liked and even adored Rowan Dore would one day tragically commit suicide at his seaside home in East Sussex. The news then, and still today, caused a shockwave that has never quite subsided for Maddie.

### *The Adventures of Don Quick*, December 1970

One could be forgiven for thinking that 1970 was the busiest year of Maddie's professional life, but this would be to miss the essential point of Maddie's character – she likes to be busy and always has done, so 1970 was not exceptional. Thriving on being busy seven days a week – there is no day of rest in the Smith household, even with a strict Catholic upbringing – has been the hallmark of her life, and 1970 was no different. When yet another small role appeared, naturally she said 'yes'.

The fact that the 1960s and 1970s were halcyon days for a small number of very beautiful and ambitious models-cum-actresses is underlined by a really vibrant black and white group photograph of Maddie with Vicki Woolf, Anouska Hempel, Liz Bamber, Gay Soper and Anna Brett. All six girls were asked to play roles in a short six-part spoof space series, *The Adventures of Don Quick*, starring the very well-regarded Ian Hendry and Ronald Lacey. Each episode was designed to be fifty minutes in length and had a satirical science-fiction base within which Hendry and Lacey could work to right wrongs across the galaxy in their 30ft-long spaceship model that had been built in the studio. More recently Maddie described Ian Hendry as 'wonderful, sad only because he was an alcoholic. But a wonderful actor and a shy, kind, considerate and modest man.'

Broadcast between October and December 1970, Maddie, who played the part of Leonie, and the girls featured in episode four, entitled 'The Love Reflector', where a distant planet was populated only by women – who, quite by chance, also happened to be beautiful. Sadly, or perhaps not, only one episode of the series survives on YouTube, and it is not this one. Clearly, this world was not able to comprehend quite what was going on, and *Don Quick* was destined for a far higher calling in a distant galaxy far, far away – some might say as far away as possible. But we are left with a wonderful snapshot of the inhabitants of the planet in episode four, all of whom were making their way through this galaxy as best they could.

## *Doctor at Large*, January 1971

Perhaps the most fun in 1971 came in the form of a new series which would leave a lasting impression on Maddie. For those reading this book who were not born in 1971 – and for those, like me, trying to remember what 1971 was all about – it may be worthwhile to look back and refresh our memories. It was the year when all the following happened:

- The Aswan Dam was opened in Egypt.
- Idi Amin led a revolt and proclaimed himself leader of Uganda.
- The South Tower of the World Trade Centre was opened in New York and proclaimed the world's tallest building
- The very first Mr Men book was published, *Mr Tickle*.
- MPs in the UK parliament voted by 356 to 244 to join the EEC; how time flies now we are out again.
- Those of us at school had to start using new shiny coins to pay for our sweets and lunches as decimal currency launched on 15 February 1971.
- The viewing public tuned in to learn all about the Romans as a brand-new comedy series – risqué and outrageous by the standards of the time – began: *Up Pompeii!*, starring Frankie Howerd, became the talk of the British press.
- Hot pants arrived in late 1971, a fashion that only lasted until the summer of 1972.
- A national survey revealed that 90 per cent of UK households now owned a television set, and the growing power of TV continued to alarm filmmakers, although that did not stop the 007 series releasing *Diamonds Are Forever* in December 1971 (we may recall Sean Connery golfing prior to starting filming in Scotland and offering to run Maddie a bath).[32]
- Mark Bolan and T-Rex hit the top of the charts with *Hot Love* and *Get It On*.
- British Leyland launched the Morris Marina, designed to save Leyland from closure.
- The BBC unveiled their latest comedy gamble, *The Two Ronnies*, which made its debut in April 1971.

1971 was also three years after Maddie had attended the wedding reception of Roman Polanski and Sharon Tate with Donald Cammell, and two years after Sharon Tate had been so tragically murdered. Charles Manson received the death sentence in the USA, although he would never be executed and would spend fifty years in prison.

We will return shortly to two of these events of 1971, but in early January of that year Maddie began rehearsing what, for her, was one of the most enjoyable experiences of her professional life – becoming a part of the television show *Doctor at Large*. The second series was designed as a follow-up to the very popular black and white series of *Doctor at Large* which had aired in 1969, and would be the second in a total of seven series based on the 'Doctor' books written by Richard Gordon.[33] As ever, it was Joan Gray who brought about an audition for Maddie, this time with London Weekend Television director David Askey.[34] Askey had already directed the first in the 'Doctor' series, so he knew the comic tenor of the books and the sort of actors he needed to characterize for this next series, where a group of newly qualified doctors embark upon the next phase of their careers at St Swithin's Hospital, where their testosterone-filled antics centre on a bevy of similarly newly qualified nurses. The handbrakes on their amorous adventures are applied by the excellently cast Ernest Clark as Professor Geoffrey Loftus and the steadfast anchor that was Arthur Lowe as Dr Maxwell – a local GP. The part that Maddie auditioned for was that of Dr Maxwell's innocent and beguiling daughter, Sue.[35]

> 'My acting was developing well now and what I felt was my arrested development during my teens had gone – the RADA course gave me the confidence I had lacked to reach out and take on more demanding roles. I think it was this that impressed the lovely David Askey because he offered me the part really quickly and I was thrilled.'

During rehearsals, Maddie found herself meeting a whole host of gifted and rising comedy stars. The group of young doctors was a perfect springboard for cheeky chappies such as Robin Nedwell, George Layton and Richard O'Sullivan, all of whom were on the cusp of successful and regular TV appearances that would be launched by *Doctor at Large*.[36] However, the main star of the show was to be Guildford-born Barry Evans. Barry had the looks of a film star and had won a John Gielgud Scholarship to study at the Central School of Speech and Drama.[37] Seen as 'a bright and exciting new actor' by the *Sunday Telegraph*, by 1979 Barry had a string of National Theatre plays under his belt, along with a handful of films. But it was playing Dr Michael Upton in the first series of *Doctor in the House* that made his national popularity sky-rocket. The sparky comedy repartee between Evans and his team of aspiring stars was brilliant, quick-witted and sharp-paced. Scripts provided by Graeme Garden and Bill Oddie – later of *The Goodies* fame – as well as John Cleese meant that each episode was bursting with innuendo and colour. However, a small insight into the troubles that would hit Barry Evans later in his career were evident to Maddie when she arrived, bounding up several flights of stairs, full of energy and excitement, to the first day of rehearsals at Stonebridge Park, Brent, north London, in early February 1971.

> 'Like my Dad, I was and still am terribly claustrophobic, so I took the stairs up three flights and zoomed up, hardly able to control my excitement, when, at the top of the stairs, I instantly recognized Barry Evans with his distinctive "Mod" haircut and look. Rather than a happy, smiling greeting which I was expecting he said "Oh my goodness, look how happy you are, well that won't last long." It was quite a depressing comment for my first morning and I have to admit to feeling a little deflated.'

Evans had a dark sense of humour that affected Maddie deeply. It is a truism that comedy and depression are partners and any comedian will tell you that they are on the edge of both for most of their lives. Sadly, the latter can often become the dominant partner, and so it would be, and possibly already was, with Barry Evans. Later, Barry would describe the rehearsals and filming for *Doctor at Large* as the happiest days of his life. He turned down offers to star in a further two series in order to branch out into films, but these never fulfilled their promise and TV work dried up. In 1977, Evans would write in a news article entitled 'Back to Stardom via the Dole Queue' how he ended up on state benefits to survive.[38] Tragically, after a few years trying to recover his early promise, Evans was found dead in 1997 from unknown causes, but with a mortal injury to his head.

Such events, however, were far in the future, and in the spring of 1971, rehearsals for *Doctor at Large* were great fun for everyone concerned. With so many quick-witted comedy actors in one place, it was bound to be laughs each and every day.

Maddie also worked closely with Arthur Lowe, whom she describes as 'a wonderfully kind and clever man'.[39] Lowe, an honourable soul of the old school, expertly guided Maddie through their scenes. The relationship between them, a careful and wise father overseeing his vulnerable and beautiful daughter, was reminiscent of her own relationship with father Bob. They both took to it seamlessly.

> 'I absolutely worshipped Arthur Lowe. His comedic timing was genius and everyone on set revered his calm presence and worldly sense of humour – he was a very clever and humble man and had already completed four series of the hugely popular *Dad's Army*, which had begun in 1968, before starting on *Doctor at Large*. I loved filming the five episodes we were in. Sometimes, after filming, Arthur and I would leave at the same time and head for the train station – a grotty place – and, on the way, we passed a scrap yard. We used to sit and wait for our trains watching the cars get lifted up on a crane and dropped into the crushing machine. I wonder even now what he was thinking, as it was a sort of metaphor for the transience of our lives – one minute in the spotlight, all polished and loved, and the next cast away for a new model and then crushed. Arthur would then take his train to Maida Vale, where he lived, and I went the other way to Kew.'

Part Three

# 1970–1972, It was all Just Amazing

## Chapter 6

# 1971: *The Two Ronnies*, Richard Harris and What Might Have Been

*'The toilets at a local police station have been stolen. Police say they have nothing to go on.'*
Ronnie Barker

### *The Two Ronnies* – What a Fine Pair – April 1971

It was a measure of the national fame and popularity that Maddie was enjoying that, during the rehearsal period for *Doctor at Large*, another invitation to attend an audition came along, and this time it was for the BBC. Maddie had recently auditioned for Hughie Green and the independent TV company Paradine Productions, which had been founded by later TV personality Sir David Frost while he was still at Cambridge University. It was Frost who saw Maddie, picked up the telephone and told Ronnie Barker to meet her in case he had a suitable part for her.

Both Barker and Ronnie Corbett had been working away in small parts here and there during the 1960s. They had first met in 1963 at the Buckstone Club in London, where Corbett was working as a waiter in between acting jobs. The pair, having been spotted by Bill Cotton, Head of Light Entertainment for the BBC, were offered a job to write their own comedy series; they both saw this as their big break and were not about to let it go.[1] So it was that when Maddie first met Ronnie Barker in her audition at the top of the BBC 'doughnut' in Wood Lane, west London, where most of the BBC offices and studios were located, it was on the recommendation of David Frost.

'I remember meeting Ronnie Barker and immediately being struck by his deep eyes. He was a very cautious and thoughtful type, not a conversationalist at all, and he had the low setting sun – typical for an early spring late afternoon – right behind him so I could hardly see what was going on! I was distracted by its beauty and the majesty of the setting. Not everyone loved those buildings, but I loved this monstrosity with a passion.

> 'With the sun almost blinding me, it reminded me of Charles Laughton's famous "monocle scene" in *Witness for the Prosecution*. Ronnie stared at me the whole time and never gave away what he was thinking. Along with Ronnie were the director Terry Hughes and the producer James Gilbert, who thankfully asked most of the questions. I soon heard that I had been offered the part of Henrietta in their mini-series 'Hampton Wick', which was the first of their very famous short stories that used to have ten minutes in each episode.'[2]

It had been James Gilbert who really brought *The Two Ronnies* together.[3] Gilbert had produced *The Frost Report* and also seen Maddie at audition and thought she would be perfect as the well-endowed but innocent governess, Henrietta, playing opposite Barker as a lecherous old baronet called Sir Geoffrey, with Corbett as his more feminine son, Edward, all set in high Victorian society.[4] 'Hampton Wick' would fit in well with the general pattern of the shows, which, according to the *Daily Telegraph*, had 'quick-fire verbal gags, double meanings and a cavalcade of naïve caricatures of British life: bumbling colonels, half-witted yokels and bosomy barmaids'.[5]

The concept behind *The Two Ronnies* was that two independent comedians came together to make a series – they were not a double-act, nor did they ever want to be seen as such, and they each continued with their own work outside of filming the show. This first series was very experimental, the two men honing their writing and acting skills as a pair who bounced off each other so well. The show featured a mosaic of music, dancing and monologues by them both – Corbett in his famous old armchair and Barker as some disgruntled civil servant or other – all surrounded by sketches built around Spoonerisms, puns, homophones and similar linguistic devices, the whole lot brilliantly written by a team of famous and talented writers. One such writer was the unknown Gerald Wiley, the pseudonym used by Ronnie Barker himself. Barker would add the work of 'Wiley' into the sifting process for sketches, as he wanted to be judged on his own merits rather than receive preferential treatment. On one occasion he even rejected his own work, saying out loud to the production team: 'Wiley has really let us down here!'

Both Corbett and Barker set themselves and everyone else the highest expectations in every part of the production processes, Barker especially prominent in directing many scenes, those with Maddie coming under special scrutiny. Playing the part of the sex-starved aristocrat Sir Geoffrey,

Barker drools over Maddie and her ample bosom, more evident now thanks to the dedication of her Kew dairy. Maddie had also begun to develop a more obvious presence, even though her still naïve innocence was what Barker was most looking for in her role.

> 'Henrietta had two jobs – the first was to record a monologue as if from a diary which was played in the background on each of the ten episodes of Hampton Wick. The second was that, as my character, dim Henrietta, I was a device to provide the foil and butt of all their jokes.'[6]

This account, taken from Maddie's own piece in the November 2023 edition of *The Oldie*, captures succinctly how Barker saw Maddie. He would ensure that her role was perfectly performed.

> 'Ronnie Barker had me practise walking up and down with a completely expressionless face. He directed my entire part and nearly all of the rest of the scenes. It may have been comedy but he was deadly serious. I had already learnt the art of simplicity in acting from a master, Arthur Lowe. He knew the vital importance in comedy of never reacting to a joke or the humour in a scene in which you are participating.'[7]

Maddie remembered that Barker had an almost obsession with the rounded female form.

> 'Ronnie Barker loved elderly, female wobbly bits. The more ancient the better. He collected hundreds – possibly thousands – of postcards and prints of Edwardian ladies in all stages of undress. They must have flowed in his direction from dealers and fairs in Ronnie's private life as the proud owner of a Cotswolds antiques shop. The most prominent features were their bosoms, encased in frills and lace. Their heavily rouged faces smiled from every page. Ron B even published a number of lavishly illustrated bedside books filled with delectable bonbons.'[8]

Maddie recalls that, due to the scheduling which required the first season of the show to open on the BBC in April 1971, all the outside filming was done in the freezing cold of that year.

> 'The main location for Hampton Wick was Doddington Park near Bath and we filmed in all weathers, and often my hands were blue with cold. On one occasion when my little make-up lady and I were both freezing in our little trailer, she could not get my over-large

eyelashes to stick as my eyes were running with water so much from the cold air outside. That wasn't the only thing I remember. As we were on location I had accommodation in a small room near some main traffic lights in the town – with a Pelican Crossing, and the "beep beep beep" of the flashing amber lights kept me awake all night.'

Ronnie Barker was an intense person, and a heavy smoker to boot. Indeed, he would soon be told to quit smoking for the sake of his health, as the cold weather filming outside in Bath gave him a chest infection and bronchitis. In their taxi which took Ronnie and Maddie to the recording studios, where she would record her dialogue, Maddie recalled his deep, thoughtful expression. They hardly spoke – his mind was always elsewhere, except when he was on stage or in front of an audience. He was a deeply private man with a job that exposed him to millions. The paradox of the comedian who could act in front of a live studio audience and deliver saucy lines such as 'Please sit down and take the weight off your chest' or 'Would both of you like to come here?', with the silent and stony-faced man in the taxi with her, could not be more obvious.

On one occasion, Maddie found it hard to do up her bodice as tightly as was required.

'One night we recorded the first show of the series in front of a live studio audience at the BBC studios in White City near Shepherd's Bush. One of my tightly corseted "treasures" as they were known became unbound and slipped out of its bodice moorings. It was a long scene. Much dialogue ensued between the two rascals [*Barker and Corbett*], with the usual lack of reaction from me. I was sandwiched between them, in their heavy disguises of Bill Sikes and the Artful Dodger, in a scene only loosely based on *Oliver Twist*. The unfortunate, accidentally released "treasure" is there on the recording for all to see. I feared for my life if I had stopped the take – and I don't honestly believe the Boys would have forgiven me.'[9]

Ronnie Corbett was the antithesis of Ronnie Barker. Petite, sporty, lively and bright, he wore his heart on his sleeve and was easy to chat to, far more light-hearted than the introverted Barker. This is what made the pairing so unique; opposites, as they say, attract.

First broadcast in April 1971, work on this first series of *The Two Ronnies* continued right through until June that year and gave Maddie a wonderful and unique insight into comedy genius. After a week of rehearsing for a live recording, both Corbett and Barker were word-perfect, whereas Maddie still struggled with learning just her few lines. Corbett was, according to Maddie, an 'impossible task-master to himself, striving almost for the unachievable in his constant fight for perfection. His slight frame contained the heart of a meticulous man.'[10]

## April and May 1971: Richard Harris and what might have been ...

Maddie could often be found at either Elstree or Pinewood studios. Both studio lots were huge and growing, and were a maelstrom of activity, business deals, networking and gossip. They were also male-dominated and sexist, where it was *de rigueur* for young actresses to have their backsides patted for good work, but many other places patted too for no reason at all. Beneath the glamour and the artistry, in the shadows – hidden from the money, jets and reputations – was a far more sinister and seedy aspect to the film industry, one that had to be understood and, where possible, contained. This had always been the case, since the earliest days of the silent moves, but it was certainly a prevalent and predatory feature of the 1960s and 1970s.

It was often in and around the many cafes and tea shops that producers and directors discussed new projects, and where old acquaintances were renewed and new relationships formed. The atmosphere of vitality and creativity was electric, the air charged with potential. These were also the places where actors and anonymous extras mixed – some weary of the business after a long career, others in the prime of their fame and popularity, and others, like Maddie, just loving every second and trying to get a break.

It was on one of these exciting and heady days in the spring of 1971 that Maddie was approached to meet a genuine star. While Maddie describes her own small star as being 'in the ascendant', that of Richard Harris was burning brightly in the night sky overhead.[11]

> 'The occasional big star would procure girls via their agents or management. Producers would be more direct and could make life unbearable for an actress unless she played footsie. But force was rare and most ingenues knew that complying could lead to fame and fortune - if you were very lucky and had a degree of talent and looks.'[12]

So it was that Richard Harris had noticed Maddie somewhere, and his management had contacted her to ask if she would like to join him for dinner. Answering in the affirmative, one evening a beautiful Rolls Royce drew up outside her parents' home in Kew. Harris' Irish charm had ensured that a bouquet of flowers was waiting for her on the seat. It was then off to the Savoy Hotel in Piccadilly to meet Harris, who had not booked a dining table – he lived there in his own apartment, eschewing his mansion in Melbury Road in Kensington. Such were the rewards of success in the film industry.

> 'He emerged from his hotel room wearing caramel leather. A long coat that made him look godlike. He was a very handsome man.'

By 1971, Richard Harris was already an international star. Harris' role as one of the mutinous sailors in *Mutiny on The Bounty*, playing opposite Marlon Brando and Trevor Howard, marked him out as a true rising star. He became an Academy Award nominee for his starring role in the film *This Sporting Life* in 1963. Harris went on to receive wide acclaim, and a Golden Globe, for his role as King Arthur in the 1967 film *Camelot*, based on the Lerner and Loewe musical. His two most recent films in 1970 had also been box office successes, with the western *A Man Called Horse* and the magnificent historical drama *Cromwell*, in which he took the leading role of Oliver Cromwell opposite Sir Alec Guinness as King Charles I. But with stardom came demons. Harris loved his alcohol and his mercurial emotional balance was susceptible to the point of memory loss – he had once left a £10,000 [£145,000 when adjusted for inflation] Rolls-Royce in a multi-storey car park and totally forgotten he owned it for 25 years; his accountant later confirmed it had been costing $400 a month with a final bill of $92,000 (£75,000).

In the spring of 1971, Harris was working on a BBC television adaptation of Paul Gallico's novel *The Snow Goose*. It was perhaps in his mind that he was growing older and needed a younger vision of beauty in his life to rouse his Irish emotions. A moving and deep tale riddled with metaphors for our own lives, *The Snow Goose* tells the story of a reclusive lighthouse keeper and his relationship with a young girl, played by Jenny Agutter, and their mutual affection for an injured snow goose. Set against the backdrop of the opening year of the Second World War, there are moments of deep joy intertwined with tragedy. Harris won a second Golden Globe for Best Movie made for Television, and was nominated for both an Emmy and a BAFTA.

## *The Snow Goose* – was this a metaphor for the relationship between Harris and Maddie?

How Harris had the time, at the height of his career, to notice Maddie we will never know, but the attraction was enough for him to spend a lot of emotional energy on their friendship. Maddie recalls that Harris treated her with 'the utmost kindness and respect', even taking time out of his hectic schedule to be with her family. Was this an indication that the 41-year-old Harris was simply smitten with the nearly 21-year-old Maddie, that he saw her as a muse or that he saw something perhaps more permanent? Or perhaps it was working on *The Snow Goose* that tripped him up? There is more than a passing resemblance of the relationship between Philip Rhayader, the lighthouse keeper, and the young girl Fritha in *The Snow Goose* in Harris' relationship with Maddie Smith. Rhayader is a recluse, and Harris was known to be an isolated figure emotionally. In later life, he would say he had 'no friends in the business'.[13] Harris went further when he spoke to a reporter from the *Daily Mirror* and said he did not like other actors: 'I don't go to their clubs, don't go to their hangouts and don't mix at all.' He would add: 'I am part of the business, but I am apart from it.'[14]

Reaching out to Maddie was thus not a case of an older man lusting after a beautiful and sought-after actress; it was much deeper than that. For Harris to want a woman in his life was a rare thing, and the carefree nature of his visits to the family home in Kew resemble those of a man desperate for normality.

More worryingly for a twenty-something actress who had seen so little of the world, Harris' mercurial Irish heart was always at war – either with himself or with others. This was part of what gave him such an emotional and tormented impact on screen – along with an addiction to drink. His strong character, further fuelled by alcohol, made for a formidable personality that would be overpowering for anyone timid, vulnerable or inherently shy. Harris' notoriety for raising hell in pubs in drinking sessions with Oliver Reed, Peter O'Toole and Richard Burton propelled his career rather than blunted it, but it came at a cost of two marriages that ended in divorce and a string of insulting spats on set with the egos of his fellow actors. This brooding sense of unrest and resentment shows itself in *The Snow Goose*, but as the titular bird is nursed back to health, so the disabled, angry and tortured Rhayader recognizes the innocence, beauty and naivety of Fritha. No doubt this was mirrored in how Harris saw Maddie, and just as the relationship blossomed in the film, so the deeply romantic Harris likely saw his friendship with Maddie blossoming in the same way. In fact, Harris wanted *The Snow Goose* to become his reality. The fact that Irishman Harris and Maddie's Irish father, Bob, hit it off so well illustrates the lengths to which he was prepared to go to really embed himself in her life, and how happy she made him.

> 'My father, of Scottish and Irish descent, was completely intoxicated by him. They chatted together about Irish poets and music, as they stood together in the garden. Then Richard leapt onto my bicycle and tore up the lawn. He was on fire. I adored him but had no idea where we would go from here in this extraordinary relationship. I had remarkably little to say for myself and genuinely wondered what this fascinating and complex man would see in me.'

Richard Harris arrived in Bob's life at what was a high point for Maddie's father.

> 'My dad could be an enormously social person when he wanted to be – in fact he was full of charm and magnetism, and people were easily drawn to him. I can recall that he was hardly ever home at one time in his life as he was always out at events and get-togethers, meetings and groups. There were also numerous evenings where, out of the blue and with no warning for Mum, the house would be filled with loud music and laughter as Bob had brought back some of his pals to listen to music of all sorts, and he played it as loud as he could through some huge speakers that nearly lifted the house off its foundations. This was the Bob that Richard Harris met, so no wonder they bonded so well and positively.'

The great freedom that Harris felt when he was with Maddie and her family was a release from the constant focus of photographers, journalists and avaricious film producers. For him, it was something of a return to his childhood. Perhaps being with the innocence of Maddie brought Harris breathing space away from the world – a world that he and others like him, such as his great friend Peter O'Toole, did not really like. If only it could have lasted forever.

In May 1971, Harris, in an echo of his deep and constrained emotional roots in Ireland, wrote a poem to Maddie, one of a number that he sent to her. In the depths of his personal expression, he tries to put his feelings into words on paper, and we can try to feel his emotional state:

> 'Time flies. It flies timelessly into a page of nothingness.
>
> 'Strangers touch with touching hands touchingly. A deep meaning. Fleeting time.
>
> 'Disentangles Gentleness. Pushing fingers into memory. Nothing will remain; Only the warm, planted wildflowers of impression. A glow in winter. A love-song sung in the palm. Reflections of a distant future mirrored in today's yesterday.
>
> 'Time washes. Nothing is removed. It only dries the eyes of the fingertip tears That smears the ripe departure.'

It is the passing of time that occurs throughout this short poem for Maddie that stirs the imagination. Harris was possibly thinking of his own mortality – especially given his notorious drinking sessions and love of alcohol. But this brief friendship was to last only a matter of weeks. Harris was just too massive a personality for Maddie Smith to feel that she could cope, let alone keep up. Any conversation with Maddie regarding her fleeting time with Harris quickly moves to regret, a life-long sadness that it was she who brought it to an abrupt end.

> 'I blame myself for what happened next. Richard was filming *The Snow Goose* - the film was Paul Gallico's masterpiece.
>
> 'Richard rang me from location late at night. He was well into his cups. He invited me to come down NOW to the location and join him there. It hurts me to recount that I was terrified; I had no idea what my parents would say and - oh foolish girl - I pretended I was seeing someone else.'

When Maddie wrote a short piece for *The Oldie*, she completed her recollections on this incident by saying: 'As I write this, it is with disbelief, as though it had happened to someone else. I was later seized with dreadful guilt and regret. The fault was entirely on my side. How very different his and my lives might have been.'[15]

In further echoes of *The Snow Goose*, just as the lighthouse is destroyed by a German bomber with all Philip Rhayader's paintings inside, so Maddie destroyed their friendship; and, just as Jenny Agutter was left with only a painting that Rhayader had created, of her holding the bird in her hands, so Maddie Smith was left with Richard Harris' poems.

We cannot tell how Harris felt when he was told she was dating someone else, but Maddie would never hear from him again.

The early 'Maddie Smith look', aged 3, in 1952. (*Image copyright Madeline Smith private collection*)

Pictured with her father, Robert, on a sunny family day at home in Kew in 1953. (*Image copyright Madeline Smith private collection*)

'I loved my ponytail.' With Mummy in her new school uniform, aged 5, in 1954. (*Image copyright Madeline Smith private collection*)

By the age of 13, Robert noticed something very unique about his daughter, with her gamine or elvish look, and asked his friend and popular model photographer Lewis Morley – otherwise known as Fred – to take some pictures. Robert was right. (*Image copyright the Lewis Morley Estate*)

In this stunning photograph, also taken by Fred around 1966, it is possible to see the natural and striking beauty that would catch the eye of Barbara Hulanicki at Biba. (*Image copyright the Lewis Morley Estate*)

*'I have been so lucky to have worked with some of the most famous directors of the twentieth century, and this began when Robert Aldrich cast me in* The Killing of Sister George *in 1968. Here I am on the left, aged just 19, dressed as a nun next to the simply wonderful Beryl Reid.'*

An early 1969 photo taken of Maddie somewhere in London, with a bright green hand-made dress and knee-high white boots. *'This was taken by a random photographer who met me on the street and asked if he could take my picture.'*

*The Vampire Lovers* became a hit almost immediately in 1970, and has been a cult film ever since. Maddie is seen with Ingrid Pitt in one of their many evocative scenes together from the movie.

Maddie pictured between actresses Kate O'Mara and Pippa Steel at the launch party of *The Vampire Lovers* at the Savoy Hotel, London, in 1970. *'Pippa was a cousin of Hayley Mills, a gentle, talented actress who tragically died young at the age of 44 in 1992.'*

On the lot at Elstree Studios in 1970. Maddie had just completed filming *The Vampire Lovers* and was about to move straight on to *Mr Forbush and the Penguins* when someone on the crew decided this would make an excellent publicity shot – and it does. Maddie is pictured on the left with the *'beautiful and calm'* Pippa Steel and Janet Key.

Maddie with champagne bottle in hand, along with Pippa Steel, Janet Key and Geraldine de Sancha during a break in filming for *Mr Forbush and the Penguins* in 1970.

*Frankenstein and the Monster from Hell* would be Peter Cushing's final film as Dr Frankenstein, with the gentle giant David Prowse as the Monster. The film was shot in 1972 but this poster is from 1974 when it was released.

Maddie is pictured here with Ralph Bates in a still from *Taste the Blood of Dracula* in 1970. A very talented actor, Ralph would tragically pass away at the age of 51.

The German fashion magazine *Brigitte* adored Madeline Smith. During 1972, Maddie was constantly flying to Hamburg for model shoots, articles and commentary pieces. (*Image copyright the Lewis Morley Estate*)

An iconic Maddie Smith image that defined the booming late 1960s and 1970s, capturing the playful freedom, colour and vibrancy of 'the beautiful people' everywhere.

This previously unseen photograph shows actor Roddy McDowall, who directed Maddie when she played opposite Ava Gardner in *The Ballad of Tam-Lin* in 1970. (*Image copyright Madeline Smith private collection*)

Studio still of the famous powder-blue dress with Roger Moore on the set of *Live and Let Die*, January 1973. It was Roger Moore himself who asked for Maddie to play Agent Caruso – his first Bond girl.

Although *Play It Again, Sam* never came off for Maddie, it did not stop her seeing quite a lot of Dudley Moore during 1969. (*Image copyright Madeline Smith private collection*)

Peter Wyngarde as style icon and self-styled sex symbol Jason King. It was Wyngarde's seductive talk about microscopic algae that was supposed to steal 21-year-old Maddie's heart in their scene together in *All That Glisters*, episode nine of the early 1970s hit series *Jason King*, still available to watch on YouTube.

Sir Alec Guinness, pictured here in a promotional still for Alan Bennett's *Habeas Corpus* in 1973, would spend every performance kissing a part of Maddie's leg for a whole year.

It was purely by chance that Maddie's father, Bob, was a friend of Lewis 'Fred' Morley. A rising star in the world of photography, it was and is Morley's hectic life taking photographs for theatre companies, model agencies and film studios that ensured Maddie's unique look was captured. Morely's pictures capture the social change and artistic explosions of the time.

*'There were always charity and fun days to attend, and here I am pictured with the lovely Ed 'Stewpot' Stewart, the Radio 1 DJ. We spent some great days together in the summer of 1972.' (Image courtesy of Madeline Smith private collection)*

*'Working with the Two Ronnies was one of the highlights of my life, and here I am pictured in a publicity still as Henrietta, ready to film another episode of Ronnie Barker's Hampton Wick in 1971.'*

The famous Roman bath scene from the 1971 film *Up Pompeii*. Always up for fun, Maddie was happy to jump in to add a touch of realism to the scene. While a make-up assistant applies those last-minute touches, we can see a very happy props man testing the bath bubbles – prior to pulling out the plug and leaving Maddie stranded in the bath.

In 1972, actor and director Lionel Jeffries offered the part of Arabella to Maddie in a film version of *The Amazing Mr Blunden*. It was the perfect part for Maddie, who is pictured here with James Villiers playing the part of Bertie, her new, and supposedly wealthy, husband.

Publicity still for *Casanova '73* with Leslie Phillips. Ding Dong!

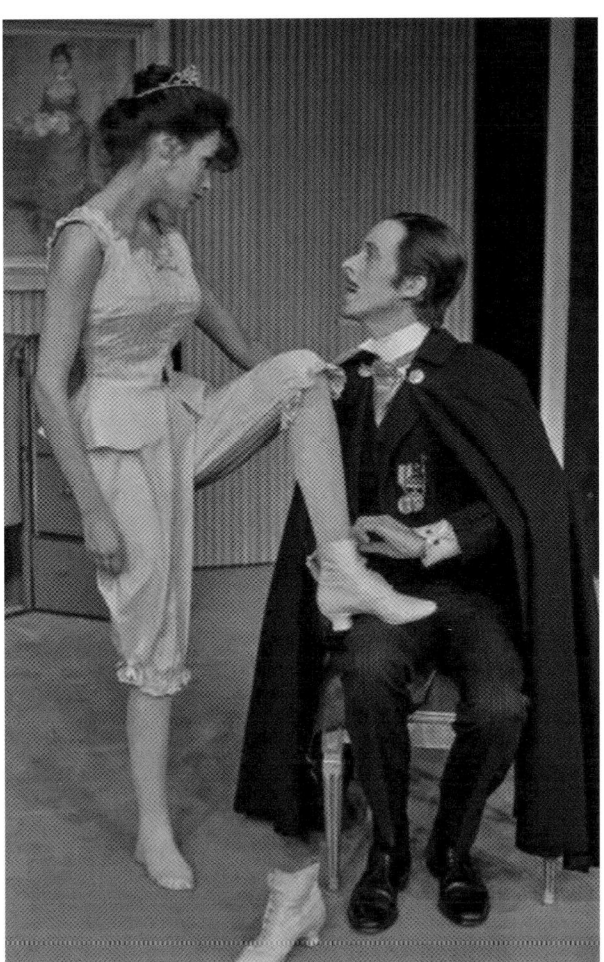

This promotional still, taken in December 1974, shows Maddie with a fine actor at her feet, the hero of *The Snob*, Peter Eyre.

Taken on location during the filming of *Clochemerle* in the summer of 1972. Maddie is pictured as Hortense Girodot, with her avaricious and manipulative parents Hyancinthe (Elspeth MacNaughton) and Monsieur Girodot (Wolfe Morris), who had fleeced the community in every way possible to become the richest family in the town.

Two of the many wonderful actresses whom Maddie worked with are pictured here in this still from the recording of Agatha Christie's *Why Didn't They Ask Evans?* in 1980. Connie Booth played Sylvia Bassington-Ffrench, while Francesca Annis was Lady Frances Derwent. Madeline enjoyed playing the villain, Moira.

Maddie pictured with her first life partner – the handsome, prolific and talented David Buck.

With Nicky Henson in 1975 during the filming of *The Bawdy Adventures of Tom Jones.*

Terry Scott was already very famous for his sitcom roles on television but wanted to try something more substantial. He is pictured here with Maddie during the Guildford run of Moliere's *The School for Wives* in May 1984.

'The Three Boys' from the 1983 Christmas special of *All Creatures Great and Small:* Peter Davison, Christopher Timothy and Robert Hardy.

Maddie is pictured in her pretty Edwardian outfit, filming with Peter Cook in 1980 on the north Norfolk coast, with the heels on her shoes puncturing the putting green – a 'what might have been' moment for her.

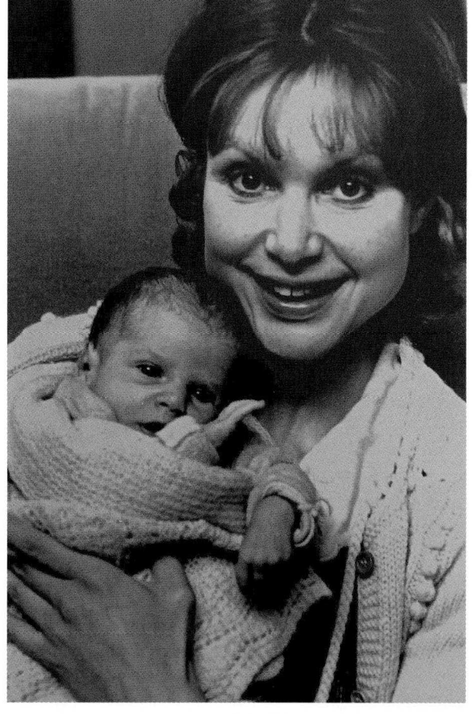

*'The happiest day of life.'* Maddie with baby Emily in 1984.

In between films and television appearances, photographers would call and, as this beautiful image from 1976 illustrates, Maddie's looks and abilities continued to move with the times.

A long-lost image from the archives showing Maddie surrounded by barbed wire as part of an advertising campaign for softer hair. (*Image copyright Madeleine Smith private collection*)

A creative LWT programme starring Ian Hendry and Ronald Lacey, *The Adventures of Don Quick*, aired in autumn 1970. Episode four was shown on 20 November, with a planet inhabited entirely by women – all British models, it seems. Maddie is seen here with (from left to right) Vicki Woolf, Anouska Hempel, Liz Bamber, Gay Soper and Anna Brett.

*'Taken in 1974 at Flat C 7, Broomfield Road – the flat I escaped to after my turbulent bust-up with Dad when he found out that I planned to give up acting in order to become a nurse. Bob said I was far too sensitive to become a nurse – and he was right.'*

The classic Madeline Smith – the face of an era.

Chapter 7

# The Wonderful Frankie Howerd in *Up Pompeii!* and 'Sloth'

'Because you are all students, so naturally, to you I'm not what you could call an academic and no way at all could you call me an intellectual. Which is why I feel so much at home here tonight.'

Frankie Howerd's opening remarks to the Oxford Union, 1990

## *Up Pompeii!*, 1970–1971

**Cassandra the Soothsayer**: Oh Woe, Woe and thrice Woe. Repent now I say or suffer the fate that befell the wicked people of Gomorrah!

**Lurcio**: Quite! Quite!

**Cassandra**: And Soddom!

**Lurcio**: I quite agree, dear – the lot of them!

It was with lines such as this that British audiences were to laugh their socks off in a new film when it was released in March 1971. The man who could collapse an audience into laughter just by saying 'nay, nay and thrice nay' (it was the way he said it) was Frankie Howerd, and this was to be his first major film – in what was hoped would be a trilogy of comedy blockbusters.

However, our story is still in August 1970, when in what was hardly a blink of the eye, Maddie left the make-believe world of Corbett and Barker – and Henrietta and Victorian bloomers – and moved on to the majesty of ancient Rome – located, as it was in those ancient days, 18 miles west of London at Pinewood Studios.

It would have been nice to film for TV in the south of France and then jet off to Italy, but as it was not BBC license payers' money being used but private capital, it was Iver Heath near Uxbridge that had to double as Imperial Rome.

The concept for the new film grew out of the initial *Up Pompeii!* TV series of 1969–1970, a collaboration between Michael Mills, Head of BBC Comedy at the time, and David Croft, screenwriter of *Dad's Army* and many other shows.[1] Then along came Ned Sherrin, the author and broadcaster, to suggest a film designed to bring large-scale audiences back into cinemas. Every film-maker was seeking the magic potion to combat the power of television, and Sherrin was given the task by Anglo-EMI to produce the film, with a budget of £200,000.[2] The idea, however, seems to have been Talbot Rothwell's, the main writer for the 'Carry On' films.[3] Sherrin saw *Up Pompeii* (the movie version somehow lost the closing exclamation mark of the TV programme) as the first of what would be a trilogy of similar titillating films starring Frankie Howerd as Lurcio, the slave who could manipulate all of Rome through his connections and mischievous activities, all served with a good dose of near-the knuckle sexual inuendo. The head of Anglo-EMI, Nat Cohen, backed the idea of this sexual romp, stating: 'I am convinced the key to recapturing large cinema audiences is a good, uproarious comedy.' There was currently no-one better at uproarious sexual comedy than Frankie Howerd – but that was in front of live audiences; the question was, could the fragile Frankie do the same on film?

It would be back to Chelsea again for Maddie's audition, this time to the home of producer Ned Sherrin, who saw her as the perfect actress for the role of Erotica – nimble, young and willing daughter of Michael Hordern (later to become Sir Michael), who would play the part of the bumbling but endearing Roman senator Ludicrous Sextus. Her brother in the film, Nausius, was played by Royce Mills. Filming began in August 1970 at Elstree Studios, which were now becoming familiar to Maddie as she began working with yet another wide range of talented and well-known figures.[4]

Hordern was a true acting great, his thoughtful gaze and forlorn face having graced many a film during the 1950s and 1960s, where a serious and 'mournful countenance' was required.[5] For Maddie, this was a new experience. Hordern, with his Shakespearean background, was a huge name, perhaps a surprising addition to a cast full of household names and British stars of television, stage and screen, but bills needed to be paid even by the most famous of actors.

> 'Michael was simply the sweetest man. He knew this was a sex romp type of film but just loved the comedy of it all, and went with it in his marvellously confused way as Frankie was telling jokes all the time – it was only when he was on camera that he looked nervous actually.'[6]

No-one could play the hangover scene in the film like Hordern. Emerging from a doorway the morning after the 'orgy had turned into an orgy', he walks through a marble hallway with the headache to end all headaches, each step echoing through the viewers' heads as much as his own. We can feel the pain and disorientation of the sort of hangover that turns anyone into a lifelong teetotaller. It is so perfectly played. Indeed, the film is worth watching for that scene alone.

However, the star of the film was nervous and superstitious. Frankie Howerd was a very anxious person, and one of Sherrin's well-founded concerns was whether the instant rapport and comedy that flowed from Frankie in front of a music hall or television studio audience would replicate on film.[7] The answer was that it did not. Howerd was full of anxieties about being captured for eternity on film and how it would be received – he was never a natural star.

> 'Frankie was of course the main star of the film but I didn't see him much on set, only here and there, though he certainly noticed me and smiled often as he rehearsed his lines. Frankie really lived up to his character's name of Lurcio, as he spent lunchtimes lurking around looking for young male company … I don't know how successful he was but he was a keen pursuer … it was either for company or sex, perhaps as a way of dealing with the stress. He was quite relaxed about his homosexuality, which was all part of his charm in an age where such things were still not talked about openly at nice dinner parties.'

Other cast members that Sherrin had placed in the film included Patrick Cargill, who would play the bored Emperor Nero.[8]

> 'Patrick was adorable and just like you saw him on television. Intelligent but aloof. I had already worked with Patrick on *Cribbins* so we knew each other well and I really felt that I was now becoming a regular performer, along with all the other well-known names of British television and film.'

The 'Carry On-esque' nature of the names of characters must have made even the established stars wince. Barbara Murray, a very familiar face in British film and television, had to cope with the role of Ammonia, mother of Maddie's character, Erotica. Barbara was a unique talent, described in an obituary as 'An enticing presence, all misty eyes and pale beauty ... Her beauty seemed to strengthen in middle age, as did the regality that placed her firmly as a lady of a certain era, but there was a delicious mischievousness in her grand voice which ensured there was always more to the characters she played than just elegance and sophistication.'[9]

It was established performers such as Barbara Murray who gave the film a degree of gravitas.[10] Like the typical Roman wife of a successful politician had to be, she was aware of her husband Ludicrus Sextus' constant indiscretions, but her own mischievous personality allowed her to play along so as not to jeopardise the family name or indeed her own position in Roman society. Barbara played this immaculately. The film may have been a romp to get British audiences back to the cinema, but it was a very well-acted romp with hidden performances of real merit – and it was possibly this that put Frankie on edge as he was surrounded by such professional actors. The film also looked good. The Roman baths used in the film had just been seen in the previous movie filmed on the set, *Julius Ceasar*, starring Sir John Gielgud; they looked quite magnificent in *Up Pompeii*, a film made on a very tight budget.

Maddie has fond memories of filming her scenes with Barbara Murray.

> 'Barbara was lovely. She very quietly got on with her part while Frankie sort of panicked and took his cues from her. In the Roman bath scene, Barbara was gently washing herself in what was meant to be a pool of asses' milk in true Cleopatra style. I think the director had expected Barbara to take off her swimming costume in order to seem naked in the water – as far down as the camera could get anyway – however, Barbara made it very clear that absolutely nothing was in fact going to be coming off. As you might expect, silly me just stood there giggling as I watched this unfold and, before I knew what was happening, the make-up department had persuaded me to join Barbara in the bath to add a touch of "realism" to the scene. I nipped away to my dressing room and returned in a large bath towel and, as carefully as I could, lowered myself into the water – God knows what it was, but it certainly was not asses' milk.
>
> 'Barbara performed her lines perfectly as Frankie sat coyly on the side of the bath and the director shouted CUT. I had been looking up to the heavens a few moments

> earlier and noticed quite a few of the lighting crew up in the gantry looking down – as you might expect in those days, there was a lot of elbow nudging and a few "oi oi's", but I just ignored it. As soon as the scene ended, however, I looked up again and even more crew members had arrived – there must have been a dozen or more and they were now armed with little cameras. I thought that they were planning to try to get a photo of me as I climbed out of the deep bath, but I was wrong – they had a better plan than that. The next thing I knew, Barbara was out of the bath, an assistant had wrapped a large towel around her bathing costume and she was off to the dressing room. I was still sitting there when I heard a loud gurgling sound and very quickly the water started to drain away, and within seconds I was sitting naked in an empty bath, to the cheers of the guys up aloft and the smirks of quite a few cameramen … the cameras clicked away as I jumped out of the bath trying to hide my modesty, to a chorus of cheers from up above – it was all harmless and great fun, but then it was a great and very funny film to be a part of.'

Naturally, a photo or two made its way to *The News of The World*, and within a few days some marvellous publicity for the new film was achieved – and a few pound notes found their way into the pockets of the lighting crew.

Other stars included the solemn Bill Fraser as Prosperous Maximus, who always opened his first day of recording, whether it was on television or film, with a bottle of champagne and a few glasses. Maddie recalls that this went down well and got the cast and crew into the right mood for what was a film of elated spirits anyway.[11] The sultry, very talented and underrated Adrienne Posta played the role of fellow slave Scrubba. Maddie remembers well the challenges that beautiful young women had in a male-dominated and sexist film industry at that time.

> 'Dear Adrienne is lovely. Friendly and very talented and certainly underrated. She was a classic case of being too beautiful. For some reason, in the 1970s especially, beauty was equated with simplicity and a lack of intelligence. The best way to get ahead was to be average looking and sombre and that seemed to give off the right waves, indicating depth of character to directors and producers. Beautiful girls were just seen as a silly playful accoutrement and it was doubly hard to be taken seriously.'[12]

*Up Pompeii* was released in 1971 to a cascade of advertising and promotion, but it fell a little short of Sherrin's hopes to flood the cinemas again, as was also the case in parts two and three of the trilogy of Howerd showcases.

'I was supposed to be in the next film, called *Up the Chasity Belt*, but I had already committed to go on tour with Patrick Macnee, but I was in the third of the three films which was called *Up the Front*. It was in this film that we had Tony Spratling, who was the amazing and famous lighting cameraman. Tony was the Director of Photography and he was brilliant. By now, I had learnt a few tricks of the trade and I would trot around the set to find him and cheekily ask him how to light me in the next shot. The more experienced and ambitious actors know how to get the best angles on their expressions and what lighting works best for a particular scene. I was ambitious too and wanted to get the best angles I could on my face, and Tony always said "yes" to me and gave me what I asked for.'

## A few more words on Frankie

Frankie Howerd and Maddie Smith would form a lasting friendship on the set of *Up Pompeii*, and a few years later they were paired together again to film some commercials for Grandee Cigars.

'Frankie hated the camera and close-ups so he would only allow himself to be shot on his own – he did not do joined up close-ups so each of our parts had to be filmed separately and then spliced together. I had to wait all day and often well into the night before he was finished, and then shoot my own parts. On one occasion, it was well past midnight before Frankie had left and we had to set up all over again for me. On one occasion, where I had to pretend to light up a cigar for Frankie, I was not taking enough notice and I set my dress alight. The flames erupted so quickly and there was quite a bit of screaming, I can tell you.'

Close-ups were not the only things that unsettled Frankie Howerd. He was also uncomfortable with the colour green and would not allow it anywhere near him.

'In one commercial, Frankie was meant to wear a green suit. It had all been especially made to measure for him but he refused point blank to wear it. The wardrobe department had to make another, this time in blue, before he would agree to filming. Frankie even had the green baize notice board in his dressing room removed or turned around as he just refused to be near anything green.

'I adored Frankie and he liked me very much. I think he trusted me and did not see me as any sort of threat. He was a one-off, hugely funny in company but on his own very gloomy and serious.'

Over ten years after *Up Pompeii*, in 1984, Maddie appeared with Frankie Howerd one more time in Bromley, Kent. They were both in *The Fly and the Fox*, a version of Ben Jonson's *Volpone* adapted by Barry Took and Alick Morrison. At the time, Maddie was in a long-term relationship and was pregnant with what would be her first and only child and playing the role of the merchant's wife. She sensed that Frankie seemed to be wearing out, being clearly unwell and not himself. The unique Frankie Howerd passed away in April 1992.

With 1970 proving to be a busy and rewarding year for Maddie, offers of roles were coming in so regularly that she was hardly at home. Her parents could only marvel at her success. Her dad was especially supportive, often giving Maddie the emotional support she needed to cope with the new world of which she was now a part. The contacts she was making ensured that this success continued, and in early 1971 she would begin perhaps her most satisfying role to date.

## *The Magnificent Seven Deadly Sins*, 1971

Throughout 1971, Maddie spent many days and weeks travelling to and from Pinewood Studios. Getting there by taxi was expensive, but she always paid for every trip herself, which possibly explains why she was constantly short of money – along with the fact that television and film fees were then so paltry unless you were the star, but that was the investment required to pursue a dream.

It was while she was having lunch in one of the cafes on site that actor Graham Stark suddenly appeared and sat down for a chat.[13] A close friend of Peter Sellers, Stark was putting together a small film based on the Seven Deadly Sins. Maddie, he said, was perfect for the part of 'Lust'. Stark had a lengthy track record of film acting appearances behind him, and was now trying his hand at direction. He was often a stand-in for Spike Milligan in *The Goon Show*, but his face is best-known to film fans from the *Pink Panther* movies, in which he played Inspector Clouseau's blank-faced, overwhelmed assistant. Stark would appear in more *Pink Panther* films than any other actor, most famously as the geriatric hotel owner whose dog was not his dog when it bit Clouseau on the leg.

Stark – who was not the first man, or woman for that matter, to think that Maddie was the epitome of lust – made the offer of the role with the caveat that there was no money in it. Instead, he said he would take some creative photo shots which Maddie could keep.

> 'Pinewood was like that in those days. There were so many productions going on around you that there were crews, producers and directors everywhere trying to catch famous faces and set up projects. It was a melting pot of creativity really, and they were always thinking about the next film when working on the current one. Graham was very nice and so gentle. I liked him a lot.'

The film was written by a range of talented comedy writers, including Graham Chapman, Barry Cryer, Ray Galton, Alan Simpson and Spike Milligan. Stark put himself down to play 'Sloth' in a section that also starred Harry Secombe, Leslie Phillips, Harry H. Corbett and Bruce Forsyth. The doleful Abraham Basalinsky – better known as Alfie Bass – was cast as 'Pride', playing opposite the fantastic Ian Carmichael as two motorists blocking each other on a road, with neither willing to give way.[14]

The 'Lust' section was written by Stark himself, who felt Maddie was the perfect actress for the part. Based on a story by the incomparable Marty Feldman, the future model, actress and socialite Anouska Hempel – whom we shall meet further on in this book – played a small part in this section, as did Bill Pertwee, famous as the ARP Warden in *Dad's Army*.[15, 16]

> 'The story was very sweet. I was meant to play a pretty girl in a red telephone box (remember those anyone?) and in the box next to me was Harry H. Corbett playing the part of Ambrose Twombly. He is dumbstruck and smiles at me through the glass, and dials the number in my box as I am waiting for a call. Pretending it's a crossed line, he manages to persuade me that he might be really sexy. He seems to know a lot about me, and I agree to meet up with him as I tell him that there is a very strange man looking at me from the telephone box next door that "looks like a monkey". The closing scene is the telephone hanging down and moving to and fro' – I loved this role but was recast into 'Sloth''.

'Sloth' at least had the advantage of having been written by Spike Milligan but Maddie was not pleased that the role in the GPO telephone box that she wanted was given to Cheryl Kennedy. Instead, Maddie now played in

Milligan's silent movie with captions about the inherent laziness of many human beings. Along with Marty Feldman, Peter Butterworth from the Carry On team and Ronnie Barker, Maddie was only there to add a moment of glamour to Cardew Robinson's inability to change beds – hardly Maddie's best moment but indicative of the need to be seen and stay current almost regardless of the part.

The film was a gentle critique of the moral vulnerability of the human condition, more a series of morality plays than an overt comedy. It had the added attraction of merging animation sequences with the live-action scenes, which was quite new, but the critical reception was mixed. Stark perhaps realized just how difficult it was to marry so many talents together.

# Chapter 8

# 1971: Working with Roger, Jason and Hugh

'My acting range has always been something between the two extremes of "raises left eyebrow" and "raises right eyebrow".'

Roger Moore on Roger Moore

Filming for *The Two Ronnies* was over and Maddie felt like she needed a break. It had been an intense period and, although stimulating, had also been draining. There is no doubt that working on *The Two Ronnies* was one of the many highlights of her career, but there was also a significant down side. Maddie harboured a deep desire to develop as an actress – especially on stage – but had found that most of her short career to date, while exciting, was drifting into the narrow confines of parts with strong sexual undertones. The apogee of this had been the most recent part of Henrietta in the 'Hampton Wick' episodes. Ronnie Barker had undoubtedly wanted someone just like Maddie to wear the French Empire style of dresses, with their low-cut chest lines and corsets tightly strung enough to make her body explode, but this was a role that again exploited Maddie's physicality at the cost of her acting ability. She was now feeling typecast and was getting to the point of having had enough. Maybe, Maddie mused, it was time to think about doing something else unless she could open up a new journey.

### *The Persuaders* and 'The Long Goodbye', 1971

The request for Maddie to attend the audition for a role in an episode of *The Persuaders* came as a surprise. Maddie had been so immersed in filming and rehearsing for working with Ronnie Corbett and Ronnie Barker, that she had forgotten that she needed to keep lining up other work – both to pay the bills but also maintain the momentum of her profile.

Robert S. Baker, the British film and television producer, created *The Saint*, which ran successfully on television between 1962 and 1969.[1] In partnership with Monty Berman, Baker developed a series based on the hugely popular series of Simon Templar short stories by Leslie Charteris. *The Saint* provided a perfect platform for Roger Moore to establish himself as the unorthodox but entitled suave establishment figure, a character type that would mark his entire career through *The Saint*, *The Persuaders* and the James Bond films – a Robin Hood figure who would also despatch the baddie if it would save lives. In total, Roger Moore would star in six series of *The Saint*. He was reportedly offered the role of James Bond more than once, but refused, given his commitments. As *The Saint* became tired, Baker breathed new life into basically the same character and brought Simon Templar into the 1970s with a new show called *The Persuaders*, which had the often-quoted strapline: 'Two worlds collide when Lord Brett Sinclair, a titled British man, and Danny Wilde, a Bronx-raised, self-made American, reluctantly join forces to right wrongs and protect the innocent.'

With an action-comedy concept, *The Persuaders* needed action-orientated and charismatic stars. After a few false starts and refusals, Roger Moore would ultimately find himself teaming up with the vibrant and charming American Tony Curtis. With an American star needed to help ease the path for the show onto network television in the USA, Rock Hudson and Glenn Ford had initially been offered the role, but it was fate that saw Curtis persuaded to become a Persuader.

Given their very different temperaments and Curtis' predilection for smoking cannabis, the relationship between the two stars would be tested across the years, but there is no doubt that they had a healthy professional and personal respect for each other. This shone through with the repartee and banter between the pair in every episode.[2] Moore had become synonymous as *The Saint*, the best role of his career so far, as not only was he in the prime of his physical life, with an almost perfect profile for any camera angle, he was also business savvy and tried to buy the rights to *The Saint* himself. So when it came to *The Persuaders*, Moore was keen to establish a strong financial interest, owning the lion's share of the production rights, while his own company, ITC, would make the series, with funding from Lew Grade and Robert S. Baker.

To garner a strong profit margin on production costs, Moore reused many of the fashionable outfits from *The Saint* – those that survived the change of decade into the Seventies. Style is style in whatever decade it is worn. Moore owned and would use the fabulous cars that the millionaires Brett Sinclair and Danny Wilde drove in the new series. These were mostly reused star vehicles from *The Saint*; again, style trumped fashion every time, with the personalized number plates changed of course. Even with these economies, Moore estimated that each episode cost around £100,000, a huge amount for the early 1970s. A substantial part of the high cost was the choice of overseas filming, which was consistently in expensive locations across Europe. Filming began, after the UK rehearsals had been completed, in the south of France in May 1970.

As they planned each episode, it was Moore who directed most of the production schedules and looked ahead for what supporting talent he needed. The cast list for *The Persuaders* was huge, including established faces such as the dependable Laurence Naismith as Judge Fulton, Denholm Elliott, Susan George, Ian Hendry, Joan Collins and Terry-Thomas. But there was also room for up-and-coming talent, and that is how Maddie came to appear on Moore's busy production schedules for ITC.[3] Across the twenty-four episodes that made up the first and only series, there were no less than eleven directors, although quite why so many were used has never been fully explained.

Maddie has never been quite sure just how she came to the attention of the makers of *The Persuaders*.

> 'The invitation to play my part in *The Persuaders* came suddenly through Joan, my agent, and without an audition. I had been seen on something or somewhere and it was so easy. There were so few of us beautiful former models now working in the film business, so it seemed like a small pool in those days. I know Sally Geeson felt the same.'

Episode thirteen would feature Maddie as Carla I, playing opposite another rising model-cum-actress named Ann Geissler – better known by her stage name Anouska Hempel (today Lady Weinberg).[4] Anouska Hempel had followed a very similar career path as Maddie when she arrived at this moment in her life, having had a small part in the horror film *Kiss of the Vampire* (1963), followed by roles in the Bond film *On Her Majesty's Secret Service* in 1969 and *Scars of Dracula* the following year. It was as if an aspiring film actress could not get noticed until they had been 'christened' by an appearance in at least one horror movie. Also appearing in the episode were

Peter Sallis and Nicola Paget, but perhaps the most notable aspect of this episode was that it was the only one of the twenty-four in the series to be directed by Moore himself. It may have been that experience that cemented Maddie in Moore's mind when, during the following year, he accepted the role of James Bond and pondered who he wanted as his very first Bond girl.

Maddie was left with a very positive impression after appearing with Moore's co-star in *The Persuaders*.

> 'I like a guy who has an air of danger about them and I adored Tony Curtis – cool guys have to have an edge and, when I first met Tony, I thought he was gorgeous. He had his own trailer for the shooting which he shared with his wife, and he once invited me in to see all the paintings that he had purchased in London – he was an avid art collector … oh my god he was handsome, clever and sexy; what a combination and very persuasive!'

In her episode of *The Persuaders*, Maddie plays one of a number of young women claiming to be the daughter of a deceased scientist who had come up with a formula for making synthetic fuel, and therefore the owner of that formula. It is up to Brett and Danny to try to work out if any of them are indeed for real, or whether the world is in fact ready for such a discovery. When Maddie rings the buzzer for Lord Brett Sinclair's luxurious apartment, there is an immediate relaxed chemistry between them, as well as a shared level of clipped Oxford English pronunciation. The eye contact between Maddie and Moore seems almost like a game of cat and mouse. Maddie's grey-blue eyes sparkle against the very 1970s soft velvet and velour blue furnishings of the apartment, and the whole opening scene between them is quite magically filmed.

The episode would air on a Friday evening, 10 December 1971, by which time Maddie was well on her way to further adventures in the following year. It would not be long before she was reunited with Roger Moore on the set of his first James Bond film.

### *Jason King*, 1971

There were two more jobs also coming Maddie's way that year. It seemed that she was never going to be short of work, which would have no doubt kept her agent, Joan Gray, very happy.

If there was one TV show that typified the new decade with its themes of liberated behaviour, die-hard misogynistic men, new dynamic fashions – with huge collars, flared trousers and heeled boots – and outrageous new 'glam' pop bands and artists such as T-Rex, ABBA and David Bowie, then it has to be *Jason King*.

The title role in this series was taken by Peter Wyngarde, whose background was, to say the very least, disputed. He was born as Cyril Louis Goldbert in either Marseilles or possibly Singapore, but that's about as much as is known about the early life of the man who was to evolve into the sex and fashion icon and talismanic actor.[5] Depending on the source you trust, he was born sometime between 1924 and 1937; even he was unable to accurately state his own age, and he changed his life and back story when he came to England in 1945, though even that date is a guess. Wyngarde claimed his father, Henry Wyngarde – who also may have been his stepfather – could have been a prestigious British diplomat, and that the father named on his birth certificate, who was a Russian merchant seaman called Henry Goldbert, was his stepfather. The fact that no Henry Wyngarde exists in any public record anywhere in the world did not stop the future *Jason King* star from claiming until the end of his life in 2018 that the elusive diplomat was his true father. The story continues through all sorts of machinations, including that Wyngarde claimed he spent two years in a Swiss sanatorium recovering from his 'wartime experiences' before studying law at Oxford, then working in a London advertising agency. If you are not confused already, which is clearly what Wyngarde hoped to do by reinventing his entire past, then it should come as no surprise that, in 1973, Wyngarde said: 'As a child it was difficult to differentiate sometimes between fact and fantasy.' No kidding!

What is true is that Cyril Goldbert changed his name to Peter Wyngarde when he arrived in the UK and appeared at the Buxton Playhouse in 1946. Clearly with a real talent and ability to assume false identities, Wyngarde is credited with appearing in *Hamlet* in London in 1951 – where Sir Alec Guinness played the lead. By the early 1960s, he had amassed quite a few small parts across films such as *The Siege of Sydney Street* with Donald Sinden (1960), and he appeared in one episode of *The Saint* in 1966.[6] In 1969, Wyngarde took a starring role in *Department S*, in which his character, Jason King, is a novelist turned super-sleuth. It was here that his moustache was first noticed, along with his amazingly coloured clothes, as he played a suave womanizer who never quite kissed the girl. Such was his appeal that the following year, producer Monty Berman offered Wyngarde a new espionage series called *Jason King*.[7]

One great asset that Wyngarde had was that his mysterious past allowed him to slip seamlessly into the role of Jason King – a smooth-talking James Bond-like character, with elements of upper-class sophistication that he may have syphoned off from Roger Moore, wrapped up in the most hypnotic fashion creations that 1970s wardrobe departments could design. Like some Regency dandy, Jason King longs to drift along with the finer things in life, dressing in ties as large as folded curtains, suits with lapels that could help him take to the air if the wind was in the wrong direction, and cravats that doubled as sheets on a cold night. Then there was his outrageous clipped accent – obviously from his days at 'Oxford'. But that was not all. Wyngarde loved to smoke heavily throughout each episode, spend vast amounts of money – no doubt from a trust fund – and drink heavily. Indeed, there was hardly a scene without a large drinks trolley nearby. It was this majestic, god-like figure that Maddie had to fawn over in episode nine of a two-part feature called 'All That Glisters' (sadly not a spelling mistake) and fight against that moustache and a suffocatingly large black hairstyle that was always notoriously perfect.

> 'I arrived on set having never met Peter before and it was straight in and on the job, where the director simply said for me to get straight on top of him with only the most minimal of rehearsal time. Luckily, we got on incredibly well straight away and he really liked me, and we kept in touch for some time after recording. I did become one of his many friends and we went out for dinner and fun many times – he was so popular and carried himself well, and loved the attention he received.'

Suave, debonair and a notorious flirt, Wyngarde loved both his on- and off-screen personae, which were in fact symmetrical. His fame was such that he was in great demand everywhere for charity gigs, store openings and business ventures. Wyngarde's promotor, Carl Gresham, was so good at his job that he promoted himself very well when he spoke about Peter in depth in his book, modestly called *The Gresh – A Lifetime in Show-Biz*.[8]

Between 1970 and 1972, Peter Wyngarde turned up for promotional events in Norway, Germany, Sweden, Cannes and, of course, Luton, where it was almost impossible for Peter's characteristic moustache to breathe for the number of screaming ladies trying to kiss it. On 10 November 1971, Peter was asked to act as chairman of a panel of judges in the Miss World contest, which was broadcast live on BBC. Compered for the tenth time by Michael Aspel, the judges included Des O'Connor, Douglas Fairbanks and our very own Maddie Smith. In retrospect, Wyngarde was not a fan of the process – it was all too practised and he wondered how you could actually tell anything about the women's personalities. But he did have a solution for the organizers: 'You'd be better taking them to bed, one by one, and judge them on sex appeal!'[9] It is heartening to learn how much time Peter and his moustache were willing to sacrifice, all in the cause of accuracy, in selecting Miss World. Quite inexplicably, his visionary ideas were not adopted!

Also notorious was that Wyngarde was difficult to direct, which may explain why in the course of the single series of twenty-six episodes, the producers used four different directors – one of whom was Roy Ward Baker, who had directed Maddie in *The Vampire Lovers* the previous year. Wyngarde was ever present and loved having the camera on every inch of his wonderful presence. Each episode contained a plethora of new faces that had to come to terms with being in the presence of 'genius'. For Maddie in her episode, this meant being seduced by the irresistibly dressed and suave King while he lectured her about microbiology, using slides under his microscope – a subject that he says he discovered 'yesterday'. As the naturally overwhelmed Maddie grapples to find any bare skin to kiss in between hair and moustache, the doorbell disrupts proceedings and saves our hero from actually having to succumb – you see, it's all about the chase. Indeed, no-one would ever capture Jason King's heart – he was just too out of reach.

> 'Underneath the terrible wig beat the heart of a very lovely saucy gentleman. We became very close friends. When I attended his funeral, I met all of his Golbdert relations – I nearly passed out, as I had no idea that Peter was Jewish, that [*Goldbert*] was his real name or how warm and welcoming they all were. Whatever his background, he had a lovely collection of people around him who loved him.'

The two episodes of 'All That Glisters' were shown on 8 and 15 December 1971, and allowed Maddie to at least have a large amount of dialogue, which was a refreshing change for her. She deals with King and his companion suitor suitably calmly as they discuss how to solve a crime from their palatial apartment in Paris – of course it had to be Paris; Peterborough would not have suited Jason King at all well.

## *The Mind of Mr J.G. Reader*, May 1971

Maddie was offered a small part in a new television series commissioned by Thames Television that was recorded early in 1971.

Based on the stories written by Edgar Wallace, this short series of six episodes was another quirky and risky undertaking trying to develop the viewing habits of the new and varied television audiences of the time – sometimes they worked, but at other times they did not. This one did not.

Filmed in black and white, which did not assist in its appeal, *The Mind of Mr J.G. Reader* was another lovely series that would be undermined by the all-important scheduling. The lead role was played by Hugh Burden, an experienced and skilled actor. Reader was a man who superficially seemed dull-witted, bureaucratic and anonymous, but underneath was a calculating mind able to detect the traits of criminal psychology, with successful results.[10] Even Scotland Yard needed to lean on 'J.G.', and Willoughby Goddard, as Reader's superior, offered a shining comic performance. Willoughby would turn up at various moments in Maddie's future, but this was the first time that they met.

Maddie played a Miss Clutterbuck in the fifth episode of the second series, called 'The Willing Victim'.

> 'We were all in on the joke, including Willoughby himself. As J.G. Reader's boss, Willoughby Goddard enjoyed the spectacle of a new secretary in each episode – it was a wonderful way of previewing and revealing new talent, and my turn came early in 1971. Willoughby was grossly overweight and had no intention of doing anything about it – he was offered many parts because of his fattened establishment characters, so why change? My character was very sweet and dressed in the loveliest Edwardian clothes, with just a touch of jewellery. I kept my back as straight as I could and played

> my reserved and genteel part well, I think. I loved it, but then I love anything in acting I suppose. Willoughby and I would work together much more in the future too.'[11]

Set in the 1920s, the costumes were certainly marvellous, to which the still photographs – which can be found online – testify, with Maddie at her most demure self. The sets too and the whole series deserved far more credit than it received. It remains another forgotten gem that can be accessed on YouTube.

## Chapter 9

# 1972: Diana Dors, Lionel Jeffries, *Clochemerle* and Peter Cushing

'And if you can get past the plummy RADA accents and the lack of nudity/blood/anything remotely frightening, you'll find a film which, while it stretches the definition of what might be called a "horror film", is certainly a delight from beginning to end (you might even get a lump in your throat, although of course you won't admit it).'

Chris Wood, British Horror Films, on *Frankenstein and the Monster from Hell*

One of the lesser-known highlights of 1971 had been an invitation for Maddie to attend a photo shoot with three very different personalities. Maddie was in her prime as a model and now very famous across the UK, so some creative spark at the *Daily Mail* came up with the idea of inviting three well-known people to try their hands at selecting different clothes for Maddie to wear that suited their personal tastes. Playwrights Galton and Simpson tried their combined hands, and sat either side of Maddie with their choices of outfits. Gerald Nabarro was a politician known for his Terry-Thomas lookalike personality, big cars and huge handlebar moustache. And alongside Gerald, who would sadly pass away the following year, was the inimitable Oliver Reed. Already a sex symbol and film star, Reed was in the process of establishing a fearsome reputation for his love of alcohol in all its varied forms. He would make no less than four films in 1971 and seemed to be everywhere. It is still possible to see one or two of his imaginative fashion choices for Maddie in photos that are available on the internet.

'Oliver was just marvellous. A cheeky, hugely charismatic presence, and trouble with a capital "T" lurked behind him all the time. I remember the photo shoot being one long chuckle from beginning to end – although I confess my memory becomes a little blurred, as Oliver had a friend or relation with him who supplied bottles of beer for what seemed like the entire day.'

Oliver was not the only 'Reed' whom Maddie would meet that year. With her wages starting to arrive in numerous little pay envelopes and cheques, Maddie had a disposable income for the first time in her life. She used to enjoy spending some – if not most – of it with saunters around the Antiquarius Market on the King's Road. Here, every stall sold the unimaginable and often unobtainable in the antiques world, but it was the small jewellery tables that always caught Maddie's eye. She had developed a love for buying beautiful and genuine Art Nouveau necklaces and bracelets for her mother, and over time she created quite a collection for Ursula. Sadly, everything would later be stolen in a number of burglaries that the Smith family suffered in Kew.

It was on one of these Saturday browsing trips that a middle-aged lady came up to talk to Maddie and asked if she would mind meeting her husband, who was at home nearby. 'Nearby' meant Chelsea, and naturally, Maddie's interest piqued and she agreed. As she arrived at the substantial Chelsea property at 213 King's Road, Maddie noticed a celebratory blue plaque on the wall announcing to visitors and passers-by that this was the home of Sir Carol Reed, the celebrated British film director. Maddie knew the name well – Reed was still perhaps the most famous of all British directors at the time, although his star had by then faded. The meeting was all very polite, and Reed was delighted to meet Maddie. His wife had been struck by Maddie's beauty, and felt she should meet her husband. Reed told Maddie that he was looking at a new project called *Angell, Pearl and Little God*, a novel by Winston Graham about the intertwined lives of Angell, a middle-aged barrister, Pearl, a beautiful girl aged 21, and Little God, who was a boxer and chauffeur. Reed felt Maddie would be ideal for the part of Pearl and promised to contact her if the film came together. In the event, Maddie never heard from Carol Reed again, but she has never forgotten the experience. It was typical of how chances for fame came and went on the ever-changing rainbow of opportunity that was the King's Road.

### *The Amazing Mr Blunden*

Maddie continued modelling throughout 1971, but by 1972 was becoming concerned that she was not being challenged enough in her career and wondered what the future might hold – never suspecting that a new film offer was about to land at her feet.

> 'Joan Gray, my agent, was married to a fiendishly handsome man called Stuart Lions. Stuart, I recall, was rarely at home and was a busy casting director and producer. I always felt that Joan was in awe of him and slightly afraid of him in equal measure. Anyway, Stuart was lined up to become one of the producers for a new film which was to be directed by Lionel Jeffries, who had just had a major success with *The Railway Children*, which had starred amongst others a young Jenny Agutter. His next film was to be called *The Amazing Mr Blunden.*'

Antonia Barber was a writer of children's fiction who resided in Kent and Cornwall.[1] Born in 1932, Barber was delighted when she was contacted by Lionel Jeffries about adapting her book *The Ghosts* into a screenplay for a new film.[2] Jeffries himself had enjoyed a tremendously successful film career, and had starred opposite Dick van Dyke in *Chitty Chitty Bang Bang* only three years earlier in 1968. Before that, Lionel played a wide range of lovable and successful roles, including with Peter Sellers in *Two Way Stretch* (1960) and the hugely popular *Murder Ahoy!* (1964), with Margaret Rutherford as Miss Marple. Jeffries was now moving into directing and screenwriting, and in 1970 had directed a very highly regarded film version of *The Railway Children* starring a very young Jenny Agutter and Maddie's lovable hero, Bernard Cribbins.

For those who were small children or young teenagers in the 1970s, watching *The Amazing Mr Blunden* would become a cherished part of their childhood. It was one of those films they were expected to want to watch, and became part of an annual tradition within many homes. Much like *A Christmas Carol* or *The Railway Children*, it was a film that taught moral values within a theme of redemption and forgiveness. It also had an ethereal and ghostly dimension, some might even say a touch of Victorian horror, within its storyline – it was good for children to watch it, and some adults could learn from it too. It was, however, aimed at a certain type of family, one that cared about making their children not watch films or television unless it taught them something. For those children in the Seventies who preferred to be smoking at the local park or riding their bikes along pavements to annoy pedestrians, this was not for them. It was a film that reinforced good family values – a tonic if you like, to reassure parents and children that they were leading their lives in the right way. These were indications of just how well Lionel Jeffries had written the screenplay.

To begin with, however, Maddie was not sure she had even been given a role.

> 'As is often the case, there is always a lot of talk but that means nothing until the formality of a contract appears, and there was a lot of waiting around as the cast was assembled with Lionel. There are so many moving parts in making a film and, while Stuart and Joan may have known that I would have a part in the film, I did not.'

One of the reasons for the delay may have been that there was some doubt over who should play the part of Bella. Until the research for this book revealed the facts, Maddie was unaware that she was nearly pipped at the post once more by Hayley Mills. Hayley, who replaced Maddie in *Mr Forbush and the Penguins*, was actually offered the role of Bella, but scheduling meant that she was unable to accept.

> 'It was bliss. Again, I was lucky and did not have to audition as I was offered the part through Stuart Lions. I think that lovely Lionel Jeffries was very glad to have me on board as I had been chosen for my innocent charm and looks. My part in the film, the part of Bella, required a naïve and innocent young lady, hoping for the very best in her dreams of the future.'

Maddie now found herself rehearsing with some of the best of British talent. Amazed to find herself sharing scenes with Diana Dors, Laurence Naismith and James Villiers, Maddie almost immediately developed not only admiration for but a friendship with Diana, one that never faded.[3, 4, 5]

> 'Diana and I had judged Miss United Kingdom not so many months before so we already knew each other pretty well, and it was a lovely mutual kiss and hug when we met for rehearsals – I was proud to be her daughter, albeit a pretend one. Diana was always misjudged by the public and the reviewers. She was actually a very fine actress who played up to what the public wanted to see, but underneath she could suddenly turn from a glamorous beauty into an evil harridan on stage – with warts made out of stuck-on rice crispies and a rasping horrible voice. Diana could play the perfect pantomime

wicked witch, but she was also very funny and modest about her skills. Her husband Alan Lake could not live without her – and he didn't.[6] Diana Dors was immensely talented and most underrated as a character actress. There was so much more to her than people realised. Alan knew it and he could not face life without her huge presence.'

The plot of *The Amazing Mr Blunden* revolves around the teenage Lucy, played by 17-year-old Lynne Frederick (who became Mrs Peter Sellers in 1977 aged 22, when he was 50) and the younger James, played by Garry Miller.[7] For Jeffries, who had already seen how serenely Jenny Agutter had played the part of a Victorian teenager under his direction in *The Railway Children*, this was a straightforward case of getting out the lace-up leather shoes, tights and smocks again from the prop cupboard and replicating her role with Lynne Frederick. Indeed, Lynne would be asked to wear the exact same blue Edwardian coat as worn by Agutter two years previously – perhaps Jeffries saw the coat as a symbol of good luck.[8]

'Lynne Frederick was very little and very quiet. I think she was much older than the part she was playing. Her mother was Iris Frederick, a very powerful casting director in her own right, and Lynne gave me the impression that she was very determined that she was going somewhere and did not have time for small talk – of course in a few years' time she would marry Peter Sellers and her life would turn out so very tragically.'

The mother of the two youngsters in the film has fallen on hard times but is rescued by the chance appearance of a solicitor named Mr Blunden, played by the wonderfully humble yet superbly talented Laurence Naismith, who offers her a housekeeping job in an old empty and ghostly manor house.

The location for the film was the village and church at Hedgerley in Buckinghamshire, with studio scenes once more at Pinewood Studios. The burnt-out shell of the old hall was in fact Heatherden Hall. The young pair learn from two other children in the garden that almost one hundred years before a tragedy had befallen the household in 1818. A certain Mr Blunden had arrived too late to save them, and their lives were put in the hands of their Uncle Bertie as their guardian, which is where Maddie arrives in the story. Bertie, an effeminate Regency dandy, spent a lot of his time smitten by and watching Bella Wickens, a music hall dancer played by Maddie.

The Wickens are working-class owners of a dingy tavern in a squalid part of old London: bawdy, poor and led by a resplendently repulsive, greasy, noisy and menacing Diana Dors as Mrs Wickens. Originally, an ageing Bette Davis was offered the part, but turned it down on the basis that she was always being cast as the eccentric and ghoulish older woman.

The Wickens encourage the relationship between their 'ballerina' daughter and Bertie, whom they suspect has a massive fortune. The deliciously naughty Bella manages to tie the knot in a splendidly filmed wedding and moves into the big house. Jeffries cast Maddie well in this part – she was the right age, had a wonderful 'porcelain' complexion and was undeniably naughty, something that Maddie was enjoying both in the film and in her private life. But Maddie recalls that Jeffries knew what he wanted and could be very demanding.

> 'One day I was in the make-up room having all the slap put on my face, plaster of Paris to give me an even whiter complexion than I already had. Just then, Lionel came in and saw me and with his terrible temper shouted at the make-up lady that he had chosen that girl (me) for her innocence [and to] take it all off! Having a terrible Irish temper myself, I could relate to how Lionel felt. But that was not all. On another occasion when I was just walking around the set, Lionel came over and told me in no uncertain terms that my deportment was awful! He sent for a piece of board from the carpenter's shop and had that shoved down the back of my dress to stiffen my frame upright, literally like a board was up my back!'

It is well into the film, when the Wickens have left their squalid pub and relocated to their new family seat, that Bertie (played by James Villiers) announces that there was actually no money; he had spent it all and anything that was left would go to the heir to the estate. Villiers would later be described in one obituary as 'one of the country's most distinctive character actors, with ripe articulation and a flair for displaying supercilious arrogance that put him in the Vincent Price class of screen villains'. Although his character Bertie was not a villain, Villiers captures his supercilious arrogance to perfection.[9] His performance has to be seen to be believed.

Having discovered there is no money for them, it is now that Dors' evil Mrs Wickens hatches a plot to murder the heir to the estate – young George – when he comes of age so that Bella and Bertie inherit what is left.

Through a miracle of time travel, the children are able to prevent their own demise, and the amazing Mr Blunden, who had arrived too late to save the children 100 years previously, can now rest and depart to the other world: 'I have suffered for 100 years ... tormented by my own conscience. It seemed more like a thousand years.'

Maddie found this role highly liberating. Not only was she increasingly confident in her abilities, but she was at last able to develop characters for herself, making Bella determined to escape from the drudgery of her existence in the slums of London. Maddie had also become far more confident with men, and her obvious sexual allure – which had already entrapped many a suitor's approaches – was no longer the only thing she would be hired for. This film established Maddie as a talented actress, and Bella is one her finest roles. While retaining her unique and attractive appearance of innocence, Maddie was able to conceal her new-found sense of excitement within fleeting – and sometimes longer – relationships.

It is easy to see how much Maddie enjoyed playing the free-spirited Bella in the wedding scenes with Bertie. Fresh from being married by – instead of to – Paul Eddington, who plays the vicar, Bella is excited and alive – freed from the clutches of the music hall, just as Maddie wanted to be freed from living at home with her parents, off to become a proper lady. Maddie plays Bella as sweet, mischievous and loyal to her devoted and long-time suitor Bertie. As a backdrop, the stately home of Langley Park in Buckinghamshire provided the perfect setting to build a sense of nostalgia of Edwardian England. Thc horses, carriages and fashions are a superb counter-point to the sometimes dark, chilling and ghostly aspects of the film, which can at times be unsettling.

Hidden amongst the cast is the outstandingly dour and Scottish Graham Crowden,[10] alongside the gritty and underrated David Lodge, who plays ex-boxer Mr Wickens.[11] It would not only be Diana Dors who stole the show for Maddie. Lionel Jeffries could be a marvellously kind and sympathetic director to work with, as Maddie discovered.

> 'I remember Lionel being so kind to the little boy in the film. He was an actor himself so he got involved very closely emotionally with us all and got down on his knees to talk kindly to the little boy Georgie. He was a highly emotional man, a rainbow of feelings, and did not get on with the producers.'

The film was released in December 1972 to widespread acclaim, at a time that the British population was also digesting an interesting raft of new pop songs that helped define the era. The pop charts of the time displayed the wide range of British musical tastes, from the jokey *My Ding-A-Ling* by Chuck Berry to the brilliant but confusing *The Jean Genie* by David Bowie, the brooding and depressing *Nights in White Satin* by The Moody Blues and – at number one – *Long Haired Lover from Liverpool* by Little Jimmy Osmond.

*The Amazing Mr Blunden* was up against a tsunami of over 250 new films in that year. Some were non-starters from the beginning, such as *Blacula* (a black African version of Count Dracula – can you imagine that being released today?), *Get to Know Your Rabbit* and *Sex Life in a Convent*. There were also home-grown films such as the impressive *Young Winston*, the less impressive *Carry On Abroad* and the totally unimpressive *Mutiny on The Buses*. The big films that dominated the box office in 1972, however, were *The Godfather* with Marlon Brando, *Deliverance* with Burt Reynolds and Bernardo Bertolucci's erotic *Last Tango in Paris*. *The Amazing Mr Blunden*, beautifully made though it is, was washed away in a deluge of reviews raving about these new films featuring violence and sex in ways that had not been seen before.

Jeffries' film had its detractors, of course – there's no point in having reviews if they are all positive – but the general view was that it was a good story, well told and finely acted by all concerned, including Maddie Smith, still growing in confidence and now with a burgeoning CV that few, only six years previously, could even have imagined.

### *Clochemerle* and France, Summer 1972

As fortune or fate would have it, the summer of 1971 was not going to allow Maddie the luxury of a restful break, and she would remain busy professionally. Having completed filming for *Jason King*, she was off to France. Although destined to be only one series of nine episodes, each of thirty minutes, *Clochemerle* was a little gem of a production, based on the 1934 novel by Gabriel Chevalier.[12] This was a book of observational humour about people's ability to display the worst of character traits – rivalry, bigotry, jealousy and conflict. Maddie describes how she found out about getting the part in *Clochemerle*.

> 'I seem to recall that this was to be the swansong of Michael Mills, who was head of comedy at the BBC and was leaving to join Thames Television. I happened to be in the BBC bar for recording something or other and Michael sidled up to me and simply said that he had seen me as Henrietta in *The Two Ronnies* and thought that I was perfect for a part in his new project that was being filmed on location in France and would I be interested? I think it took just over a second for me to exclaim "YES" and beam from ear to ear, with a little jump in the air too.'

In collaboration with Bavarian Film, the BBC commissioned legendary writers Ray Galton and Alan Simpson, who had scripted *Hancock's Half Hour*, to create a script for TV. In 1969, Galton and Simpson had been approached by the BBC and asked if they had any ideas for a new series, and they recalled that they had once been to a small 'fleapit' of a cinema in Sutton, Surrey, watching a low-budget film that had stayed in their imagination. 'At that time, we were in love with all things French. The newly discovered world of wine, haute cuisine, the country, the language, and above all, cinema. The marvellous comedies of Jaques Tati, Fernandel, Raimu, Bourvil, et les autres.'[13]

The BBC spared no expense on this project, an all-star cast being assembled with a staggering thirty-two different characters: 'The use of British brogues and regional accents built a sense of truth far more readily than the more customary (and logically inexplicable) cod-French and broken English, and a host of familiar faces brought intelligence and obvious enjoyment to the acting.'[14]

Listed among the familiar faces were Roy Dotrice, Hugh Griffith, Wendy Hiller and Cyril Cusack, all of whom were already well established in their own careers, adding a significant sheen to a production which also boasted lovely sets and costumes.[15] Wendy Hiller, for example, was an Oscar-winning actress and a powerful presence on location. With her nearly sixty years of experience, one reviewer described her as 'a no-nonsense actress who literally took command of the screen whenever she appeared on film'.[16] Maddie would watch and learn from these wonderful professionals, but also came to meet a batch of new faces similar in age and career profile to her own, such as Amanda Jenner, Christian Roberts and Georgina Moon.

In addition, the charming Academy Award-winner Peter Ustinov was employed to narrate over the scenes of life in an imaginary rural French village. This small community was torn apart by a decision by the mayor, Barthelemy Piechut, played by Cyril Cusack, to construct a new public urinal in the square outside the church and in front of the windows of Justine Putet, a spinster and virgin of the town. In a stroke of genius by the casting director, the virgin and spinster would be played by the formidable Wendy Hiller.[17]

For Maddie, travelling to such a beautiful part of France in a gorgeous summer was just magical – and she was being paid to do it. Filming and rehearsals took place in and around the tiny village of Colombier-le-Vieux in the Ardeche, just to the south of Lyon. Maddie played the role of Hortense Girodot, the innocent and beautiful daughter of the ugly and overweight Hyacinthe Girodot and her fat, even more ugly father, a solicitor and notary who had fleeced most of the village and grown fat on their troubled lives. The Girodots were the richest family in Clochemerle, and viewers were expected to marvel at how two such awful people could have given birth to such a beautiful daughter in Maddie Smith. 'As local physician Doctor Mouraille (Peter Madden) observes, "One can only assume the family chromosomes finally rebelled at producing such ugliness"'[18]

Narrator Peter Ustinov provided a master class in gentle mockery of the individuals which is worthy of listening to all on its own. Maddie was filming in France for two weeks – a period not without its highlights, both on and off the sets. It was cheaper to keep the actors in France rather than travelling to and from the region, and Maddie remembers that two hotels were booked – one for the established stars and another for the also-rans. As she was still very new to television work, Maddie was on the same floor as Bernard Breslaw of 'Carry On' film fame in the also-rans hotel. She has fond memories of Bernard opening his door just as she was walking past and peeking out to say a very chirpy 'good morning' in true 'Carry On' style.

Having struck up friendships with many of the actors on set, Roy Dotrice decided that it would be fun to travel around in his ancient but very collectible Rolls Royce, which he had driven down to the location especially to tour the region, hunting down all the best restaurants.[19] Fifty-year-old Roy was at the height of his popularity, charming and a very well-known face. Maddie naturally accepted his kind offer, and together, with the sun and gentle breezes on their faces, Roy and Maddie found the best Michelin-starred restaurants they could. Better still, Roy paid all the bills. Their friendship was a close and fun-loving interlude in what can be a hectic life of passing ships. Maddie fondly recalls the carefree chats on picnic blankets, savouring a bottle of red wine as they overlooked the French countryside.

*Clochemerle* was a fantastic experience for Maddie and a huge success for Michael Mills. It was such a hit right across Europe, where similar petty town officials existed everywhere, that it was widely translated into many different languages. The term '*clochmerlesque*' has entered the French lexicon to describe petty parochial squabbling – indeed, I have heard the same term used in Britain. Overall, Maddie is delighted to have been involved in the making of such a magical programme.

> 'It was an amazing experience and I loved every minute of filming in France – the quality of the cast and crew was overwhelming and a real tribute to what the BBC could put together in its prime ... what a privilege to be part of such a wonderful project which has sadly now been forgotten.'

## *Frankenstein and the Monster from Hell*, 1972

The contrast between projects that an actor often has to cope with could not have been made starker than in that summer of 1972, when Maddie had to change her entire mindset from the beautiful scenery and easy way of life of rural France over to a murky laboratory where Dr Frankenstein was creating yet another monster. In a return to the Gothic traditions of the Hammer horror film genre, *Frankenstein and the Monster from Hell* was at last a film where Maddie did not have to take her clothes off, be ravaged by a female vampire or display her eye-watering decolletage.

After spritely, elegant daughter of the richest family in the village of Clochemerle, Maddie was cast as Sarah, the mute daughter of Adolf Klauss, a corrupt and unsavoury director of an insane asylum. Playing a mute character presented some challenges for Maddie, who had to work on numerous facial expressions to communicate her emotions during the film. The most positive reviews would comment on how well she achieved this.

'Although it did not always receive the positive reviews that it deserved, this was a sweet little film by Hammer Films, shot in nice autumnal colours at Elstree Studios, and the story was actually pretty good. It was a challenge for me and it was hard working with no script and yet being in so many scenes. This was Peter Cushing's sixth and last film where he played Baron Frankenstein; he was now 59 and he was not in the best of health.'

The monster was played by David Prowse, who would later go on to play Darth Vader in the *Star Wars* film series, and his makeup required for the monster was extensive. Playing a monster who showed emotional and psychological distress at seeing his own image required Prowse to work hard at interpretation of emotions, and the combination of mute monster and mute young girl gave this film a great deal more pathos than most of its ilk.

'There was a melancholy air to making this film. Audience taste was changing and less and less people were willing to sit through the type of Gothic horror that had been the Hammer trademark. The director, Terence Fisher, had been injured in a car crash before we started filming and he was quite ill and walked around on set with a walking stick so that sort of dampened everyone's spirits and to cap it all, Peter Cushing, who was very quietly spoken anyway, made no small talk; his wife Helen had died the previous year and he was still grieving. He seemed to be wasting away as he just wasn't eating; I knew about such things because I had struggled at school with anorexia when I was younger. When I saw him for the first time I remember thinking that his skin was so thin it looked like parchment.' (*The Northern Echo*, April 2017)

Although a film about human tragedy needed to be played with a sombre underlying tone, this was all for real – perhaps too real – and although the movie was filmed in 1972, it would not be released until 1974.

### 1973: *Take Me High* with Cliff Richard ... please!

In complete contrast, as 1972 spilled over into 1973, Maddie was offered yet another small but notable film role, this time alongside the famous pop star Cliff Richard in *Take Me High*. The whole tenor of the production was noisy, colourful and vibrant, as the following online review captured many years later:

> 'Birmingham itself is as much of a character here as any of the lead actors and in so many ways, the extensive location filming adds to *Take Me High*'s brilliance … A lot of time is spent in the city, the roads surrounding Gas Street, or at the canal basin – getting to the heart of a very vibrant and busy working area. If that isn't enough, the film's climax captures a superb period snapshot of Birmingham's New Street, complete with a cast of thousands, supported by aerial camera work.' (WeAreCult.rocks/burger-me-take-me-high)

Cliff Richard was still one of the UK's biggest pop stars, recording many hit singles throughout the 1950s, 1960s and 1970s that helped define an era. Cliff's forays into films seem to be completely forgotten now, yet it was these happy, carefree and very well-produced movies that were probably his best work; and *Take Me High* was the best of the best. Although Cliff's film work has been drastically undersold, this remains a hidden gem, so much better than *Summer Holiday*. It is a film that would cheer anyone up on a dull autumn afternoon and remind them that they were once youthful, joyful and knew what excitement felt like – just like that cast of thousands of young people in the film.

Directed by David Askey, who had also been the creative genius behind *Dr At Large*, the film was equally fast-paced, focussing on the social interaction between the new young generation and their suffocatingly 'stuck in the 1950s' elders. It was thus in many ways a reflection of Maddie's own situation at home.

> 'Cliff was so gifted. I could often hear him rehearsing his songs in his dressing room and boy did he have a naturally great voice. He also played his guitar and we all would congregate outside listening to him in a freebie concert before filming began. Cliff is a warm, kind and gifted guy and we all loved him.'

Although Maddie – described by one reviewer as 'divine' in her role as Cliff's on-screen wife, Vicki – had only a small part in the film, she makes an early impact on Cliff's character, so much so that he sits in his car and sings himself a pretty depressing melody. Also in the film were George Cole as a local councillor, Richard Wattis and Anthony Andrews in a first big screen appearance, all of which gave the film the polish of a really good romantic comedy. Sadly, it did not excite the cinema-going audience, and Cliff decided that this would be his final film.

### *Carry On Matron*

With a plotline where a gang of thieves attempt to steal contraceptive pills from the beautifully named 'Finisham' Maternity Hospital, this could only be one of the 'Carry On' films. Directed by Gerald Thomas, *Carry On Matron* – the twenty-third in the series of thirty-one films in the franchise – was one of only two in the entire string that featured the whole cast of main characters. Here they played roles such as Dr Prodd, Sir Bernard Cutting and Dr F.A. Goode (you may need a moment to think about that one), which makes this film something of a masterpiece – if that is not an oxymoron – for fans of the 'Carry On' genre. Given where Maddie was in her career and her obvious talents at this time in her life, it should not come as a surprise that the role of Mrs Pullitt came her way.

> 'I was only on set for half a day in *Carry On Matron* – partly because my character did not have a lot to do in the film, but also because the speed with which a "Carry On" film was made was hectic; the cast and crew were shuffled around so fast it was hard to keep up. These films were all made on a shoestring budget and it was down to the cast of really talented character actors to make each movie a success – as little as possible was spent on locations and sets, and even less on salaries!'

Maddie recorded her part without any problems and was invited to join the troupe for their next and future films, but in another accident of fate she was already committed to touring in a play with Terry Scott so had to decline.

> 'Looking back, I loved my short time with the Carry On crew – they were such fun and for me, at the start of my career in films and theatre, it was simply amazing to be standing having a cup of tea on set with so many famous faces. I hated touring – I never liked the constant driving to new locations and variable accommodation – it made me feel uneasy but it was a job and I had to take it. That's how it is for the vast majority of people in the profession.'

Although Maddie did not know it yet, another location was on the near horizon, and this time it would be an opening that most young actresses – both then and now – could only dream of: she was going to get an offer to become a Bond girl in Roger Moore's very first Bond film, *Live and Let Die*. It would be back to Pinewood, back on cold sets in January 1973, in a role that would provide her with fame forever after. Before that however, the telephone needed to ring just one more time at home in Kew. It goes without saying that nothing in Maddie's career was predictable. And it should not be a surprise to learn that her telephone number at this time was RIC 2007 – an incredible coincidence. However, it had never crossed Maddie's mind that she was about to receive a call on that number from Roger Moore himself.

# Part Four

# Dreams Can Come True

# Chapter 10

# Becoming a Bond Girl, *Live and Let Die*, January 1973

'Let me tell you this. On screen, Roger Moore always plays the perfect English gentleman, polite and kind. Well let me tell you something else… off screen, he was all that and very much more. He was simply the nicest person you could ever wish to meet. Many years after *Live and Let Die*, I attended a party or reception to celebrate the anniversary of The Saint. We had not met since 1973 and when Roger saw me, he stopped talking to his guests and walked straight towards me, arms open wide, for an embrace as if it were yesterday that we had last seen each other. That was Roger Moore.'

Madeline Smith

Maddie was actually wondering whether she ought to move from acting into nursing while the cast and crew of the latest James Bond film were assembling in January 1973 for its final shots. When she answered the phone one evening it was to be asked by Roger Moore himself if she would like to play a role at the start of the film. One wonders if he in fact noticed the RIC 2007 number that he had dialled.

Although Maddie was elated, the mistake should not be made of thinking that the worldwide interest in the Bond films was the same in the late 1960s and early 1970s as it has been in more recent times. Indeed, by the time of the release of Sean Connery's final Bond film, *Diamonds Are Forever*, in 1971, the brand was in need of resuscitation. The off-piste choice of George Lazenby for the 1969 007 film *On Her Majesty's Secret Service* had seen interest wane and box office takings drop by nearly 50 per cent. In a desperate measure, Connery had agreed to reprise his role one more time to bring back some stability, in return for a sizeable increase in his fee. But then Bond producers Albert ('Cubby') Broccoli and Harry Saltzman realized they needed to make the right choice for their next 007 to save the Bond brand for the future – it was that serious.

In choosing the immaculately well-groomed Roger Moore, the producers struck gold. Roger was thrilled to become Bond, which seemed like a natural extension of his hugely successful role as *The Saint*. The fact that he felt honoured to be offered the role was part of the reason he would go on to complete seven Bond movies over the next twelve years, earning over $1 billion for his producers. Moore was a superb and natural fit for the role, but it was not just Roger himself that would attract new audiences to the world of James Bond. It would be a combination of Moore himself, the beautiful and varied locations, the people around him, the new gadgets and the new iconic status that was to be attached to the Bond movie theme.

The main filming for *Live and Let Die* had all been completed by the time Maddie was called for her scene.

## The Locations …

Although Roger Moore had been immobilized by kidney stones early on in the movie's production, which caused a small delay in the schedule, filming began on 13 October 1972. Roger kept a daily diary which he intended to make into a book after the film was complete, and that diary provides a complete picture of all that took place throughout the months of filming. (He recounts a series of exciting foreign and exotic locations, from the United Nations on 46th Street at First Avenue in New York City, to other venues around the Big Apple such as Harlem, idyllic Caribbean islands, New Orleans, the Everglades and the mighty Mississippi.)[1]

Finally, after all the other scenes had been shot in faraway places and were ready for editing, the suntan creams had been packed away and watches had been reset to GMT, it was Maddie's turn – in an icy-cold Pinewood Studios that resembled an aircraft hangar just off the M5.

## The People …

Probably the most important decision of many that the Bond producers had to face was the choice of director. Guy Hamilton had been selected to direct *Goldfinger* in 1964. Despite the movie being a huge box-office success, Broccoli and Saltzman dropped Guy but brought him back to direct

Connery again in 1971 in *Diamonds Are Forever*, which doubled the takings of the Lazenby film two years earlier. With finance being the bottom line, it seemed wise to retain Guy and he was offered the opportunity to direct *Live And Let Die* and its new star, Roger Moore, in 1973.[2] He would come to be known as 'the General' for the way in which he handled the nearly 100 members of the crew in the complex filming on the Louisiana waterways.[3]

When Maddie met the 'lovely and kind' Guy Hamilton on set that icy-cold January morning, she had no idea of who he was. Hamilton was an English director who had been drawn to the film industry when he was a young boy in France, where his father was press attaché to the British Embassy in Paris and a captain in the King's Own Royal Lancaster Regiment. Hamilton attended Haileybury School in England before returning to France at 16. It was as a 17-year-old clapperboard boy at the Victorine Studios in Nice that Hamilton discovered his passion – but first he and his family had to escape from the invading Germans to North Africa at the beginning of the Second World War.

Upon reaching England, Hamilton was commissioned into the Royal Navy, where he served in the 718th Torpedo Boat Flotilla, ferrying secret agents to France and picking up pilots shot down at sea. It was this experience that would later feed into his direction of *Goldfinger*. Awarded the Distinguished Service Cross, Hamilton once said that he wanted to be a film director before the age of 30, which he 'squeezed in just' when he went on the direct *The Colditz Story* in 1955. He also directed *Funeral in Berlin* starring Michael Caine in 1966 and smash-hit iconic war film *Battle of Britain* in 1969. A hugely experienced and successful film-maker, Hamilton may have come across as a gentle director to Maddie, but he was exceptionally tough and always wanted value for money. 'In the making of Bond films, we are some of the meanest toughest film makers. If we spend a million dollars it had better be up there on the screen.'[4]

Maddie was offered the part in *Live and Let Die* because Roger Moore had remembered her from *The Persuaders*. As we have seen, Moore directed only one episode of the twenty-four that were made, and this just happened to be the one in which Maddie Smith appeared. By fate or good fortune, Roger felt she would be ideal for Agent Caruso, a part that required more than just beauty – it needed a playful and mischievous quality.

> 'I was so very lucky. I did not even have to audition whereas today there would be a thousand willing young actresses wanting this part to start their careers.'

Agent Caruso was Moore's very first Bond girl, meaning the role has always held a special place in Maddie's affections, she having been chosen out of all the amazing women who he could have selected.

> 'The beautiful Jane Seymour had been to all these wonderful, stunning locations and filming for months whereas I was called for my scenes to something akin to an aircraft hangar just off Junction 5 on the M4 and Pinewood Studios. But I was still Roger Moore's first Bond girl and that made it all much more special to me. I took an early morning mini-cab, which I as ever paid for myself, and arrived to find a little enclosed area with panel boards that was the set for Bond's luxurious bedroom apartment. If anyone tells you that the film-industry is all glamour, they had never been in a frozen cold bed with Roger Moore dressed in just their knickers. I should of course be grateful that Roger remembered me from my part in The Persuaders and wanted me to play Agent Caruso.'

Moore – who despite being an international film star had a very self-deprecating attitude towards his own acting ability – records that he had a very busy day at Pinewood on the January day before he filmed his scene with Maddie. All the costly and dangerous overseas location filming had been completed, and the numerous hospitalized stunt men had all survived, so it was now back to cold, grey and wet England to complete the early scenes of the film on a set. Roger records a number of events on what he called his 'HRH Day', including hosting a lunch for Prince Mohammed bin Talal, brother of King Hussein, together with six of the prince's bodyguards and two Special Branch officers. As can be imagined, it made for a tricky day as Roger showed the prince his prop guns on set. There would have been a few concerned security men reaching inside their jackets for their loaded guns as Roger waved his imitation Smith and Wesson .44 Magnum hand gun around. Then it was home to change for another HRH moment, meeting the Duchess of Kent at the Royal Albert Hall for an evening fund-raising concert. As Roger said more than once, it was hard being Bond – the acting was easy, it was all the rest that came with it that was draining.

Before Roger Moore left Pinewood that evening, he noticed that Maddie Smith was also there, and recorded: 'Madeline Smith was in the studio today being photographed in a fetching negligee. I called "Goodnight, darling," to her as I rushed off for the concert and she called back: "I'll see you in bed tomorrow," which is one way of saying goodnight.'[5]

The next day was recorded in Moore's diary as 'B Day 75' – meaning the seventy-fifth day of filming as Bond. He noted, revealing the typical values of the 1970s: 'B Day Seventy-Five was the day I bedded my third Bond bird: a lovely Italian secret agent played by voluptuous Madeline Smith.' [Maddie was his first Bond girl as far as cinema audiences were concerned but, in reality, her scene was shot last.][6]

In the scene, after returning from a mission in Rome, Bond has been romancing his young Italian contact in a suite of rooms. As the camera hovers over the bed, Maddie is slowly revealed, having spent the night with Bond and still swooning on his chest. The time is 05.48, Bond glancing at his stylish LED digital watch after a knock at the door heralds the arrival of his boss. 'M' walks in, played by the fatherly Bernard Lee.[7] This was the second time in a few short weeks that Maddie and Bernard had been on set together, having only recently completed *Frankenstein and the Monster From Hell.* With characteristically subtle Bond movie innuendo, 'M' congratulates 007 on his handling of the 'Rome Affair', noting that the Italians, while very impressed, were quite worried that one of their agents had strangely disappeared. While the two men fumble around the coffee machine in the adjacent kitchen – 'M' not able to use it and Bond trying to use it to deflect 'M' from noticing that the half-naked missing agent was quickly scraping up her hastily discarded clothes from the floor – Maddie makes her way (through the freezing cold of the set) over to Bond's wardrobe. The ever loyal and faithful secretary Moneypenny, played by Lois Maxwell, has just arrived and looks on in her usual mystified way, retrieving 'M's coat from the closet with Maddie looking up with her cheeky, fluttering eyes.[8] The precursor to the famous subsequent watch scene with Maddie's zip was Bond using its magnetic power to slide open the metal door handle on the wooden door to the wardrobe.

All of this was filmed in a glamourous, semi-Italian-style way in carefree and yet hectic shots. Yet there was little glamorous about the temperature on set – it was January 1973 and chillingly cold, and no-one had thought of warming the sheets of the king-sized bed supposedly set inside a cosy flat.

> 'The bed was freezing cold and when I get there, Roger was in his shorts and already shivering under the sheets and gorgeous green silk quilt. As I got in with him, dressed in just a pair of frilly knickers that you might find on a three-year-old with nappies underneath, the shivers ran straight through me … brrrrrrr … hardly the right temperature for me to be saying "one more time again Mr Bond!" I wanted to shiver as I crept across the floor into the wardrobe with nothing on except my Victorian frilly pants – Ronnie Barker would have been thrilled!'

Poor Roger was even colder than Maddie, as he had to keep nipping out of bed as part of the various scenes to answer the door and make the coffee, all the time pretending to be warm as toast. Filming was meant to take one day, but it actually took two. There was a lot of hanging about in dressing gowns as scenery, lighting and cameras were moved around. Last to be shot was that final iconic scene for all lovers of the Bond genre with 007's magnetic watch.

> 'I wore that awful powder-blue dress with the huge enhanced cups and Roger was to gently take me in his arms and apologize – in such a way to suggest that they still had unfinished business – after all it was barely 6 am in the film! It was then that he used his magnetic watch for the second time to gently unzip the back of my dress without touching it – amazing. But the truth was there were two or three people at our feet, out of shot, each pulling the fabric down in a different direction – even the lovely Roger Moore could not make my zip come down all on its own…'

Roger also captures the scene in his diary:

> 'It may seem like money for jam pressed close to the beautiful Madeline Smith and taking her clothes off into the bargain, but on the twentieth take your arm is aching, you've got cramp in your left foot and your right knee is going to sleep. Part of the trouble was that Madeline's dress just would not fall far enough down; probably due to her self-supporting anatomy. Julie Harris, the costume designer, had to go down on her knees off camera and gently pull the dress down. As the watch is by no means magnetic, Crackers [?] was also down there on his knees with his hands up Madeline's skirt pulling a hidden wire attached to the end of the zip – so the floor around our feet was getting pretty crowded.'[9]

Eventually, Maddie's dress gave in. The scene then ends with a beautifully written piece of Bondesque. Caruso: 'Such a delicate touch…', followed by Bond murmuring 'Sheer magnetism, darling.'

This scene has become set forever within the lexicon of Bond filmography. Yet it is difficult to imagine many men getting arm ache, cramp in their left foot, a sleepy right knee and twenty-nine attempts to pull down Maddie's zip – even if they were given the chance to try.

Throughout the bedroom scenes, Roger Moore's third wife, Luisa Mattioli – whom he had married in 1969 – was present, standing with her arms folded at the bottom of the bed, as if on guard. Maddie recalls that she never left the foot of the bed.[10] She had nothing to worry about, though, as Roger was a perfect gentleman, both on and off the set. Luisa was vital to Roger's book about creating the film, as it was her camera that took many of the original stills that had never before been seen.

### The Watches … stand by all Bond 'techies'!

The watch mostly closely associated with Maddie's scene was of course the magnetic one – but there were in fact two watches in that opening scene in the film. As Bond wakes up, he is able to cleverly show us the time in red LED digital numbers that he lights up by placing his finger on one side of the watch. This is a Pulsar P2, which was technically advanced for the time but only had the ability to show the time. There were no gimmicks, and its simplicity still makes it a sought-after watch by those desiring to be seen as a closet spy or looking for an antidote to the computerized age, unable to cope with more buttons and dials on their wrist than a Formula 1 racing car. In 2020, the actual watch was auctioned, along with an on-set photograph, a wedding telegram and a letter, for £11,250, having been in the possession of the productions prop master since 1973.[11] This was no gadget from Desmond Llewellyn's 'Q' in the special toys department of MI6, but simply James Bond's preferred overnight watch. To magnetically unzip a dress from behind, free a boat from its moorings, escape from a crocodile swamp and deploy a circular saw to cut through ropes tied around your wrist, Bond would need a different watch.

Step forward the ever-reliable Moneypenny in her beautiful orange woollen coat to introduce the new watch to the audience. While Maddie hides in the wardrobe (which is possibly why she cannot remember Roger Moore having two watches at all!), Moneypenny tells Bond – now dressed in a cream silk dressing gown, naturally monogramed 'JB' – that his repaired watch has arrived from Q Branch. Bond gives it a shake and then magnetizes 'M's coffee spoon. This is no ordinary watch. As described by Christie's auctioneers when it came up for sale on 17 September 1998, this is an:

'Especially converted Rolex Oyster Perpetual Submariner with a black dial, pierced numerals, Mercedes hands, rotating black bezel with five-minute indications and saw-tooth edge protected screw down crown and screw back in stainless steel oyster bracelet with deployant clasp.'

Now this *is* a watch that Q Branch had created for our hero, and it is seen throughout the film – along with yet another watch. This was a standard Tissot Seastar PR 516, which was possibly Roger Moore's own personal watch that he forgot to take off during filming as there was no reason for it to be there. For collectors, these items are the Holy Grail of Bond props. The Rolex Oyster Perpetual went to auction with an estimate of £4,000–6,000 and sold for £21,850 – and that was in 1998.[12]

**The Music …**

On the second and last day of filming, Roger received a small tape and tape recorder – it was the demo for the all-important theme for *Live and Let Die*.

> 'There was a break in filming and Roger took this opportunity to go and collect a small tape recorder - one of those new ones for the 1970s - small and flat, and he laid it on the floor and asked everyone to gather around - and he meant everyone on the set. He pressed the button and out came the opening bars of the new theme tune for the film:
>
> 'When you were young/And your heart was an open book/You used to say "Live and Let Live" (You know you did / You know you Did / You Know you did)"
>
> 'and it was simply amazing - a real rock and roll, banger of a song, different to any Bond film score that had gone before and sung by a popular band not a female singer as they had all been in the past. Roger said "The music is going to make this a great film" - and he was right.'

It is safe to assume that few – possibly only Guy Hamilton – knew just what a bumpy route it had been to get this tape with that song, sung by Paul McCartney and Wings, on the floor of the Pinewood studio just as the film was about to wrap up.

In his memoir *All You Need is Ears*, Beatles producer George Martin told the tale that 'Cubby' Broccoli listened to the demo tape of the song and thought it was very nice, but wondered which female star they were going to get to sing it.[13] McCartney had been approached to write a film score and, together with his wife, Linda, and George Martin, a song in three sections emerged, written in one day – very different to any Bond theme that had gone before. A solo piano and voice is followed by a pounding rock refrain, and the song then moves into a strong and vibrant instrumental. Martin could see that a large orchestra would be needed, and he wrote the parts for over fifty instrumentalists. There was also a short fourth element written by Linda that gave a reggae section the Jamaican feel.[14] Martin wrote that he worked closely with Guy Hamilton to ensure that each scene had music that conveyed the right emotional feel. Impressed by the orchestration of the song, Broccoli and Saltzman offered George Martin the opportunity to write the music score for the whole film, and the collection of pieces became one of the best of the entire Bond movie series.

Without realizing it at the time, Maddie Smith had become famous. She was now part of an exclusive club of female actors who can claim to have been Bond girls, sharing membership with such names as Ursula Andress, Daniela Bianchi, Honor Blackman, Claudine Auger, Diana Rigg, Britt Ekland, Tanya Roberts, Fiona Fullerton, Halle Berry and Eva Green. Who would not want to be a member of that club? Just think of the reunions!

In 2022, Maddie gave an interview to journalist Portia Jones where she was inevitably asked about the way Bond sexualizes women. She responded:

> 'We were willing participants; we were all in on the joke and we were having fun'[15]

Jones responded:

> 'Bond has come under fire in recent years from fans, media and even those involved in the franchise. Time has been called on Bond's chauvinist roots it would seem, with directors and producers starting to ditch the misogynistic scenes and outdated stereotypes.'[16]

But Maddie was happy with the way things have moved:

> 'Times have changed, "the dolly" has gone. The subservient scantily clad ingenue who rolls over for Bond is now an antique. She will be his equal in cunning and intellect, as ready with a gun as he.'

For those who want to know even more about the making of *Live and Let Die*, Roger's production diary, entitled *Roger Moore as James Bond 007: Live and Let Die*, was published in paperback by Pan Books in 1973. It is a comprehensive, day-by-day record of how the film was put together, with lots of stills taken by the ever-present Luisa Mattioli. Nonetheless, the last word on the movie should be left to Maddie:

> 'I was always thrilled to be a part of the film and being a Bond-girl changed my life and has stayed with me all my life. I had no idea what it would one day come to mean – it didn't mean very much in 1973, but I would gain all the allure of the Bond girls that were to come and I gladly take my place in that grouping.
>
> 'I think our opening scene set the tone for the rest of the film. It was light, chic and did not take itself too seriously, and people could see that this was a totally new version of the old James Bond they had come to know.
>
> 'But the best thing about the film was its pacing. It was a fresh take on Bond – Connery was hard-edged and brittle whereas Roger brought a slower-paced, laid-back and devil-may-care style to the role – he gave Bond time to enjoy the finer things in life, and his suave and sophisticated personality gave Bond the new image it so needed. Roger will always be the absolute best Bond for me. Just as we were hugging and saying goodbye, Roger said to me that this [*the film*] was nothing – and that working with Alex Guinness on the West End stage, which was now about to begin, would be a real job.'

# Chapter 11

# Starring in the West End with Sir Alec Guinness in *Habeas Corpus*, 1973

'He had a big soul wrapped up in a little packet'
Maddie Smith on Andrew Sachs, 2025

If 1972 had been a year of great achievements and experiences for Maddie, then 1973 was all set to be even better.

The manic year of 1972 had ended with a pre-Christmas bout of self-doubt, mild depression and determination to become a nurse. This was not something new. For some months, Maddie had been pondering following her inner voice, which kept suggesting that she should be working to help people, working in medicine and realizing one of her childhood dreams.

'St Bartholomew's was the training hospital of my choice and I had been accepted.'

Maddie had gone so far as being fitted for her uniform and making plans to study nursing while living at home. Then, out of the blue, her father Bob confronted her with a newspaper image and 'Carry On' film-style headline claiming that bombshell actress Maddie Smith was becoming a nurse. The shock this caused in the family home exposed a deep emotional rift between Maddie and her father, who seems to have momentarily lost control and thrown her out. Arguments between parents and their children are common, but this was different. A build-up of inherent and unspoken tension, mixed with her father's conviction that she was making a big mistake, boiled over. Maddie moved out.

'Despite the deep rift with my father, I had set my mind on an independent life and I did want to go into nursing – in fact I was looking forward to it, despite what my dad and the papers had had to say.'

But Maddie did not move far. The red mist may have descended, but she had not lost track of reality. She needed to be near home; she needed the comfort of having family close by, and was not ready to live on her own. Three doors down from the family home there was a top-floor room available, and Maddie managed to move all her belongings out over two days – boxes and bags came out of one house and went into another on the same street. But there was a problem. Maddie only had enough money for one month's rent, and the telephone – her lifeline for jobs – was not working. The move was exciting and frightening at the same time. It was at this very moment that Joan Gray changed Maddie's future by arranging Roger Moore's call. She had a choice – she could move into nursing and follow that dream, or follow another. Perhaps the clincher was that there was also a new role in the air – the possibility of a part in a play with Sir Alec Guinness that could end up in the West End. This, plus the need for a second month's rent, made the decision for her. It had not been easy, and despite the wonderful life that Maddie has since enjoyed, there is still a small part of her that wishes she had become a nurse.

Although still concerned that her roles would never develop far from the sexualized stereotypes that she had largely played in her career so far, she was feeling far more technically able to act, and hoped that these two new offers would enable her to show a deeper side of her ability. *The Amazing Mr Blunden* had taught her a great deal about character acting and presence, while *Clochemerle* had added a lustre to her CV. Hammer film work, such as the recent *Frankenstein and the Monster from Hell*, also assisted in paying the bills, and she now sensed that perhaps the tide was turning. The part in *Live and Let Die* and hopes for the Alec Guinness play promised to further enhance her bank balance.

> 'Once I had accepted the two parts, a warm blanket of comfort wrapped around me. I would be able to keep my small flat as I could now pay the rent for months on end and not worry about how to buy food and clothes.'

By the early Seventies, Alan Bennett was a dramatic new presence in the world of the theatre.[1] Bennett, who read medieval history at Oxford, contributed to the early stages of *Beyond the Fringe* in 1960, meeting Jonathan Miller,

Peter Cook and Dudley Moore. It was *Beyond The Fringe* that triggered his love for the stage. Unwittingly perhaps, Bennett and his comedy colleagues were the bridge between the Goonish surrealism of Harry Secombe, Peter Sellers and Spike Milligan, and the far sharper political satire of the later 1960s. Bennett's first play, *Forty Years On*, was staged in the West End in 1968 and was well received. *Forty Years On* was quickly followed by *Getting On*, starring Kenneth Moore, which opened in 1971 to more positive reviews praising Bennett's revealing and sometimes harsh exposure of the parts of life British society liked to sweep under the carpet, such as sexual inadequacy, loneliness, jealousy and guilt. Bennett himself described this new play as 'an attempt to write a farce without the paraphernalia of farce – hiding places, multiple exists and umpteen doors'. This was certainly the case, the stage populated by only four Bentwood chairs during rehearsals; to declutter the stage further, director Ronald Eyre reduced these to three. The resultant exposure of the actors and their lives was brutal, with nowhere to hide for the lecherous curate, ubiquitous char, henpecked husband and frustrated wife, and nowhere to express themselves except through their words.[2]

*Habeas Corpus*, Bennett's third full-length play, further explored these themes. When it opened in the West End, it was described as 'a gorgeously vulgar but densely plotted farce'.[3] As with any play, no matter how good the words were on paper, its success would depend on the cast and the director to bring it to life. As far as the latter was concerned, Bennett was fortunate to enjoy the close friendship of the 44-year-old director Ronald Eyre, who, as a fellow Yorkshireman, could relate both to the characters and the pacing of Bennett's work.[4] Eyre had quickly carved out a strong reputation during the 1960s, making his directorial debut with *Titus Andronicus* at Birmingham Repertory in 1963. With credits behind him at the Royal Court Theatre for *Three Months Gone* and The Royal Shakespeare Company at The Aldwych Theatre in London – both in 1970 – Eyre was ready for a new challenge. Maddie got on with both Eyre and Bennett really well.

> 'Ronald was lovely. Quiet and professional. And Alan Bennett trusted him implicitly. In fact, during rehearsals, which were in the Crypt of St James' Church in Piccadilly during February 1973, Alan attended every rehearsal, but I don't recall him ever saying anything. He sometimes slept on the top of an upright piano or perhaps he was just listening with his eyes closed, and he always had cakes for the entire cast settled on his tummy.'

Maddie knew well beforehand that she had a part in the play (Felicity Rumpers), and was already learning her lines ready for rehearsals when *Live and Let Die* was filming in January 1973. Hence Roger's comment to her in bed together that 'This job is nothing compared with your next one.'

> 'Roger Moore was in awe of Alex Guinness – his modesty was no act. It set Roger apart in my estimation, then as now.'[5]

## A cast that could only have been imagined

At their very first meeting, Eyre asked Maddie, 'Why have I been given you?' This was a genuine enquiry, as Maddie had yet again not been called for an audition but was automatically chosen by the production company, which in this case was Stoll Productions Ltd. Its manager, Michael Codron, a highly talented and successful impresario, had insisted that Maddie play the part.[6]

The first rehearsals at St James' Church saw Maddie introduced to a collection of very talented actors, including one or two very distinguished ones.

> 'The cast of *Habeas Corpus* could only have been imagined – it was simply a wonderful collection of experienced and talented actors and I loved meeting them all. Chief amongst them was of course Alec Guinness in the role of Arthur Wicksteed. But there was also the lovely Andrew Sachs, who played Mr Shanks. Lovely Andrew was already working with John Cleese making short films for various businesses on marketing, health and safety, that sort of thing, and they were already good friends, which of course would blossom in *Fawlty Towers* when it began two years later in 1975.'

By the time rehearsals began in February 1973, Sir Alec Guinness was already a giant in the worlds of theatre and film.[7] He had appeared in his first play in 1934, nearly thirty-eight years before Maddie stepped on to the West End stage with him, and had been knighted for services to the arts in 1959.

In the theatre, Guinness was unsurpassed in the number of roles he played – nearly eighty in his lifetime – and regularly played leading Shakespearian parts at The Old Vic and on Broadway. He was in demand throughout his life. Although the theatre was his first love, it was his film roles that gave him the greatest success. By 1973, he had become famous for roles in films such as *Kind Hearts and Coronets* (1949), in which he played eight different characters, *The Lavender Hill Mob* (1951) and a further five Ealing comedies. For his portrayal of Colonel Nicholson in the 1957 film *The Bridge on The River Kwai*, Guinness won both an Academy Award and BAFTA Award for Best Actor. A demanding and challenging actor, many more blockbuster films followed, including *Dr Zhivago* (1965) and as Prince Faisal in *Lawrence of Arabia* (1962).

Guinness was a notorious workaholic, but it is unclear what drew him to Bennett's new play, playing the GP Arthur Wicksteed. Perhaps it was the pathos of the part – a husband only too aware of his own mortality and his fear of regret. Alongside Guinness was Margaret Courtenay as his wife, Muriel.[8] Margaret was another major name in the theatre. The previous year, while Maddie was playing a series of small roles, Courtenay was playing Lady Macbeth at the Old Vic in London. She had recently appeared with Peter O'Toole, Richard Burton and Elizabeth Taylor in the 1972 film *Under Milk Wood*.

In Phyllida Law, mother of Emma and Sophie Thompson, Maddie would also be working closely with another experienced and skilled actress.[9] Playing the part of Dr Wicksteed's sister, Constance, the always impressive Law was working hard to be a mother and to build her stage career. Maddie recalls a no-nonsense actress who was kind and pragmatic.

> 'A few days after the opening night, I remember I shared a dressing room with Phyllida and she had an array of "good luck" cards all around her mirror. She took them all down, saying she had no ego at all, and just looked into a plain mirror. Phyllida was an inspiration to me, a very elegant lady and a great example to me.'

Another visitor to that dressing room was a very young Andrew Sachs.[10] At the start of his stage career, Andrew was already a close friend of John Cleese, working on short business films that Cleese was producing as part of his new company, founded the previous year, called Video Arts. Along with screenwriter Anthony Jay of *Yes Minister* and *Yes, Prime Minister* fame, Cleese developed a very profitable business and offered work to many of his contacts in the acting profession. These little gems of films can still be found on YouTube and elsewhere.

An undervalued but vital member of any cast is the understudy, and Maddie was very fortunate to have the beautiful and delightful Wendy Shutler in this role for *Habeas Corpus*. As Assistant Stage Manager and understudy for both Phyllida and Maddie, Wendy's role was indispensable. She became – and still is – a best friend to Maddie.[11]

Sachs had auditioned and was offered the part of Mr Shanks, a salesman and fitter for an artificial breasts manufacturer – possibly a very sought-after job in the 1970s. Maddie remembers his unique way of using up time when not needed in rehearsals and to contain anxiety during performances.

> 'During our run in the West End I saw a great deal of Andrew. He would always be dropping in to see Phyllida and I in our dressing room, which we shared for a year, and just sit down to chat while he did his macrame – this was a sort of craze that had recently taken off. It was amazing to watch him "knit" with string, making all sorts of things including string bags, which helped him to stay calm until he sparked into life on the stage.'

Maddie and Cleese's paths often crossed, through the accomplished variety of roles as a writer and actor that he managed, though they rarely met.

> 'I do recall the surreal experience of sitting in a make-up chair for Yorkshire Television preparing for *Stars on Sunday*. On my left was Gracie Fields and on my right was John Cleese!'

Maddie felt Sachs was kind, considerate, vulnerable and giving. Never comfortable unless he was working, Maddie refers to him with a warmth and depth of emotion.

> 'Andy was a little genius, always thinking about his role, endlessly practising – he would go out onto the stage every night before a performance and rehearse his part with Phyllida Law. She played a flat-chested spinster who had ordered a set of artificial breasts and Andy, being the salesman, would do a little dance and mime around her holding the aforementioned items. He was a genius, a total professional, a big soul in a little packet.'

Adding further lustre to what was already a very strong cast was the writer and comedian John Bird.[12] John played Sir Percy Shorter, president of the British Medical Association and one-time sweetheart of Muriel Wicksteed. The farce that unfolded was deep, with a scalpel-like edge:

> '*Habeas Corpus* was in my view the best play that Alan Bennett ever wrote. It may have been a plain set with nothing but three chairs, but the costumes were elegant – I wore a pretty 1950s-style pink dress with pearls and Phyllida always looked perfect.
>
> 'Alec Guinness and Ron Eyre got on like a house on fire, and Ron was kindness itself to everyone, regardless of their reputations. With a set of just three chairs and some flats, the play was ahead of its time and was very challenging for everyone, and not just Andrew Sachs wanted to rehearse every night before a show. Phyllida Law, who had to dance a tango with John Bird, would almost always be at the theatre early to go through their lines and steps together. This was not a film where you could have twenty-nine takes to make a zip on a dress fall down; it had to be right every time and on time every night. It could be nerve-wracking as well as exhilarating.'

The celibate Canon Throbbing – a character name that could have been taken straight out of a 'Carry On' script – was played by Roddy Maude-Roxby.[13] Roddy was, and at the time of writing still is, a comedian, painter, ad-libber, mask-maker and poet. He had won the Theatre of the Year Award for Best Comic in New York in 1968.

Perhaps the most evocative role in Bennett's play was that of Mrs Swabb, the cleaning lady, a part so well written that Bennett wanted to play it himself, and did indeed dress up and get the chance the following year. However, it was the unique Patricia Hayes who was offered and accepted the role.[14] Hayes was already a very familiar face on television, having performed in a wide range of productions, and had appeared in her first film back in 1936. By 1973, she had played supporting roles in dozens of films.

Hayes was the subject of Eamon Andrews' *This is Your Life* in April 1972. As she arrived for rehearsals for *Habeas Corpus* the following February, she was still finding the right position in her home to place the BAFTA she had won in October 1972 for her title role in *Edna, the Inebriate Woman*, under the direction of Ted Kotcheff. Joining Patricia in being recognized by BAFTA that year was some memorable acting talent, including Dirk Bogarde for *Death in Venice*, Peter Finch for *Sunday Bloody Sunday*, Dustin Hoffman for *Little Big Man* and John Hurt for *10 Rillington Place*, along with Glenda Jackson, Jane Fonda and Rosemary Leach.

> 'Although Patricia was mostly known for her comedy roles, she could also play pathos and do it superbly, and in a play that needed actors who could talk about pain through their lines to an audience, Patricia was simply the best.'

Maddie got to know Patricia very well and they became longstanding friends right up to her death in 1998. One of the unique attributes that characterized Patricia Hayes was her sense of independence – idiosyncratic and certainly vexatious, she could easily unsettle anyone, which Maddie felt was part of her unique presence.

> 'Pat had a seeming frailty and wistfulness that hid a very independent and determined lady who had suffered much in her sixty years. One day, in conversation over tea, she told me that when her husband walked out for good, she caught sight of herself in the mirror and said out loud. "So that's how somebody looks when her husband leaves her!"'[15]

That small vignette from Patricia might well have been a scene in *Habeas Corpus*, a deeply painful and seemingly hopeless situation from which she pulled herself through. She was made for parts such as that.

> 'Evidence of her unique character can be seen in her daily routine, which included parking her little car before a performance and then wandering past the closing Berwick Market. Patrica made no secret of the fact that she would go through the bins looking for discarded objects. Her dressing room was full of objects garnered from the bins, including an old red telephone. Frugal, yes; careful, yes, and understandably so; but mean, absolutely not.
>
> 'I can remember an actress who had fallen on hard times because she had not been paid and she owed hundreds of pounds in rent and bills. It was Patrica that gave, not lent, her the money and never asked for it back - although I think the lady concerned paid back every penny. But that was Patricia, a heart and soul of gold.'

Two more dissimilar actors playing mutually supporting leading roles one could not imagine – the strictly professional, disciplined and uncompromising Sir Alec Guinness opposite the unpredictable, unsettling Patricia Hayes. Maddie looked on for many hours during days in rehearsals as Ronald Eyre struggled to get the two leads to work in harmony. Alan Bennett, more often than not, lay asleep on the piano in rehearsals, but he must have been aware that a constant set of rewrites was needed as Eyre adjusted the script to make it fit both the timing of the show and the characters. Thanks to Bennett's foresight, all of the original scripts, plus the handwritten rewrites, notes and final typed script, can be studied at the Bodleian Library in Oxford, where they were donated as part of the Alan Bennett Collection.[16] Maddie recognized the stark differences between the styles of the two main characters.

> 'As an actor, Sir Alec was a genius; he was equally faultless as a company leader, but Patricia's occasionally impulsive behaviour was irksome to this detailed perfectionist. Her bohemian lifestyle and wayward eccentricities were not to his well-honed, sophisticated tastes. For Alec, image was everything.
>
> 'Patricia was unique. A true character in every sense. As Mrs Swabb, she wore a small straw hat – scarcely noticeable. One night, well into the run at the Lyric Theatre, a green hat similar to a phosphorescent lettuce lit up the stage. Patricia had seen no reason to reveal it to Alec before the show, and he was incandescent. She never wore that hat again.'[17]

During rehearsals, Patricia just could not manage her accent, which was meant to be strongly northern. Eventually, after many hours of her failing to capture the accent, Ronald and Alan Bennett agreed that she could play the part in a Cockney accent. There was relief all round, with an immediate release of Patricia's many talents into her monologues, moves and entrances.

Meanwhile, the rest of the cast were largely left to their own devices – some slept, others read, Andrew and Maddie watched. On one of her trips home after a day of rehearsals where there had been no time for Maddie's parts to be run through, all focus having been on Patricia and Alec Guinness, she came to realise how exposed she felt.

> 'I used to wander up and out of St James' Brass Rubbing Centre to the Piccadilly underground and wait for a District Line train. At Hammersmith, I stood there looking at the tracks and thought to myself, if I was so inclined, I could see why desperate people throw themselves on the tracks. That feeling of hopelessness came from the increasing fear that I had just not been given enough attention in rehearsals. I could sense what it would be like to jump. Thankfully, I was not in that place in a deep way, but I was frightened and anxious that opening night was coming in Oxford and I had done very little time with Alec, or anyone else for that matter.'

Maddie's part opposite Alec Guinness was a steaming fantasy from the imagination of Arthur Wicksteed, lusting over lost opportunities and relishing a passionate relationship with Felicity Rumpers – a beautiful woman who was actually engaged to his hypochondriac son. We can surmise that Guinness had to dig deep to act his way through his part opposite Maddie, who was often scantily clad. He was enormously respectful, but was nevertheless embarrassed.

> 'Alec was very awkward with me. It appeared to me that he could not deal with pulchritude from women and the roles we were playing, and this showed itself every night when it came to a scene where he had to lift my leg and kiss my knee. It was all very sexless; he was at his best remembering his lines and showing pathos, but I suppose the real struggle he was having with me was part of the reason he was picked for the part. He symbolized the restraint and unresolved sexual desires of most men of a certain generation in those days.'

Alec Guinness would continue in the role until 11 February 1974, when Robert Hardy took over as Arthur Wicksteed.

After the rehearsal period had ended, the whole production opened at the Oxford Playhouse on 23 April 1973, continuing there until 5 May. According to Maddie, 'audiences were lean but were not hungry, and reviews were less than glowing. Alec nearly walked.'[18] When the play moved into London and opened at the Lyric Theatre on Shaftsbury Avenue, two very special people were in the first night audience, adding to the high anxiety and fear that Maddie was feeling: both her parents, Robert and Ursula, were sitting in the stalls.

## Opening Night, Thursday, 10 May 1973

The music for *Habeas Corpus* was scored by Carl Davis, and the fairground and Wurlitzer style he adopted added to the farcical nature of the play as each performance kicked off at exactly 8.10 pm with Maddie scampering down some concrete stairs to make her entrance. However, on the opening night, knowing that her parents would be there, her anxiety – which had been building gently for weeks – now accelerated into an overload of adrenaline. As a restorative, Maddie reached out for that traditional and well-known remedy for first-night nerves: a large glass of red wine. Glugged down with minutes to go, Maddie walked a little more gingerly down the steps, with the Wurlitzer music filling the air, and out into the full glare of the spotlights and the eagerly waiting crowd. It was soon after this that Maddie's knees locked in absolute fear.

> 'I did not really know what I was doing, and out of nowhere I could not move my legs – the combination of wine, adrenaline, panic and feeling under-rehearsed meant that I just seized up. After the show my Mum and Dad came to see me and congratulated me of course – they were both very proud – but Dad said "your knees locked up, didn't they?" – was it that obvious?
>
> 'When I told him that I had had a glass of red wine for Dutch courage, Sir Alec called me a very foolish girl and told me that I must never do that again.'

Despite Maddie's first-night nerves, the show went on seamlessly. Even someone as great as Sir Alec Guinness suffered from nerves, as happened about a month later when they were all well-tuned to their parts.

> 'Alec honed and fine-tuned his performance, underplaying his part to perfection. You could honestly never take your eyes off him. Nerves caused him to ask the management to remove distracting programmes being waved about by members of the audience or placed in his eyeline on the plush box sills. The cardinal sin for Alec Guinness was an actor or anyone else watching from the wings.'

The first reviews in London were generally favourable. Jack Tinker wrote in the *Daily Mail*: 'To say simply that this is the funniest new play to shake the West End out of its present abysmal lethargy is to do it and its outrageously talented author the disservice of understatement. Others, however, were more pointed. John Barber commented in the *Daily Telegraph*: 'The antics raised hysterical laughter in an audience who did not seem to mind their repetitiousness or the latent spleen.' But within a month, audiences started to wane.

> 'After we had run for a month in London, Sir Alec peered through his customary spyhole in the curtain when "Beginners" had been called, and said, "They're all Japanese." Things were so bad in the afternoons that we were given freebie tickets to pad the theatre. He [*Sir Alec*] and Maggie Courtenay would time the sadly deserted Wednesday matinee to see how fast they could play it.'

Not everything ever runs smoothly in any play, and Maddie remembers one incident in particular which had a rather painful conclusion. Playing

Lady Rumpers, Maddie's mother in *Habeas Corpus*, was the formidable Joan Sanderson, who later achieved fame as the deaf resident that almost drove Basil Fawlty to despair.[19]

> 'She had one particularly long, long … very long monologue dealing with how I had been conceived. It was very funny, as all of Alan Bennett's work is, and Joan was an old-school actress – she had the part word perfect, the timing was superb, as were the vital comedic pauses. She was brilliant. But a year in a play is a long time and one evening, as I sat at her feet listening to this account yet again, I happened to utter under my breath a sort of impolite "hmmm". She paused momentarily and looked me straight in the eye. Really, Joan Sanderson was the archetypal Girls' School Headmistress – unapproachable and unimpressed by youth, and, to her, I was a youth. Well, we walked off stage to the usual applause and the next thing I knew was that she suddenly turned around and whacked me hard across my chest with her pointed handbag. It hurt, I can tell you, and was a shocking reminder to me that actors like Joan, and Alec Guinness of course, were professionals and perfectionists, and not even the slightest murmur was allowed when they were delivering their lines. It was a lesson for me I can tell you, and I don't think I ever spoke to Joan again, even though we performed together for months after.'

When Maddie Smith is asked what she remembers most about the play, if there was one scene above all others that stood out, she instantly relates the final lines spoken by Sir Alec Guinness:

> 'The masterstroke was the finale of the show, when Alec, alone on stage, performed a macabre dance of death of his own devising. Dressed in top hat and tails, Alec then utters his last lines before the spotlight is cut:
>
> "This is my prescription: grab any chance you get; because if you take it or leave it, you end up with regret. Put it this way: whatever right or wrong is, he whose lust lasts, lasts longest."'

The original cast played all week every week from May 1973 to February 1974. Audiences did thankfully and deservedly improve, given that this was the peak of Madeline's career to date, a memorable experience where she had acquired the confidence to do and want more of the same. Being alongside so many talented and brilliant people meant that it was a joy to take the train into town every day, go through the anxious state that every performance brings, deal with the nerves and then go out and, for Maddie, be free. The stage is where she has always felt at home, unfettered by the cares of this world and able to express herself. It is only off stage that she has had to begin acting.

Part of Michael Codron's production style was to ensure that his cast and crew felt valued. Throughout the period of both rehearsals and the run in the West End, he invited everyone to a series of parties to unwind the natural tensions that built over time. Sometimes it was on a boat on the Thames, at others in a hotel. Maddie recalls these evenings as having no expense spared, with a real sense of unity and fun between the whole company. Reflecting on all the advantages that Maddie enjoyed as a result of her role in *Habeas Corpus*, it comes as quite a shock to learn that, when she was offered an extension to her contract, she turned it down.

Life often offers opportunities when they are least needed, when people perhaps foolishly fail to recognize their significance. So it was for Maddie. A woman with her fair share of regrets, she now reflects on this decision with a mixture of self-critical anger and confusion.

> 'I don't know why I did it. The play was such fun and it worked like a clock, and Michael spoke to me asking to extend my contract on from February 1974. I had mentioned this in a conversation with Phyllida and she said, "one year in any play is enough, darling; I'd go and try something else if I were you" – so I did, and I began regretting it the very next day. Suddenly, 1974 loomed ahead of me and I had to decide where I was going next.'

As for Felicity Rumpers, that part now went to Sharon Maughan, wife of Trevor Eve (later to be the star of the detective series *Shoestring* from 1979). Sharon's first night, playing opposite Robert Hardy in the Sir Alec Guinness role, was on 11 February 1974.

It had been a very hard year, and even more so when it is considered that other jobs were also squeezed into Maddie's schedule. There was barely time for romance, fun or men, but one relationship that did develop before *Habeas Corpus* ended came in the form of a young actor named Martin Potter.

Margaret Courtenay played the part of matchmaker when, one evening in the dressing room before a performance, she mentioned to Maddie the name of a ridiculously handsome young film actor whom she had met in passing and who had asked about Maddie. In his looks, Martin Potter had genuine claims to have been descended from the best of the Greek marble portraits of Alexander the Great. Indeed, Martin possessed such classical and handsome features that the great Federico Fellini had selected him to play the starring role of Encolpius in his new 1969 film *Satyricon* – replacing the masterly and also strikingly handsome Terence Stamp, who was unavailable. Up to this point, Martin had only played various small roles on television, and the film could and should have catapulted him into a wonderful career. By the time Margaret Courtenay had her little chat with Maddie, Martin had completed another four movies, including a role as Prince Yussoupov in the epic *Nicholas and Alexandra*, which had been released at the end of 1971 and had starred Michael Jayston and Laurence Olivier.

> 'I thought he sounded nice and Martin and I met on a date towards the end of 1973. He was a beautiful Yorkshireman who today would undoubtedly be a gay icon for his looks – he probably was then too actually. We hit it off immediately. Martin was charming, fun, incredibly handsome and we went out dancing and partying – both doing well in our careers, and both young and carefree.'

This was a real relationship – for the short time it lasted. Martin was slightly older than Maddie – which was high on her list of wants – and they were both at similar stages in their lives, but there was a problem. Martin was a highly emotional personality, finding it hard to cope with all the attention that Maddie received when they were out together.

> 'It was very sad but I quickly sensed that the lovely Martin was too sensitive for the times and lives we led. I was too young and got lost in the moment and did not want to be tied down – while the Adonnis that was Martin Potter simply seemed to get depressed about it all and we only lasted a brief but very memorable six weeks. Martin was just such a lovely man; when we parted, we sadly never spoke again. I think we were just casualties of the profession we were in and the frantic timetables we had – I was always rushing here and there to get back for a performance of *Habeas Corpus* and we simply did not have the time we needed to get to know each other properly. It was wonderful sort of having a boyfriend at last – and such a catch as Martin – but the timing was just not right for us and I often wonder what happened to Martin.'

## Chapter 12

# 1973–1974: Richard Briers, John Fortune and *Casanova '73*

> 'When I first set out on my little career in 1966, the freely available drug use, flower power and fashions of the 1960s dominated my early life – I was a young teenager in what seemed to be a world without boundaries, fun parties, hedonistic lifestyles, pain, art and passion. The 1970s changed everything. Somehow the world just became a lot more serious and in control of the new liberal world we had been a part of creating, and my career mirrored this with a serious workload; now it was mass production of television programmes, films and the creation of new household names and stars almost every week. The 1970s were boom years for absolutely everything.'
>
> Maddie Smith

Performing on the West End stage for a year was hard but exhilarating work – it was also a very serious business. Maddie had matured quickly in this new world of opportunity, where her looks and her agent Joan had combined to create the actress that was Madeline Smith. Maddie's short time with Martin Potter towards the end of 1973 had nearly resulted in a serious relationship. *Habeas Corpus* not only got in the way but was in many ways also a watershed, a time when Maddie had moved from a young, curvaceous innocent – bumbling along in the vibrant world of fashion and entertainment – into having a professional career, with all the responsibilities and offers that this would bring. Working on a single play for almost a year can be rather mind-numbing, so Maddie had managed to double-up rehearsing for and performing in *Habeas Corpus* with other roles. These opportunities had come along before completing her contract period in the West End on 11 February 1974.

## *Crown Court* and David Buck

The first of these was rehearsing and appearing in a March 1973 episode of the popular lunchtime programme *Crown Court*. This was a series produced by Granada Television that played across the entire ITV network, which had begun broadcasting only a few months earlier on 18 October 1972. Each series of three episodes in one week followed a new case in the fictional community of Fulchester, with an equally fictional case (although some were undoubtedly based on real cases) tried over three half-hour slots on successive days. *Crown Court* had a twist in that each jury for each new case was composed of members of the public, and they delivered an unscripted verdict at the end of the case.

The studio comprised a single room – a court room – and in order for viewers to absorb all the evidence, and often quite fractious cross-examinations, they had to watch all three episodes, which naturally solidified the viewing figures, much to the satisfaction of Granada. There was a very tight rehearsal and recording schedule, and casts varied week by week, all of which made *Crown Court* one of the most successful and memorable ITV series of the 1970s.

> 'I had been in Manchester where I had been recording a quiz programme with Michael Aspel and Michael Parkinson, and when I arrived home, Joan had called and said to get myself over to Golden Square in Soho early the next morning to start rehearsals straight away for an episode of *Crown Court*. There was no audition (again) and Joan had agreed it all on my behalf. There were meant to be three days rehearsing and learning quite a lot of dialogue, but the first day had to be aborted as the actor playing the role had a part that was thought to be too close to a real-life event for them – thus I arrived on day two and it was all very pressured.'

Part of the magical chemistry of *Crown Court* was the guest appearances by some very familiar names, either of the time or in the future. Ben (later Sir Ben) Kingsley, Colin Firth and Peter (later Dr Who) Capaldi can all list appearing in an episode of *Crown Court* amongst their television credits.

Once the rushed rehearsals were over, Maddie had an equally mad dash back to Manchester and the Granada TV studios on Quay Street. These were no ordinary studios. Granada House, with a large red neon sign on the roof, dominating that slowly rejuvenating part of Manchester, and the studios actually predated the BBC 'doughnut' in Shepherd's Bush by five years, having opened to live and recorded broadcasts on 3 May 1956. The studios at Granada were in constant use and produced some of the nation's best-loved television programmes – *Coronation Street*, *University Challenge*, *A Question of Sport* and *World in Action* would all start and end their lives in these buildings before they closed in 2013 and moved to Salford Quays.

March 1974 saw Maddie arrive for a whole day of filming. For *Crown Court*, all three episodes of the court case in question were filmed on one day, allowing for continuity in the exchanges in the development of the case and helping the jury follow events and the evidence. All the cast members had to be ready for their episode.

Maddie was offered the role of Patrcia Blake, a witness in a case called 'Falling Stars' which aired later that month. She was cast alongside the lovable Scottish actor Graham Crowden (whom she knew from *The Amazing Mr Blunden*) as Ben Haggerty and a very young Jonathan Elsom as Marcus Golding QC.[1] In scenes from the case that remain, Crowden dominates as he always did with his deep, booming voice and world-weary wrinkled lines, while Maddie seems demure, naïve and confused – which in places she was, having had to learn three days' worth of lines in only two days. However, Maddie also struggled to stay focussed on that particular day of recording because she could not help noticing that also in the cast was a devastatingly handsome actor named David Buck.[2]

> 'I always looked forward to watching *Your Life in Their Hands*, which was a medical programme shown in the evenings, and this was where I undoubtedly developed my desire to become a nurse. However, my guilty pleasure was actually to watch an actor that I positively drooled over called David Buck, who had narrated and starred in episodes of *Tales of Mystery and Imagination*.'

*Tales of Mystery and Imagination* was a popular programme that ran for five series from 1966, when Maddie had just started her modelling career with Biba. Often referred to as Gothic television, the series was produced by Thames TV and was an anthology of classic horror and supernatural dramas, including haunted houses, troubled families and mysterious goings-on.

The first two series starred David Buck as Richard Beckett, and he took on the parts of various characters in the stories. Maddie now found herself in the same room as David, and their connection was instant. It was Graham Crowden who was the first and most vocal person to comment on what was an obvious chemistry between them.

> 'At times during the recording that day, David would deliberately be a little off-hand with me as a way of getting my attention, acting as if he really did not like me. It was dear Graham who took him to one side and told him to calm down and stop putting pressure on me.'

Being a wise old owl both in life and on screen, what Crowden actually told David was to relax, 'because everyone here can see that you two are made for each other', and the dour Scot was right. Buck was already well established as a television and film actor, most recently having played a leading role in the 1969 war movie *Mosquito Squadron*, cast alongside David McCallum of *Man from U.N.C.L.E.* fame. Now aged 42 to Maddie's 23, there was a substantial age gap between them, but Maddie was always drawn emotionally to older men.

Once the recording was complete, Maddie faced the challenge of getting back to London from Manchester. With more than a touch of serendipity, step forward David Buck and his little orange Honda bubble car. David, who had been playing the part of Derek Glyne in *Crown Court* and was clearly completely bowled over by what he saw, offered Maddie a lift home that evening. David had been aware of Maddie for some time, having loved her role as Henrietta in *The Two Ronnies*.

> 'It was a foggy night, but what should have seemed like an eternity from Manchester to London, driving slowly cooped up together in a small bubble car, actually felt like minutes. We talked and laughed the entire way home and that was it – I was in love, and trusted and adored David from the first second I met him.'

This was not going to be a short-lived infatuation on either side. From this moment on they became an 'item', and would remain so for the next fifteen years until David's sad passing in 1989.

## *Ooh La La!* and a 'Pig in a Poke', 1973

Despite seeing a lot of David over the coming weeks and months, they both still had to find work, which was a lot easier for Maddie as she was in great demand.

Maddie's agent, Joan Gray, had many connections – it was connections that provided the majority of the work, after all – and one of these was with a director on the staff of the BBC named Douglas Argent.[3] Argent had been commissioned at the start of 1973 to get a cast and crew together to make a third series of *Ooh La La!*, which had initially aired as two series back in 1968. Based on the plays of the French dramatist and writer of comic farces, George Feydeau, this was a sequence of beautifully staged and resourced plays which, in the first series, had been composed of twelve thirty-minute episodes. For 1973, there were to be six one-hour programmes, which would feature not only an outstanding cast but superb costumes and make-up:

> 'This was an era when the BBC really dominated the short dramas and comedy for television and they spared no expense with this series. The cast was brilliant and full of talent, such as the wonderful Patrick Cargill (whom I had recently worked with on *Cribbins* the previous year) but also the superbly talented Joan Sims. Joan has always been characterized by her roles in the Carry On films, but she had a far wider appeal and ability than that and her earlier work was just outstanding. But what she had, almost to perfection, was comedic timing. Anyway, I absolutely loved the high Victorian dresses, hats and make-up; it was all so gentile and highly fashionable. The BBC at that time was not keen on short-cuts - the production was what counted, not how many administrators it took to run the corporation.'

Douglas Argent was, according to Maddie, a tall, heavily built and handsome man. He would not only be the director of the new series, but was also one of three producers – another being Patrick Cargill, who would feature in all the episodes. Argent was also a friend to Joan Gray, which no doubt assisted in her client, Maddie, being asked to appear in episode two of the new series.

> 'By now I was quite well known on both the BBC and its main rival, Thames Television. My role in *The Two Ronnies* had made my face well-known, and these parts would tend to be offered to one of what was a small number of talented and beautiful young actresses all trying to make their way in the rapidly expanding worlds of film and

> television. It depended on what the director wanted by way of character – if it was sexy and smouldering, it might be the gorgeous and lovely Caroline Munro; if it was sparky and funny, then they might contact the talented and stunning Judy Geeson; and if they wanted demure and naïve, they would no doubt have me on their list somewhere. We were a small, tight-knit group of young women who all faced the same challenges in what was very much a male-dominated and often ruthless world, and we tried to support each other whenever we could.'[4]

The original suite of plays were written by Feydeau in the period between 1881 and 1916. As far as the BBC was concerned, they had been adapted and translated for television by two of the best in their field – Ned Sherrin, whom we may recall had been instrumental in getting *Up Pompeii* off the ground as a film in 1970, and the outstanding Caryl Brahms, who was well-known for her film, radio and television scripts, as well as her collaborations with Sherrin. The pedigree for this series was thus already very strong.[5] The BBC was confident that it could attract a range of guest performers to take on parts in each episode. Rather like the earlier series of *The Persuaders*, well-known names were keen to keep their profiles alive by being seen in something as elegantly staged as only the BBC could do, in a production that meant they would be seen outside their usual comfort zone. In Maddie's episode, entitled 'Pig in a Poke', Joan Simms was accompanied by rapidly rising star Richard Briers.[6]

> 'Both Joan and Richard got on like a house on fire, and they set each other off all the time, laughing away and cracking jokes throughout rehearsals. Making a film means there is always a lot of waiting around while sets are being moved or even built, costumes are changed, more takes are needed and so on; but in television, especially those with a live audience, it was all far more immediate. Anyway, there was still time to sit and watch and listen as these supremely talented actors played their parts and delivered their lines effortlessly. However, much as I adored the costumes, neither Richard nor Joan were comfortable in theirs. Richard said once that no matter what they dressed him in he always ended up crumpled, and I know that both he and Joan looked forward to a good drink at the end of the day, either at home or in the BBC bar nearby.'

Reuniting with Patrick Cargill gave Maddie the chance to work with a man she once described as

> 'a quiet, calm and self-effacing man not at all impressed with his own fame. By the early 1970s, Patrick was an actor of choice with Thames Television, with a large following. He could be funny and unrecognizable at the same time. A wonderful gifted man.'

By a miracle of timing, Maddie opened at the Lyric Theatre in *Habeas Corpus*, with her parents in the audience, on Thursday, 10 May 1973, while only two days later, on Saturday, 12 May, her episode of *Ooh La La!* aired on the BBC. Maddie Smith – model, actress and film star – seemed to be everywhere.

## Richard Briers ... deserves a special mention

Performing together in 'Pig in a Poke' would not be the last time that Maddie and Richard Briers would meet. They and their other halves – David Buck for Maddie, and Annie for Richard – had formed an instant rapport and saw each other socially, on and off, as time went on. Seven years after 'Pig in a Poke' had been recorded, Briers decided that he wanted to try his hand at directing.

> 'Richard gathered around him a collection of people he liked and whom he valued as talented actors to work together in a play that was called *Tons of Money*, and we were to open at the Thorndike Theatre in Leatherhead on 20th January 1981. It was such fun, although in those days we had stinking winters - not the pretend ones we have today - so it was freezing cold, wet and snow had fallen, all of which affected the ticket sales. The lovely Patricia Brake was also in the cast and we became immediate friends - she had earlier played the part of Ingrid, who was Ronnie Barker's daughter in *Porridge*.'[7]

Although from Somerset, with a girls' school private education and a member of the RSC at 19, Patricia Brake was once described by Clive James as playing Ingrid 'with all the lowlife zing that cockney sparrers of stage and screen are traditionally supposed to display but never do' – a mark of Patricia's skill as an actress. However, despite the strong cast, not even the adored and close friend of Alan Bennett from Oxford days, Jonathan Cecil, could reverse the opening slump for the production, and it closed after only three weeks on 7 February.[8]

> 'Throughout rehearsals and the short-lived production, Richard's wife, Annie, was always there supporting us all, and of course Richard himself, who ground his teeth to powder in frustration at this dismal and what came to be terminal ambition to be a director, and he returned to acting with huge success. It was at this time that, twice a week, I would take swimming lessons as I was not yet able to swim and wanted to keep in shape. So it was that, on a Monday and a Wednesday, I would often arrive at the theatre soaking wet and, unable to control her inquisitive nature any longer, Annie asked why this was. When I told her, she instantly asked if she could join me. Richard and Annie Briers lived near to Kew so we were pretty close to each other and we got on so well. The joint swimming classes would go on to last ten years, during which time I became married and a mum.'

Chatting to Maddie Smith can be at the same time both exhilarating and exhausting. With a memory like an octopus with three brains, Maddie is able to recall the minutest of details about her life, regardless of which particular day in 1964 you might be asking about. Like a never-ending Yellow Pages (if you remember those) of contacts, it seems that Maddie knows someone related to everyone. This is underlined by the fact that even her swimming teacher was famous – although sadly for all the most negative of reasons. For those of us old enough to remember July 1986, the name Susannah or Suzy Lamplugh might ring a bell. The poor girl disappeared on 28 July and was never seen again. Her mother was a swimming teacher, and yes, it was she who taught Maddie and Anne Briers to swim.

> 'Anne and Richard were always dear friends of mine. When my husband David Buck died in 1989, it was a terribly sad and distressing time, as you can imagine, but I was forever grateful for the compassion and time that both Richard and Annie gave to me. On the day of the funeral, it was Annie who shared the car with me and Richard who opened the bottles back at our home for the guests – they always kept an eye on me. They were genuine people, a rarity in any decade.'

But these difficult days – days that we all face and know will come at some time – were well in the future; 1973 was still, for Maddie Smith, a time of fun, laughter, ambition and wonderful experiences in her chosen career. To illustrate just how far removed the future gloom is in our story, we now move on to the autumn of 1973 and the almost irrepressible Leslie Phillips.

## Hands up … who remembers Mary Whitehouse?

The term 'almost irrepressible Leslie Phillips' is sadly accurate for this next episode in Maddie's life, as Leslie was indeed about to be repressed by a reaction against his own latest adventure to smother us all in his charm and bathe in the glow of his distinctive voice.

## The *Casanova '73* saga, Autumn 1973

Written by the well-established and much-loved Ray Galton and Alan Simpson, *Casanova '73* was designed to be a sitcom to showcase the undoubted talents of the smooth comedic genius of Leslie Phillips.[9] Although they were never to exceed what was probably the apogee of their success when they wrote *Hancock's Half Hour* – for both television and radio – between 1954 and 1961, they would go on to write *Steptoe and Son*, perfectly capturing their sometimes bleak view of the world in what was a very black and almost realist comedy. The previous year, Galton and Simpson had seen *Clochemerle* very well received, and now hoped that *Casanova '73* would see a revitalization of their work. It was specially written with Leslie Phillips in mind, and as Leslie notes in his autobiography *Hello*, he was very pleased and thought the writing took his established role as posh philanderer to a new level.

*Casanova '73* was directed by Harold Snoad, whose work with *Dad's Army* had been so impressive that the BBC felt he could produce another successful series. Snoad recruited a range of female actors to place Phillips, playing Henry Newhouse – hence the clever 'Casa Nova' title – in his customary position of well-intentioned but unlucky Lothario, using his catch phrases 'Ding Dong!' and the distinctively drawled 'Hello!' The elegant Jan Holden played his bemused but knowing wife, Carol.[10] With her stunning blue eyes and arresting looks, Holden was the perfect foil for Phillips and his philandering. Also cast were Yolande Turner as Connie, Cyd Hayman as Miss Dropmore (those 'Carry On' epithets just kept surviving), the tall and elegant Astrid Frank as Miss Germany and Maddie Smith, who played Tessa Finlay in episode six. Recordings were a hoot. Maddie remembers Phillips as a true professional, as well as a kind and polite leading man, and everyone enjoyed turning up for rehearsals before recording in the studios.

'Leslie was warm and generous with his praise and a total delight. He loved acting and actors, and enjoyed the entire experience, which is what he exuded in all the parts he played, whether on television or film – he was a dearly loved performer by all his audiences. Leslie reminded me of Roger Moore in looks and manners, and he was equally generous, often taking the whole cast out for a meal in St Martin's Square after rehearsals on a Sunday night followed by the live recording – it was all such fun and I felt endlessly lucky to be in this position.

'There was only one incident that I recall that blackened the whole experience, and that was one evening when the comedy banter was moving at quite a pace and suddenly lurching down the stairs with his headphones on and thundering towards me like a charging buffalo came Harold Snoad. He accused me of "treading on everybody's lines", which meant he felt I was being too rapid with my responses and not allowing enough time for the laughs from the audience, but I certainly was not. No one else said anything, but to do it the way he [Snoad] did in front of a live audience was quite humiliating – especially as I had just been on the West End for a year and I had numerous television shows under my belt. Unfortunately Leslie was not around at the moment, as I am sure he would have leapt to my defence. Part of me felt like the youngest member in a classroom where the teacher wanted to bully someone to make a point. It was very hard restarting my part. I do remember that and I was embarrassed and almost tearful. It was just not a professional way to do things. There were plenty of other ways of getting his point across other than a public humiliation'

The plots were light-hearted comedy very much in line with the tone of the day – sexist, but in a gentle 'Leslie Phillips' sort of way, with as much celebration of the battle of the sexes as actual combat.

As Madeline sings 'I could have danced all night', accompanied by a grand piano, Phillips' Henry Newhouse imagines her changing into varying stages of undress as he sips on a large brandy. By episode six, however – in fact after only three episodes – the conservative activist Mary Whitehouse had made *Casanova '73* the next target in her clean-up campaign against social liberalism. Whitehouse saw this as the main cause of the emerging permissive society – one in which Maddie, and any other child born in the first five years after the Second World War, had been living for her entire life.[11] As the founder of the NVLA (the National Viewers' and Listeners' Association), Mary Whitehouse was on the lookout for any new attempt by the media to broaden the appeal of sexually explicit programmes. She had already attacked comedian Dave Allen as 'offensive, indecent and embarrassing'; divisive as she was, Whitehouse was not afraid to speak her mind.[12]

The BBC was naturally very sensitive to what its audiences felt about its programmes, and pressure built very quickly. The first episode of *Casanova '73* was aired on 13 September 1973, from which point on Mary Whitehouse campaigned against it. Although not cancelled, after the second episode, the series was rescheduled from its prime-time slot of 8.00 pm on Thursdays to Mondays at 9.25 pm, which ensured it would not be successful enough to be recommissioned, the last episode of seven being broadcast on 29 October. Leslie Phillips had been torpedoed by Whitehouse and her NVLA. Interestingly, the opening in the schedules created by removing *Casanova '73* was filled by Magnus Magnusson and the quiz show *Mastermind*. It was this unexpected opportunity that is generally accepted as having made *Mastermind* an instantaneous hit, as Magnusson would admit to Leslie Phillips some years later. Phillips was hurt by the whole saga. Whitehouse saw herself as a one-woman Aswan Dam, protecting the British nation from a flood of immoral liberalism. However, as Phillips correctly observed, had the show been aired only three years later, then the BBC would have been quite willing to keep it as a prime-time show, the dam against sexual liberation having finally burst by that time but these were the times television was exploring – where were the new boundaries?

## 1974 and *The End of the Pier Show*

As 1973 ended, there was a significant wind of change in the air for television output, with 1974 set to become a major year for new productions.

The BBC had ambitions to expand its viewing figures, and the various independent television production companies were also rising to the challenge. Combat was most definitely joined in the battle for dominance in the rapidly expanding television output. It was a year of massive investment in comedy, with shows such as *It Ain't Half Hot Mum* being launched. Meanwhile, Maddie was still on the stage in the West End in January 1974.

During a year in which Abba won the Eurovision Song Contest with 'Waterloo' and Roger Moore returned as James Bond in *The Man With the Golden Gun*, a whole raft of new television programmes were announced. Ronnie Barker became a regular on the BBC with *Porridge*, which first aired in September 1974, while ITV weighed in during the same month with *Rising Damp* starring Leonard Rossiter. As if 1974 was not packed with enough home-grown new material to attract audiences, the Americans got in on the act with the first series on British television of *The Waltons*. Children's television became a real investment opportunity too, Chris Tarrant waking up youngsters early on Saturday mornings with *TISWAS*. It was also the year that saw Ceefax launched; the computer age had sown its very first seeds.

Against this onslaught of new prime-time television, one might think that a set of six Victorian play parodies airing each week on the second BBC channel would stand little chance of catching the eye – and you would be right. Scheduling went against *The End of Pier Show* from the start, with a triple whammy of being on BBC2, on a Sunday and – the coup de grace – being screened at 11.05 pm. While not quite the graveyard slot, it was definitely passing by the gates of the crematorium. It deserved better than that, on all three counts.

Salvation of sorts came in the form of the cast and direction, which contained some new and talented faces, as well as some innovative approaches in the production techniques, which helped make this one of the stand-out yet sadly most undervalued series of its time.

Directed by Andrew Gosling, *The End of the Pier Show* was a curious and magnetic mixture of what had gone before in terms of surrealist and saucy comedy. It mirrored the intellectual comedy of the *Cambridge Footlights Review*, with a pinch of the animation techniques of *Monty Python*, a sprinkling of the zany slapstick of an Edwardian music hall and a spoonful of *The Goon Show*. The last of these ingredients certainly suited Peter Sellers, who made a guest appearance in the first episode as a confused but endlessly happy Adolf Hitler on the 09.36 train from Didcot Parkway.[13] Maddie featured in all six episodes of the first series, including playing the part of Eva Braun to Sellers' Adolf Hitler. *The End of the Pier Show* began airing on 17 November 1974, the first series running through to the sixth episode on 4 January 1975.

However, *The End of the Pier Show* was designed not just to be an endless run of surreal comedy. Just like a music hall act, each of the players had to be multitalented and play several different roles in each episode, alongside guest artists. For the viewer, it was a chance to marvel at the abilities of these professionals as they performed, it seemed, specifically for you. In Maddie's case, these roles offered a freedom of expression rarely experienced before. If one is fortunate enough to be able to find copies of these early episodes, it is easy to see that she was able to maximize her beauty and strong sexual appeal within a character that she was able to quickly build on screen. Maddie was developing into quite a versatile actress. The scripts were mainly written by the hugely talented John Fortune, who starred in seven of the episodes and was a perfect foil for Maddie's roles, which spanned from Old Mr Crabtree the train conductor to Cinderella in an episode called 'Not Quite Right Upstairs'.[14] Alongside Fortune was the very versatile John Wells, whose dry and aloof wit was perfectly played.[15]

> 'I remember The End of the Pier Show as a very happy and liberating experience. The director was Andrew Gosling, who was one of the first to use blue screen while he was directing, and the dozens of lovely artwork captions were created by the illustrator Bob Gale.
>
> 'This musical comedy was really ahead of its time and very good with super funny scripts, but it did not receive the support it needed from the BBC, who were possibly scared of not having the sort of radical audiences that would adore this sort of work – there was no Channel 4 yet, and that would have been a perfect platform for this comedy rather than it being a little BBC2 secret late at night.'

The composer and conductor Carl Davis – who had been involved in *Habeas Corpus* – also played a number of parts and wrote new songs for each episode, which Maddie was more than capable of singing with her pure voice. However, the acerbic John Wells felt, tongue in cheek, that *The End of the Pier Show* was 'a programme for dirty-minded insomniacs'. Just as Edwardian music hall contained close-to-the-mark innuendo and smutty references, so the two series that composed the show enshrined this sense of fun and ironic surrealism. Fearless in trying to entertain while pushing boundaries, *The End of the Pier Show* deserves to be watched and remembered as a classy programme of its time.

Ask the average fan which Maddie Smith role they thought of as most prominent in their memory, and the top answer would probably be her part in *The Vampire Lovers*. However, a surprisingly close second might be her advert for Super Soft Shampoo. Acting was and is such a precarious existence – dependent on the prevailing winds of opinion and the fickleness of public interest – that when offers come along to take alternative work in advertising, it is simply impossible to say no. So it was that Maddie made her series of adverts with Frankie Howerd for Grandee Cigars, and these were followed by appearing in one of the most famous of all hair shampoo adverts in 1975 – one of a very popular series for Super Soft. Carried off by a Viking who crashes through a dusty Saxon farmhouse door, we hear a delightful squeak from Maddie as she is lifted away to Norway over the shoulder of a Nordic warrior. It is as charming to see now on YouTube as it was back in 1975.

## *The Snob* at the Open Space Theatre, Tottenham Court Road

There was one other role of note that came Maddie's way in 1974, the rare opportunity to play a part in a presentation of *The Snob*, written by Carl Sternheim (1878–1942). It was rare because plays by foreign writers are always hard to produce and adapt in the UK. Although Sternheim was a popular playwright and novelist in Germany, his work remains virtually unknown in the UK, and is certainly not performed in large venues – which is why director Charles Marowitz, with his small, privately run theatre, could afford to try a performance. Sternheim was a satirist mainly focussed on the moral sensibilities of the German middle class in the late nineteenth century. Marowitz felt this play might resonate with views of the English middle class, and decided to present it at the Open Space Theatre on Tottenham Court Road. Sadly, the site of the Open Space Theatre has now been demolished, but it was a vibrant and important part of 1970s London culture.

Marowitz and Maddie had of course worked together before in *Blue Comedy* in 1970. It was a mark of the high regard in which he held Maddie's ability that this often brutally honest director wanted her to perform again:

> 'I had remained friends with Charles since Blue Comedy and we had kept in touch. He was a fine but very demanding director. Sometimes he would expect his cast to sit and rehearse through the night to learn their lines for a performance which might be happening the very next day. It was not unheard of for actors to be sacked and replaced with someone else within 24 hours; in fact that happened to me in *The Snob*, where a cast member I had been working with was suddenly told they were not right or good

> enough for the part and someone new suddenly arrived out of nowhere. That's something else that could not happen today.'

The play opened in May 1974 and ran through the rest of the year, with occasional performances as and when the cast could be brought together from other work and when the promotions department told Marowitz enough tickets had been sold. In the archives of the Victoria & Albert Museum Theatre and Performance Collection, virtually every scrap of paper associated with the Open Space Theatre can be viewed. Within the archive boxes is plenty of evidence that it was marketing, promotion and finance that weighed most heavily on Marowitz's mind, as the whole thing ran on a shoestring budget. It was very much a return to the roots of dramatic art in Tudor London, where bands of players worked hard to earn a pittance and opened their doors to everyone and anyone who wanted to watch.

*The Snob* was still running on 30 December 1974, as a beautiful press photograph attests, showing Peter Eyre as the hero Christian Maske, kneeling at the feet of Maddie. Peter, an established performer who had featured in both film and stage productions since 1965, was ideal in this role with his tall, aristocratic gait and handsome looks.

For Maddie, the whole experience was exhilarating. Once again, Maddie had been given the chance to work with Marowitz, an icon of the 1960s and 1970s and part of London's theatrical history. Although she may not have realized it at the time, Marowitz was trying to break through boundaries and open up the theatre to everyone by performing plays that were affordable, different and available at different times of the day and night. Although he had demanded a lot from her in *Blue Comedy*, that was traditional theatre with a modernist twist – the Open Space was not traditional theatre. In *The Snob*, Maddie was part of an attempted cultural revolution that would ultimately fail. This was largely because EMI Records, who developed the Open Space site, failed to deliver on their promise to provide alternative premises for Marowitz to carry on his work. In the subsequent vacuum, the large commercial theatres regained control and the Fringe as it existed in London was dead. The work of Marowitz was described as follows by the *Independent* newspaper in his obituary on 14 May 2014:

'He [Marowitz] was a key player in the evolution of the Fringe, and his work as a director, playwright, critic, teacher and as mastermind of the Open Space Theatre kick-started the careers of a long parade of exciting actors and writers. And even if most traces of those dog days of the 1960s and 1970s, when lunchtime, late night and touring plays could all be seen in shoeboxes above or below pubs, have long since blown away, his influence lives on.'

There was one further incident that would make 1974 a year to remember for Maddie. A few weeks after their initial meeting on the set of *Crown Court*, Maddie and David Buck had become an item. David had been well received by Bob and Ursula Smith, and was soon regarded as a fine addition to the family – tragically, as time would tell, it would not always be that way. At the time, Maddie still lived in her flat just a few doors down from her parents' home.

Stars from the pop music and film industry never made a move to meet someone themselves. Instead, they would ask someone from their management team or their agent to make contact, and that's how Maddie was asked if she would like to go out with Rod Stewart. It was spring 1974 and Maddie was living happily with David Buck, but she still said yes. Rod was already a star, both as a solo act and with The Faces, and had enjoyed two huge hits in recent years with *Maggie May* and *You Wear It Well.*

'By then I had a flat mate to help manage the rent and the bills, and she was frantic with excitement as this huge limo drew up outside our flat to pick me up – in fact she hung of the window shouting "take me, take me not her!". The car trip was quick and we arrived at Rod's favourite pub – in those days, stars like Rod and even The Rolling Stones were very approachable and sometimes just gave a quick song or two in the pubs. Rod's favourite place was at the top of Kew Road and was called the "Blue something", and when I got there, Rod was sitting having a drink with his manager and the three of us spent the evening chatting away in this noisy pub.

'Rod was a true gentleman. He said he didn't play around and that he really liked me and wanted me to be his girl. This was a bit of a shock as it was the first time we had ever met – he was very direct and wanted an answer. I suppose looking back that I could have played it differently, but I just told him that I was already going out with David. Rod was great about it and a truly lovely guy, just as he is now. We parted really amicably and I never saw him again – although I have admired him ever since.'

Part Five

# Changes in Direction…

# Chapter 13

# Spinning Plates, 1976–1990

'If you want to be happy, have zero expectations of others, take 100% responsibility for your life, and be grateful for what you have.'

Kevin Costner

When Kevin Costner wrote these words, he summed up in one philosophic sentence what a lifetime of experience had taught him. The Hollywood actor captured the essence of our basic needs in order to be happy. Maddie Smith would probably want to add one more truth to the three that Costner identifies: never be alone. Throughout her life, Maddie has tried to avoid being alone. She is a warm and engaging personality who needs someone to relate to, and there have been many temptations to believe that she had found exactly the right person to be with. In 1974, Maddie's relationship with David Buck was still very new. Had the synchronicity of life been different, then Maddie may have met Rod Stewart before she met David, and who knows where that might have led.

By the end of 1974, that 'Maddie Smith look' had evolved through a number of changes. No longer the pencil-thin goggle-eyed innocent model or the sultry and seductive excitement of Bond girl passion, Maddie was now a capable actress. She had a CV that now spanned at least two pages of film productions, stage performances and television appearances, and she retained the beauty that had wowed hundreds of thousands of admirers. Indeed, Maddie's youthful energy and sparkling eyes have endured throughout the years, and still very much act as a handbrake on the drift into old age. Maddie Smith has never been old, and she never will be. As she often remarks in our conversations, she has a passion for every minute of every day, her only sad times being when she is not busy.

### 1976 and *The Bawdy Adventures of Tom Jones*

Maddie's friendship with David Buck was to blossom during 1975. Her parents, Bob and Ursula, sensed that David was not just passing through their lives, as had Paul Eddington and Richard Harris, but was going to become a fixture. Time would prove them correct. Maddie and David moved in together as a couple, but there were career paths to follow and money needed to pay the bills, so their early relationship was very much one of passing ships in the night.

> 'Sometimes David and I could go for days without seeing each other. There were no mobile phones, and the best we could do was to try to stick to travel plans scribbled down on pieces of paper and left on kitchen tables. David could be incredibly busy at times, and when he was not recording somewhere he would be upstairs, creating and writing his own work.'

David was a sought-after actor, and was also becoming well known for his radio recordings and original plays. Back in 1973, David had been on stage at The Haymarket Theatre in Leicester where he had played the role of the Recruiting Officer in *Captain Plume*. In December1973, he cast himself in one of his own first plays for radio, *The Ballad of Cock Lane*, which the BBC purchased as a 'Monday Play'. In May 1975, David took on another radio role in another of his own plays, *Pact*, which he recorded for 'Thirty Minute Theatre'. Two years later, David was performing in *The Resurrectionist* for the BBC World Service – where another part was played by, you guessed it, Maddie Smith, although the two of them did not meet. In 1978, David was in *The Sunset Touch* at The Theatre Royal in Bristol, which was closely followed by two roles in 1978. One was at The Palace Theatre in Watford in *Otherwise Engaged,* while the other saw David back at the BBC and there was more radio work on offer.

> 'David was always busy doing something although work offers could be sporadic, but I remember his excitement when, in 1978, he was offered the role of Dr Watson in thirteen episodes of the BBC radio production of Sherlock Holmes. David played opposite the fantastic Barry Foster and this kept him really busy and challenged that year.'[1]

Job offers kept coming for Maddie, and a new film was on the horizon. The Hammer horror film genre was fading fast, and instead all manner of screenplays were being put into production as the film industry adapted to try to lure audiences away from their television sets.

Before Maddie had left school, a young actor took his first gentle steps into the studio lights – the year was 1964 and his name was Nicky Henson.[2] Many might remember Nicky Henson's exposed hairy chest, complete with an animal tooth gold necklace and a yellow shirt opened down to his navel, as the playboy lover in an episode of *Fawlty Towers*. Nicky's appearance and ability to sexually excite Sybil and irritate Basil Fawlty in equal measure once caused Nicky to say that his tombstone would one day read, 'Here lies Nicky Henson – he was in one episode of *Fawlty Towers*.'[3] But he was far more than just a hairy chest. By the time Maddie was discussing her own role in a new film in 1976, Nicky had been married to Una Stubbs for six years (they had divorced in 1975) and had already made fifteen films, including *Witchfinder General* in 1968 and playing the role of Jimmy in *There's a Girl in my Soup* with Goldie Hawn and Peter Sellers in 1970. His list of credits on stage were even more impressive – in 1974 alone, he had played roles in six plays, including *Hamlet*, *A Midsummer Night's Dream* and *The Taming of the Shrew*, across numerous London theatres. Nicky Henson was a truly gifted and underestimated actor.

> 'I remember Nicky Henson with great affection. He was quite something to look at, very handsome and attractive, but I only had David on my mind then so I was not attracted to him. Many were though, and I know he was "busy" on the relationship front, but that was not a surprise as he was charming and polite to everyone.'

*The Bawdy Adventures of Tom Jones* was written by Jeremy Lloyd and directed by Cliff Owen, who specialized in British comedy films. Owen had already successfully directed Peter Sellers and Lionel Jeffries in *The Wrong Arm of The Law* (1963) and two films for Morecambe and Wise, so he was an obvious choice to direct this new comedy.[4] Based on Henry Fielding's riotous novel about the amorous misadventures of a handsome and dashing young man in eighteenth-century England, *The Bawdy Adventures of Tom Jones* showcased some of the best of British film talent at this time. It portrayed some of the more lascivious aspects of Georgian England – aspects that certainly took place but about which British society in the 1970s knew very little. A certain kind of handsome yet cheeky, energetic and romantic man was needed for the leading role – and it was offered to Nicky Henson.

Maddie was asked to play the role of Sophia, alongside Arthur Lowe, who was cast as Dr Thwackum. The film allowed for a delightful reunion with Lowe, who Maddie describes as one of the three most influential men in her life, alongside Paul Eddington and Trevor Howard. Maddie had also met Trevor Howard before, but here he was now playing her father in the film.

> 'Trevor Howard liked his booze but he would always arrive on time on set, crisp and alert and ready to go. He would have learnt all his lines and expected everyone else to have done the same. By February 1975 when filming began at Pinewood, Trevor was a big star and I had to pinch myself in our scenes together that here was little me, playing his daughter Sophia.[5] It was just amazing and all part of a career full of such magical moments which I have carried with me throughout my life. But being Pinewood, it was naturally freezing cold again – I think that part of Buckinghamshire has a sort of microclimate similar to the north Russian Steppes because it's always bloody freezing there. Not only was the set cold, but the outside location scenes were even worse! Trevor had a remedy, however, and that was to distribute a nice warm brandy at lunchtime, which was very welcome I can tell you.'

Films have no time for long rehearsals. Actors learn their lines, turn up, run through the scene a few times and then the cameras start rolling.

> 'David would often drive me up to Pinewood or to barren frost-covered fields in the early morning, and I would be doing my own rehearsals in my head before we arrived on those freezing cold mornings. David would hang around for a while, maybe say hello to familiar faces and then it was time to get on.'

The casting budget may have been significant, but so too was that for the costumes, helping create the impact that was required in the masque ball. Flamboyant scenes with coloured silks, velvet breeches and fabulous furs, topped off with the most stunning hats and masques, made for a wonderful spectacle. All the costumery came under the control of 'Bumble' Dawson, who, uniquely according to Maddie, fitted and made the costumes on the cast members. This was hard and skilled work, but made for perfectly fitting costumes as opposed to something off the shelf that had to be let out or, unusually, tucked back in.[6] Beatrice Dawson was no ordinary costume designer. Immensely talented and trained at the Slade School of Art and Chelsea Polytechnic in London, Bumble – as she was affectionately known – was nominated for an Academy Award and three BAFTAs during her lengthy career. Her first job was supplying all the costume jewellery for the 1945 film *Caesar and Cleopatra*, starring Claude Rains and Vivien Leigh. From these magical beginnings, Bumble Dawson went on to work across film and stage during the 1950s and 1960s, her design work being described as 'audacious and expressive, taking real risks with colour and historical verisimilitude'.[7]

Bumble lived with her cats and cat figurines in a small flat in Maida Vale, central London. Sadly, *The Bawdy Adventures of Tom Jones* would be her final film as she passed away the following year aged only 68. Among her last pieces of work were the stunning costume for Joan Collins as the highwaywoman Black Bess and all the other amazing clothing for the film. Maddie remembers that she had a most beautiful wedding dress designed by Bumble for her scene in the church.

> 'Bumble had designed a spectacular dress for the wedding scene and I felt like a fairy-tale princess. The wedding was meant to be on a sunny spring day when it fact it was a frozen cold February morning. On the way into the church in an open-topped carriage we and all the extras were bitterly cold; the churchyard had been "planted" with hundreds of plastic daffodils!'

Apart from Trevor Howard, Terry Thomas and Joan Collins had also been attracted to take part in the film. Maddie recalls a nice scene she had with Joan.

> 'Joan Collins, who, like Trevor Howard, was really at the height of her Hollywood fame, was kind and charming on set, with no airs or graces – the truly great stars were very humble in my experience, and Joan was especially adorable and easy to work with. We would meet many years later and she immediately recognized me; she had not changed a bit.'[8]

Nicky Henson portrayed Tom Jones, giving him both a rustic charm and a mischievous yet naïve personality as those around him tried to manipulate him. He achieved these to good effect under the very relaxed directing of Cliff Owen. Henson was another potential big star who never quite achieved the accolades that he deserved. Maddie recalls his humour and humility when, in the many times spent waiting on set, he could be found in one of the location's caravans, playing cards with members of the crew. He was just one of the lads. Henson once said of his part in the film:

> 'The movie was so cheap, they decided to do all the bed scenes in one day! So all they did was change the sheets and the bedspread! So, in one day, I went to bed with Georgia Brown, Geraldine McEwan and Joans Collins!'

Many years later, Maddie would bump into Nicky Henson quite by accident a few months before his death in 2019. He had been battling cancer for several years.

> 'It was so sad to see him like that. Nicky was a very physical actor. He had been taught at RADA to be a director first and foremost, so he knew all about stage presence and how to dominate a space, but here he was pale and unable to walk very easily. That charming handsome man had been replaced completely – how terrible that illness can be – I had seen it first-hand ten years before.'

*The Bawdy Adventures of Tom Jones* had been a fun film to work on, and although box office receipts did not match expectations, the film was not a failure. Joan Collins often said she saw this film as a rare chance to have fun and play comedy, which she found much harder than fear.

## *The Black Knight* and *Fern, The Red Deer*, January–April, 1977

Maddie was busy with lots of advertising work in 1977, including one project for Midland Counties Ice Cream. During the photo shoot, one of the managers subtly approached and asked if Maddie would be interested in sampling his product – sadly, it was not one of their ice creams that he had in mind. This type of thing happened all the time for Maddie. Ten years after the opening phases of the new permissive society, all that had changed were the chat-up lines. One of the most popular ice cream treats of 1977 was a plastic see-through cone with two gobstoppers at the bottom and ice cream on top. This was known as a Screwball – perhaps this was what the executive had in mind all the time.

Far less seedy was an offer to join Edward Fox, Sinead Cusack and a young Simon Williams in a television play called *The Black Knight*. Rehearsals began in January 1977, with Maddie cast in the role of Peggy. Based on a novel by Ethel M. Dell and adapted for television by John Kershaw, this made-for-television play was the third episode in a series of six that were produced for Thames Television under the title of *Romance*, and was set in Medieval England. Each fifty-minute episode was an adaption of a famous novel and the series was aired from March 1977.

> 'Having met James Fox all those years before, it was lovely to work with his brother Edward, who was totally different. Edward Fox was and is every bit the gentleman he so often plays in film, on stage and on television – he was just lovely and I have fond memories of that little one-off episode.'

Offers for work were now arriving all the time, and Maddie said 'yes' to almost everything she could. In a whirlwind of excitement, fun and adrenaline, she next filmed a production for the Children's Film Foundation, which had been founded in 1951 and, by the 1970s, was making six films a year, designed to be shown on Saturday mornings for children. Each film was an hour in length and took around two weeks to shoot. With an eye to the future, and her interest in films and television programmes for children, Maddie leapt at the chance to play a role in *Fern, The Red Deer*, portraying Mrs Gordon. Written and directed by Jan Darnley-Smith, Maddie recalled that she played opposite Mark Eden, a very familiar face in films such as *Dr Zhivago* and later on *Coronation Street* (playing the villainous Alan Bradley).

Fame does not always attract the most welcome of publicity, and there would be a few occasions during her career prior to 1990 – when she decided to take a break to bring up her daughter, Emily, who was born in 1984 – when even the mild-mannered Maddie Smith got annoyed. One such occasion began during 1977, when she was clearly eye-catching and catching the eye. Cartoonist Jack Edward Oliver decided to select Maddie for a series of cartoon strips which tended to emphasize the sexuality that she brought to her roles, as well as her obvious beauty.

Oliver worked for a series of small publications, including *Whizzer and Chips*, and his off-the-wall, provocative style was admired by many, including John Lennon. Oliver – nicknamed However, for no reason that has ever been explained – had a particular fascination, possibly even an obsession, with Maddie Smith. Representations of Maddie would appear several times in his work. When she found out and complained to him, Oliver responded as most satirical cartoonists would, publishing a whole strip about her complaint before deciding to stop altogether. His prolific work is now almost forgotten, but in the modern age, where satirical comedy is almost dead, it does no harm to look back at his work and chuckle at his poking at anything remotely pretentious and his barbs against the corruption of the establishment. Strips with titles such as 'Chairman of the Bored', 'They've Got a Lot of Gaul' and 'On Strike While the Iron is Hot' may not always have been funny, but they were different, reflecting a time when opinions were able to be freely given without fear of retribution.

In the summer of 1977, yet another offer arrived via Joan Gray. This time it was to appear with Leslie Crowther in an episode of ATV's *Big Boy Now!* Written by Ronnie Taylor, this was one of the first comedy series to catapult Leslie Crowther into public consciousness. Crowther would later be a forerunner of Michael Aspel, Terry Wogan and Bruce Forsyth as a game-show host. The first series of *Big Boy Now!* had been a hit. Maddie appeared as Debbie Longhurst in episode three of the second series:

> 'Leslie Crowther was a lovely man. So very kind and gently funny – he never made a joke at someone else's expense and was easy to work with. These were short twenty-five-minute little shows and uplifting to watch – all very simple situation comedy. I was just pleased to keep being noticed across so many stations. Sadly, all but three of the fourteen episodes were lost, and these, I think, are stored in the British Film Institute archives in London.'

## *Shut Your Eyes and Think of England* with Donald Sinden, The Apollo Theatre, Shaftsbury Avenue, November 1977–November 1978

The Theatre Playbill and Programme Collection is the largest acquisition in the Belknap Collection for the Performing Arts, housed at the University of Florida in the USA. Founded in 1958 by Sarah Yancy Belknap, a New York librarian, her collection contains over 60,000 items – programmes, posters, stage designs, music scrapbooks, photographs and scripts – covering the nineteenth and twentieth centuries in Europe and the USA, all stored in 111 huge archive boxes. For some obscure and unknown reason, it is in the Belknap Collection in Florida that the largest collection of scripts and programmes are to be found for a play performed on the West End stage between 1977 and 1979 – *Shut Your Eyes and Think of England*. In rather similar fashion to the Bodleian Library in Oxford, where, you might recall, Alan Bennett donated his entire archive – including materials on *Habeas Corpus* – the Belknap Collection in Florida tells its own story about a largely forgotten and now dated play that deserves a little more credit than history has so far offered.

Set in Sir Justin Holbrook's penthouse apartment, a variety of guests pop in and out in the best tradition of British farce. A complex set of twists and turns could lead either to the collapse of the stock market or, in a prophetic vision, the passing of control of England to the Middle East. Written by John Chapman and Anthony Marriott, the play was produced by John Gale and premiered in Birmingham and Brighton in October 1977 before moving to the West End, where it opened on 15 November 1977.[9]

After a busy first half of 1977, Maddie prepared to join an impressive cast which gathered for rehearsals. The role of Stella Richards was perfect for Maddie. A gorgeous 'lady of the night' (and most other parts of the day too!), with plenty of giggles and light innuendo, Maddie was ideal for the role. It could so easily have been difficult to play, but Maddie, with her infectious smiles and presence, was just perfect. This was another West End experience to remember for Maddie, playing opposite the deep, plummy voice and charm of Donald Sinden in the lead role of Arthur Pullen.[10]

> 'Donald was hard to ignore; as soon as he stepped onto the stage you saw him and no one else. Then aged 54, in a white open-necked shirt, every lady's heart pulsated. My mum would often wait for me at the stage door, which was great, but I knew she was there more to catch sight of Donald than me. Donald loved European women with glossy hair – strange how my mother's hairstyles would change. Donald had just completed a series in 1975 for London Weekend Television, so it was a major coup to lure him

> onto the West End. It ensured we would have strong audiences – he was greatly loved by the British public.'

Also cast for the run at the Apollo Theatre were Frank Thornton as Sir Justin Holbrook, Peter Bland, Jan Holden, Patsy Rowlands and Willoughby Goddard, whom we met in Chapter 8 when he performed with Maddie in *The Mind of Mr J. G. Reeder*. It was a fun reunion for Maddie. A very grand old school actor who was great with character parts, Willoughby Goddard had a large body to go with his larger-than-life personality, mostly built upon peanut butter, which he ate by the spoonful, and bottles of port.

> 'Willo once said to me that he could eat and drink more than anyone else because he had a larger space to fill. One evening, when his wife came visiting to his dressing room, he dumped his vast collection of empty port bottles and peanut butter containers in my rubbish bin to blame me – I'm pretty sure his wife was not fooled. Willo was a fine actor and I liked him very much.'

Frank Thornton was an immensely experienced film and theatre actor, and by 1977 he was carving his name in television history with *Are You Being Served?*, which had first been screened earlier that year.[11] Although immensely 'above board' in every respect, Frank did have a soft spot for Maddie Smith. He was always polite and respectful to all the cast members, as one might expect, given his roles on stage, film and television. One night, however, he dropped his guard and came out of his freezing cold dressing room in his dark-blue underpants and, square on with a naked chest, he squeezed Maddie's shoulders and said 'David Buck is a very lucky man'.

Fifty-five-year-old Frank had also been cast in *Up The Chastity Belt* with Frankie Howerd back in 1971 and *The Bawdy Adventures of Tom Jones* the previous year, so he knew Maddie quite well. His film credits ran right back into the 1950s and 1960s, with dozens of supporting roles. Frank reunited with Maddie on the stage as if they had never been apart. He was loved by everyone that worked with him, a consummate professional who made his mark in Maddie's heart.

> 'Frank was so sweet. He was once so kind to come with his wife Beryl to watch me front a children's show called *The Pied Piper* on the South Bank. These shows had been created

> by the genius that is Terry Trower, who was a one-time Thames TV composer. I was reading an Oscar Wilde fairy story for 7-11-year-olds called *The Selfish Giant* and I made myself cry – these fairy stories are incomparable and I recommend to any grandparent that they buy them for their grandchildren. I was so touched and I was overwhelmed that Frank came up to me afterwards and told me that he thought that I had done a good job.'

Peter Bland was one of those faces that are often associated with the era but people can't quite put their finger on why.[12] Peter was a Scarborough lad and made his way as a supporting actor, mostly in comedy with *Dave Allen At Large*. His presence in *Shut Your Eyes and Think of England* provided an anchor to a well-paced farce that had the potential to spin out of control. Maddie also remembers the beautiful Jan Holden. Jan had worked with Maddie on *Casanova '73* and had a long string of film credits to her name, as well as being in hit TV shows such as *The Champions*, *The Avengers* and *The Saint* with Roger Moore. With her sparkling blue eyes and tall, elegant presence, Jan had been through her own version of hell when her marriage had broken down in 1973, leaving her raising three daughters on her own. Jobs and appearances in Rep and in the West End were vital to her ability to survive as an actress and mother – something that Maddie was pondering herself. Patsy Rowlands, cast as Joyce Pullen, was another of those faces that helped to define an age on television even though many fail to recall just who she was.[13] Born in Hove in East Sussex, Patsy was already a veteran of nine 'Carry On' films.

> 'Patsy was adorable, humble and very funny, and she and Jan Holden got on like a house on fire.'

The Apollo Theatre on Shaftsbury Avenue was home to many wonderful plays, and Donald Sinden was without doubt perfect in his role in this one in 1977. Donald's voice was described by one obituary writer, after his death in 2014, as follows: 'To hear him full spate is not unlike being shot between the eyes by the world's largest plum.'

Donald chased around the stage in full flow so well, and with such perfect comedic timing, that he was nominated in the 1978 Society of West End Theatre Awards, sometimes known as The Olivier Awards, for his role in

*Shut Your Eyes and Think of England.*[14] The nominated category was for comedy performance of the year, and Donald was up against some really talented competition: Sheila Hancock for *Annie*, Geraldine McEwan for *Look After Lulu* and Ian McKellen for *The Alchemist.* It was McKellen who took the award – but Donald Sinden's nomination was a great tribute to the power of the player as well as the play.

Maddie played her role for a year but, remembering what Phyllida Law had told her in her dressing room during *Habeas Corpus* – that a year in any play was enough – she felt that the time was then right to leave the production. Her part in it was not very demanding and could not be developed, so it was time to look again at where she could place her name. However, Maddie was becoming restless for something else. Memories of her stilted education, the pain of becoming a pariah in her own school and underperforming in her examinations, still lingered. Maybe – just maybe – there was a part of her that remained unfulfilled.

### 1978, *In The Looking Glass*

Before making a final decision on whether to apply to study full-time, and in between major work, David and Maddie did what all acting couples have to do – they economized on expenditure in the fallow times while trying to stay current and in demand. This was relatively easy for Maddie, as she had become a very well-known face on British television and accustomed to taking on all sorts of roles at short notice. She had also just completed a full year on the West End stage.

While Maddie had been working at the Apollo Theatre in *Shut Your Eyes and Think of England*, a triumvirate of John Fortune, John Wells and Carl Davis had been trying to persuade the BBC to let them have a second go at a series similar to *The End of The Pier Show.* Despite its dismal positioning in the scheduling, *The End of the Pier Show* had attracted a cult-like following, very much in keeping with the post Monty Python era of surrealist comedy. At this time, disco and nightclubs were everywhere, young people wanted change and new ideas, *Star Wars* had premiered on a low budget but made millions for George Lucas, and the Hippie movement was well advanced, so blending these social movements together in another exploration of what technology could bring to television production seemed a popular idea. The BBC agreed and gave the go-ahead for *In the Looking Glass*.

Maddie was thrilled to be invited back. In surrealist comedy, actors need to have an ability to communicate a quirky personality – something that helped to release the unconscious mind. Maddie possessed this quality then, and still does. No one sitting chatting for two or three hours with Maddie can quite guess where her mind will take her next. Although physically present, her mind races ahead, leaving a rather blank look – this was, and is, part of that endearing, pleading, Maddie Smith look, as though the screen has frozen but the computer is still running behind the scenes, looking for answers. John Fortune and John Wells, who co-wrote *In the Looking Glass*, could have auditioned any number of aspiring young actresses to add glamour to the show, but they needed that certain something that they saw as unique in Maddie Smith, so decided to stick with her.

The two Johns also decided to use the same production team that created *The End of the Pier Show*: director Andrew Gosling and producer Ian Keill, with music again by Carl Davis. Maddie would appear in all six of the newly commissioned, highly bizarre episodes.

Guests this time around included Bob Hospkins, John Bird and Valentine Dyall, and the storylines seemed to want to shock and unsettle the viewer into the parallel universes of the two Johns' imaginations. For example, the viewer settles down to a cup of tea in London suburbia only to find themselves on an inter-galactic space liner, or they join Maddie chatting away to her father, who is determined to dig a hole through his sitting room floor to the centre of the earth – given the state of the nation at the time, 'why not?', you might ask. As one reviewer has since described the series,

> 'The cast usually sported 1930s fashions and hairstyles, spoke in RP [received pronunciation] BBC English and were very obviously products of the Kippsian world of privet hedges, Dunromin semis and tea in front of the wireless.'[15]

## *All Creatures Great and Small*

Once the recordings for *In the Looking Glass* had concluded, 1978 was far from over for Maddie. Indeed, Joan contacted her to ask if she would be interested in another TV role, this time working with Christopher Timothy, Peter Davison and Robert Hardy in *All Creatures Great and Small.*

The chance to be a part of the second series of the show, which had begun attracting large audiences earlier that year, was an exciting one. Recording took place at the Pebble Mill studios in Birmingham. In an episode titled 'Pride of Possession', Maddie plays Angela Farmer, a rather sweet and retiring widow with a sick dog. Young vet Tristan, played by Davison, is attracted to Angela while he is deciding that the dog needs an injection. Rejecting his advice to lay the dog on the table, Angela – misguidedly – would rather cuddle the animal in her arms – you can see where this is heading. Of course, this leads to the injection being put in Angela's arm by mistake. Maddie's character lives to tell the tale, and the relationship between them is shown developing in a scene in her home, Tristan being his usual clumsy self. Maddie played this part so well that many viewers believed that their romance was for real. At the end of the episode, viewers were left wondering what would happen next, Angela having invited Tristan around for tea. However, time passes slowly in Yorkshire, and it would be some years before fans of the series would find out what happened.

## Off to University and my BA degree, 1979–1982

As the 1980s approached, Maddie's longing for something more in her life continued to grow and she sought greater personal challenges. Life with David was good, and they enjoyed each other's company. It was a natural love and friendship, and neither had to compromise on their dreams or desires. For Maddie, however, the longing to return to some form of education masked a deeper truth – that she had loved school, just not a certain teacher. She wanted to try again to prove to herself that her ruptured education – destroyed by illness and being deprived of her desire to act – could be repaired. She was surrounded by books at the home she and David shared. With David having graduated from Cambridge, Maddie felt a little inadequate, a situation she decided to resolve by sacrificing her blossoming career and returning to education.

With David's support – which was essential as she would have to forego many job offers if she enrolled in full-time education – Maddie applied for and was accepted on a degree course in English at Goldsmiths, University of London, near Greenwich. The course was to start on 7 October 1979.

> 'When I left school in July 1967, it was never intended to be a goodbye to education. Working in the delightful Kensington fashion boutique of Biba was a joyful stop-gap for resuming my A-level studies. Then came the long chain of events in the late 1960s in which the only classes I intended were in acting. I had fallen in love with the profession and I had a passionate affair lasting about eight years. It began to pall only when interesting roles fell away. I was also now living with lovely actor/writer David Buck and our shelves were groaning with books; I had lost the ability to read. Looking back, I think the high doses of mind-numbing medication had a lasting effect on parts of my brain, even though I was quite happy learning my lines. In 1978 I retook A-level English without any tutor, hopping over to Senate House before rushing back to the West End for the matinee performance of *Shut Your Eyes and Think of England*. With a successful result, I applied to various colleges of the University of London to study English, and was thrilled to be invited for an interview by the acting head, Stan Tottman, who said he would take a risk with me. I was so excited I didn't even accept his offer of looking over the college, and floated home on a cushion of happiness.'

## A new world – paying the bills, 1979–1982

However difficult life can become for an actor who loses the ability to drop everything when a job offer comes in, there is always the trusty game show to fall back on. Maddie would have to rely on these over the next three years. Her profile would undoubtedly fade, and so would the offers of parts, but the game show offered a lifeline.

> 'Acting and actors, and the profession as a whole, can be brutal, and many a talented individual has been unable to cope – even in Shakespeare's period, your face needed to fit, and if it did, then the parts would always come your way. Memories are short and producers are always looking ahead for new faces and new material to woo audiences. The 1980s were nowhere near as bad as today, when absolute rubbish can be made into a television series and there is no need for talent, but it was still tough if you became forgotten. I was lucky. I had spread my wings so far that I was well-known across all the main television networks. It is then that television producers add your name to a very long list of performers, and when your chance comes to shine on a game show, you have to grab it with both hands or you don't get invited again.'

There was a time when the television game show filled the schedules. *Blankety Blank, Bullseye, The Golden Shot, The Price is Right, Give us a Clue, A Question of Sport* and of course *The Generation Game* provided broadcasters with guaranteed audience ratings, newspapers with continuous stories and actors and celebrities with much-needed income. Game show hosts such as Bruce Forsyth, Leslie Crowther and Michael Aspel grew in status to become national treasures, the schedulers pushing everything aside to provide them with prime-time viewing slots. Maddie hoped that she could maintain her public profile through being invited on to these game shows while bringing in a modest amount of appearance money to help David, who was shouldering much of the burden alone.

From the very beginning of her degree course, Maddie was fortunate in that she was offered non-stop work. The first was a part in the made-for-television film *Why Didn't They Ask Evans?* Filming should have been completed before Maddie started at Goldsmiths, but in an awful twist of fate, there was a national strike of television technicians, which meant that Maddie began term having to rush away every evening to rehearse.

> 'It was a fabulous part and production, with Eric Porter and the incredible John Gielgud. We rehearsed in St John's Church, Waterloo, and the rehearsals were so memorable – to be surrounded by these wonderful actors seemed like a gift from heaven; they were so good at their jobs. The later crime novelist Lynda La Plante was an actor in this play under her stage name of Lynda Marchal, although her real name Lynda Titchmarsh. Lynda played the role of Evans. Connie Booth was also cast, and the two sleuths of the show were Francesca Annis and James Warwick. Francesca was gorgeous – absolutely lovely, modest and quiet, and we had an immediate bond. Their job was to identify the murderers – one of which was me. It was such a relief to be the villain for a change as opposed to the often rather wet parts I was landed with.'[16]

*Why Didn't They Ask Evans?* was released in 1980. It was a time of 'power dressing' with huge shoulder pads for men's and women's jackets with low set buttons, extravagant red and yellow leather jackets, acid-wash jeans, graphic T-shirts, head bands and leg warmers. Music was going through another transformation, with Michael Jackson's *Thriller* the top album of 1982. Meanwhile, Madonna had arrived on the scene with her songs about female empowerment, and Prince sang about his *Purple Rain*.

In 1980, *E.T. the Extra-Terrestrial* broke box-office records, while Michael J. Fox was going *Back to the Future* in 1985. Another blockbuster in 1981 was *Raiders of The Lost Ark*. With movies such as these, cinema audiences were back in huge numbers across the world in the early 1980s. The release of *Chariots of Fire* in 1981 signalled the start of a renaissance in the British film industry, showing that it could compete with Hollywood. *Chariots of Fire* won three Oscars at the fifty-fourth Academy Awards ceremony in 1982. *Dallas* was the number one show on television through much of the Eighties.

In the news, 1981 was the first year of the London Marathon, which attracted 7,000 runners, President Ronald Reagan survived an assassination attempt, Peter Sutcliffe (the Yorkshire Ripper) was found guilty of the murder of thirteen women, riots broke out across the United Kingdom, Bucks Fizz won the Eurovision Song Contest with 'Making Your Mind Up', and in the November of that year the actress Natalie Wood died – apparently after falling off a boat skippered by her husband Robert Wagner, fellow actor Christopher Walken also being on board. And who could forget that Prince Charles and Lady Diana Spencer were married at St Paul's Cathedral in London on 29 July.

## *Betjeman's Britain*, August 1980

> 'On Monday 25th August 1980, most people were asleep when *Betjeman's Britain* was aired at 10.40pm on ITV.'

So wrote Maddie Smith in an article for *The Oldie* magazine in 2023, describing her second meeting with Peter Cook – the first being back in 1965 at the cold and draughty BBC studios at White City.[17]

In the summer of 1979, Maddie was preparing to begin her English degree at Goldsmiths, which would begin in October. Thankfully, a new job offer that came along was scheduled for August, so it would not interfere with her studies. After October 1979, to accept acting work it was sometime necessary to feign illness and miss study time – an uncomfortable but necessary strategy if she was to earn an income and maintain some sort of acting presence.

The genesis of the idea to bring some of John Betjeman's best work to life had been the release of an LP (long-playing record, for those of you still in short-trousers) called *Banana Blush*, upon which the poet himself read his poetry out against a background of subtle and gentle brass-band music composed by Jim Parker.[18] Parker was no stranger to poetry, he and his gaggle of musicians and speakers performing in pubs, crypts and basements – in fact anywhere that would host them. It was the creative mind of director Charles Wallace that stumbled across them in the late 1970s.[19]

However, ITV commissioning editors did not just throw money at the vast array of projects that were presented to them, and the majority were rejected. It took over two years for Wallace to secure the attention of Philip Garner at Anglia Television, who regarded the arts output of the network as being 'sorely neglected'. He felt that a programme reminding the nation of the work of their Poet Laureate would solve that deficiency.[20] A contract for Maddie to work with Wallace was agreed, and she duly travelled for filming at Sheringham Golf Club on the north Norfolk coast. Accommodation for Maddie, Peter Cook and the whole crew was provided free of charge at The Links Hotel. What could be better? Peter would play the dedicated golfer and Maddie his put-upon caddy in Betjeman's poem *Seaside Golf*, for which filming began in a sunny August 1980.

Although Maddie had once been unsuccessfully wooed by Dudley Moore, it was his comic partner Peter Cook whom she deeply adored for his humour, his gentle demeanour and his good looks. They hit it off from the moment they met.

> 'It is not for effect that I say he is the funniest man off-camera that I have ever met.'[21]

The connection between Maddie and Peter was a real one, but his mind was always somewhere else; he almost seemed to rise above the usual amorous intentions of male actors in Maddie's experience.

> 'My idol did not disappoint when we came to make our film in 1980. Peter made me laugh so much – with "business" that was not even in the script – that I actually felt quite ill with hysteria. Peter could have carved out a successful career as a mime artist. To amuse me, he performed some ridiculous antics with the wing mirror of our ancient prop car, fiddling around with a cloth and copious amounts of spit and polish. Dear, silly Peter.'[22]

The next day, however, Maddie became quite shocked at the state of Peter when he arrived for filming.

> 'When I greeted him on the second day of filming, it was obvious that make-up could not hide his pallor. Peter looked ghastly. He told me that he had dreamt of murdering his friend Dudley Moore. He felt Dud had deserted him with his ambitions for stardom in America. Pete had himself tried to make it in the USA, but with patchy success. He returned, much chastened, to these shores.'

There may have been more to his pallor that morning than just a bad dream – he had apparently spent the entire night awake, chatting to the hotel's commissionaire. To make matters far worse, the film in a second camera had been slightly out of focus with the first and the two could not be spliced together, which meant whole scenes had to be reshot on another day – this time, two months later, the October cold and cutting winds sweeping across the golf course as they do in those parts. Maddie was now a full-time student at Goldsmiths and had to create a small space in her routine to get to Norfolk to complete the re-shoots.

> 'Peter's costume had not been retained – so none of the previous footage could be used. Once more, I was required to wear high-heeled shoes on the green – which, in normal circumstances, would have had us expelled from the club for life. Peter was apoplectic at the breach of custom. Rightly so. In real life, he was a consummate golfer (in one inspired moment, he campaigned for Hampstead Golf Club to host the US Masters), and he knew and observed the etiquette. I walked on tiptoe – not easy on grass already sodden by east-coast October rain storms.'[23]

The few images that remain of the filming over those two sessions show Peter and Maddie in wonderful Edwardian costumes. Both actors relished each other's company and clearly shared a similar sense of bizarre humour. Perhaps they could have become more than just friends, but their careers and life generally pulled them in different directions.

> 'My hero Peter asked me for my phone number. There being no mobile phones, I gave him the direct home line, with a warning that the call might be answered by a man.'

Apparently, Peter hung his head at that moment and sighed, Maddie having of course being referring to David. She did – and still does – wonder what might have developed had she been free, but it was not to be. Just like her time with Richard Harris, fate took a hand and guided Maddie in a different direction.

> 'Inevitably, I never heard from Peter, and within a matter of a few years he had become a bloated and tragic figure, dying in 1995, aged only 57.'[24]

What drove Peter Cook to self-destruction was no doubt the combination of many factors, all emotional and psychological. He always seemed to be the most sensitive of men, which was how he was able to bleed into his comedy a deep pathos and hatred for the establishment. It was no accident that he was a moving pillar behind *Punch* magazine or that so many of his characters on screen mocked the perverse, hypocritical and entitled English upper-class. But for Maddie, the rupture between Peter and Dudley Moore was the key reason behind his problems.

> 'He was haunted by Dud's apparent desertion, defection, to the United States. I believe theirs was the "marriage", and that Peter never recovered from the "divorce". In fact, I believe it killed him.'

## *Have You Anything to Declare?*, Spring 1981

Just as Maddie drew breath and looked forward to her second semester at Goldsmiths, another job offer came her way. Having decided to study full-time, the most Maddie should have accepted was some limited and short-run television work. However, this offer was a full-blown play, *Have You Anything to Declare?*, with Brian Cox in Manchester.[25]

Yet it was not Brian Cox that attracted Maddie to consider saying 'yes', nor was it the chance to work with director Braham Murray. It was not even the money, although David and Maddie needed more of it, just to survive. In an admission that she finds it uncomfortable to admit, Maddie says she was attracted by the prestige. Outside London, the Royal Exchange Theatre in Manchester was as good as it gets, and the opportunity screamed at Maddie as something that may not come around again. Many others had been –

and would continue to be – attracted to working in the quirky seven-sided building with its unique history. After some agonizing discussions with David, Maddie decided to ask the university authorities – specifically her endlessly supportive tutor, David Margolies – for permission to miss a term while she seized the opportunity that her ego craved.

> 'Looking back, I was crazy to have said "yes". I know I am the first to advise younger professionals to follow their dreams, but I was trying to follow two - studying and my love affair with acting. This was selfish and greedy, and put me and my body under huge pressure. The rehearsals were demanding, and very early on I began to yearn for the tutorials on Chaucer or some other great English writer that my fellow students were learning about while I performed each evening, then went back to a cold lodging with Brian.'

It was not all bad of course. The audiences were strong, and Brian Cox was another actor she got to work with who had a wonderful stage presence. In the play, Maddie had a whole scene to herself with Brian.

> 'I once told Brian that when he came out on stage the sun begins to shine - he was magnetic and, like all truly gifted stars, had enormous charisma, where less was more and he seemed at one with the audience. I was enthralled every night.'

Back at Goldsmiths, new best friend Janette took notes and wrote essays, passing copies to Maddie for her to catch up on when she got home. Even now, it is an emotional scar that Maddie can still touch and feel.

> 'I had yearned to return to education, and when I was in Manchester I just wanted to get home and back to university. I failed to connect with the rest of the cast - I did my job, and quite well I think, but my mind and spirit was elsewhere. On one occasion I began a scene that was the next one on - it was a disaster and had to begin again. When there was a day off, I thrashed my little rusty Mini at 90mph down the motorway to get home as quickly as I could - then spent the night reading the essays my bosom pal Janette had given to David. It was no good, and I was so relieved when it came to an end after three months. The whole experience was poisoned for me.'

Maddie was offered to continue her role when it moved on to the equally prestigious Roundhouse Theatre at Chalk Farm, Camden, but this time she said 'no'.

## It was the game show that paid the bills

A year earlier, on 7 October 1979, Maddie had collected her cheque for fees and accommodation from the bursar's office at Goldsmiths University, and paid it into her bank account. That was how students received their grants in those days, and that cheque would be Maddie's only income for the time being unless she could find a way of spinning plates and maintaining her studies whilst completing some small-scale acting work. Now well into her English degree, Maddie's name appeared on a production list for a 1981 edition of *Give Us a Clue*, one of the nation's favourite game shows, hosted by Michael Aspel.

> 'I got the call to come along and take part in my first game show, which was episode 9 of series 4 of *Give Us a Clue*, which aired on 10 November 1981. Alongside me was bubbly Sally James of *Magpie* fame on children's TV and actress Annie Ross, while playing opposite us were Ian Lavender from *Dad's Army*, the actor Henry McGee and singer and composer Denis King.
>
> 'The game shows really were great fun, and it was lovely to be in a studio again after so many gaps. It was also nice to feel that one had not been forgotten. After all, I was just taking a short career break and had no intention of giving up. The live audiences and recordings kept us all on our toes and we had some tremendous fun, and of course the small fees we all received helped to keep the wolf from the 1980s door.'

Maddie was so popular on *Give Us a Clue* that she was invited back later in the same series, playing against Graeme Garden, the comedian Jim Davidson and former England rugby captain Bill Beaumont. One can only ponder whether some of her tutors at Goldsmiths watched her appearances and wondered how she could complete their essay on time when she was in Manchester appearing with Michael Aspel, but no one ever mentioned a thing. Again, David and his little car were pressed into service to drive her there and back.

As the early 1980s unfolded, the ultimate game show invitation that any celebrity could receive was for *Blankety Blank*, hosted by Terry Wogan, with his sardonic and ironic doleful quips. Just as his wonderful morning show on Radio 2 was not about the music but about being with Terry, so *Blankety Blank* – a show that made no sense at all as a game – was all about listening to the genial Irish host. Terry made the whole experience a little more worthwhile – despite the game. Sadly, later hosts – perhaps with the exception of Les Dawson – seemed to be under the impression that *Blankety Blank* was actually a good game show, which spoilt the whole effect that Terry Wogan was able to weave into the programme.

> 'Yes, I am proud to say that I was invited back onto *Blankety Blank* more than once and I lived to tell the tale. They were in fact fun to make. It was lovely meeting old friends and making new ones, as the world around us was changing so fast.'

Both 1980 and 1981 were punctuated by more offers for television work, and Maddie now saw a way into an area that very much appealed to her – children's television.

### 1981: Into children's TV with Clive Doig's *The Deceivers* and *Eureka*

As Maddie approached her end of second year examinations at university, so programme creator and innovative producer Clive Doig was working on a new idea for a television series called *The Deceivers*. With a background in vision mixing and creating innovative programmes for deaf children, Doig's work included *Jigsaw*, for which he won a BAFTA in 1981. Interestingly, Doig also had a background in deep-state rebellion, describing the BBC of the 1960s in his online memoirs as follows:

> 'The BBC was a stuffy, bureaucratic, authoritarian organisation with old-fashioned managerial ideas, mainly due to its heritage of RAF and senior servicemen.'[26]

During late 1980, Maddie had to do more juggling of her university work alongside working on *The Deceivers* with Doig and Jeremy Beadle, who was proving to be a very talented presenter. Doig was also working on *Jigsaw* at the same time and saw *The Deceivers* as a natural extension of that programme, which would run for fifty episodes and six series on BBC1.

Each episode of *The Deceivers* dealt with a series of deceptions to encourage children to learn, question and investigate. Using a mixture of comedy, drama and narration, *The Deceivers* was an interesting series for more seriously minded children, but BBC schedulers placed it at 6.00 pm on a Tuesday evening on BBC2, which ensured that it did not attract a large-scale young audience when it first aired on 6 January 1981, directed by Richard Simkin. Maddie enjoyed the new challenge and could see herself doing much more in this line of work.

> 'Clive was and is a total genius: warm, loving and with probably one of those rare brains that never stop creating. Not a man for satire, but he knows how to make programmes that entertain and educate young people. His work for television galvanized many young men's minds.'

With *Eureka*, Clive Doig was on firmer ground, and strong reviews and viewing figures meant that this would run for four series and accumulate thirty-two episodes. Again devised and written by Doig and Jeremy Beadle, the series told the stories behind famous and familiar inventions. For Beadle, this was the first real niche that he had found for himself in what otherwise had already been a difficult life of part-time jobs and disappointments. With Doig he found himself able to produce grown-up material for children that was just as fascinating for adults, and had he not moved on to *Game for a Laugh* and *Beadle's About* then he might have achieved an even more popular standing with the national audience.[27]

> 'Jeremy and Clive came rocking up to me in a BBC canteen and immediately sat me down and asked if I wanted to work with them – I almost screamed "yes!" Jeremy was just madcap – full of knowledge and silly facts, and he and Clive just bounced off each other. It was like a small family and I still feel the same way. It was a special time with special people.'

Maddie was part of an ensemble cast that also included Sarah Greene, Sylvester McCoy (later of *Dr Who* fame), Bernard Holley and Philip Fox.[28] The cast was supplemented by a series of new presenters – Jeremy presented series one in 1982, and he was followed by the ever-popular Sarah Greene in 1983, with Paul McDowell and the inventor and lip reader Wilf Lunn taking on series three and four respectively. *Eureka* was one of the most successful programmes for children that the BBC ever produced.

> 'Sarah Greene is still a proper girlfriend to me. She was at that time a presenter on BBC as well as an actress, and we hit it off immediately. She and I have remained strong

> friends ever since. We often reminisce about those days which, from a complicated world today, seemed so much simpler and [more] innocent.'

Having managed to balance her academic studies with accepting work offers for the entire three years of her degree course, Maddie still had the major challenge in the spring of 1982 of preparing for and completing her final exams.

> 'I knew ahead of time that I had to make a timetable with Clive Doig because I would be writing exams at exactly the same time as having to dash away to record an episode of *Eureka*. Although I was still young and used to a frantic and anxious state, the stress eventually caught up with me and made me so ill that, one evening, David called a doctor to the house. It was touch and go whether I went to hospital, but I told her straight that I was taking my finals and my stomach pains would have to wait. I carried on, and my trusty and rusty little car shuttled between the university and the BBC studies in White City for a whole month. I couldn't sleep, and sat up through many a night either reading my books or learning my lines. Clive was a gem in what he did for me - he could easily have recast me but we got through it.'

Graduation day came in the summer of 1982 at the Royal Albert Hall, where Maddie filed past her great heroine, HRH Princess Anne. For Maddie Smith, the world now seemed very different. Her Bachelor of Arts degree in English had not been achieved without cost – she and David had struggled financially for three years to keep their heads above water, and personally there had been desperate times when academic work clashed with the need to take on what jobs were offered. But she felt vindicated and had loved every minute of every seminar and tutorial. She felt fulfilled in a way that she had never been before – a gap in her emotional and psychological life had been filled. It had already been a very busy year, but there was more to come during the remainder of 1982.

### *The Bagthorpe Saga* and *A.J. Wentworth, B.A.*

Maddie had still been working at the Manchester Royal Exchange with Brian Cox, having persuaded Goldsmiths to agree to a three-month break, when she got a call to play a part in *The Bagthorpe Saga.* The director in

Manchester, the influential and creative Braham Murray, allowed Maddie to depart the play, with the proviso that should she not be back in Manchester on an agreed date, she would foot the bill for an understudy. Maddie recalls the time precisely, because the 1980 summer Olympics had just begun in Moscow, where the USA had boycotted the event in protest at the Soviet invasion of Afghanistan. Earlier that year, there had been the siege at the Iranian Embassy in London and the Solidarity movement had begun in Poland, presaging the collapse of communism in that country. In music, Pink Floyd were at number one with their hit album *The Wall*, while Jack Nicholson was starring in cinemas in Stanley Kubrick's hit movie *The Shining*.

The adventures of the eccentric Bagthorpe family formed the basis of a series of ten novels by author Helen Cresswell, which were published from 1977 onwards. From the perspective of new material for children's television, these adventures and the individual personalities involved were ideal material for a drama series. A mix of satirical and often farcical adventures created an atmosphere for the relentlessly dysfunctional but highly intelligent Bagthorpe family to show their true characters. Maddie was offered the part of Aunt Celia in three of the six thirty-minute episodes, which were broadcast between 25 March and 29 April 1981.

> 'Recording for these little episodes was great fun and filmed in Tetbury, just off the M4. For the first time, I was able to work with Angela Thorne, who played Laura Bagthorpe, while I played the part of Aunt Celia. Angela was so kind and gentle, and she took the ageing Dandy Nichols under her wing. In later years, Angela would become very famous for her role as Marjory Frobisher in *To the Manor Born* [1979–2007] – but I knew that she had been nominated for an Olivier Award for playing Margaret Thatcher in *Anyone for Denis*. Angela was a truly talented actress and I have many happy memories of our short time together. The leading role went to Edward Hardwicke, who already had a huge reputation behind him for his role in *Colditz* [1972–1973] but also his numerous roles as part of Laurence Olivier's National Theatre. I loved playing the dreamy, head-in-the-clouds and artistic Aunt Celia.'

The Bagthorpe series was ahead of its time. It was so well written that the programmes can be watched again today and the humour is as hilarious now as it was then. Who wouldn't enjoy watching a grandma who was a serial cheat at Scrabble, or a very creative child who was also a talented arsonist?

The books are still in print and would make superb Christmas gifts to encourage that elusive act of reading among the young.

> 'It was [filmed in] a very hot August and in one scene we are meant to be devouring a picnic. At the start of the week it looked yummy and was full of colourful icing on the cakes, but as the week drew on and the wasps flew around us as we pretended to scoff away at the buns, I noticed the holes getting bigger every day – how none of us were stung I just don't know. By the end of filming a few days later all the icing had been devoured by wasps and it looked like something out of Miss Haversham's tragic wedding feast from Charles Dickens. Mind you, I remember well that I was driven around to different locations in a very eccentric and speedy little red sports car, which made the whole thing great fun.'

For her part as Aunt Celia, Maddie had to give her character an ethereal quality, playing 'a potter and poet who believes in fairies with a dreamy quality'. It was a magnificent piece of casting. For good measure, Aunt Celia is described by the children as beautiful and 'very tasty'!

It had been some time since Maddie had sat on a bench waiting for a train with one of her acting heroes, Arthur Lowe, after filming for *Doctor at Large*. It was therefore a lovely surprise when she was given a role in a new series called *A.J. Wentworth, B.A.*, which starred Arthur alongside film stalwart Harry Andrews.[29] Directed by the multi-talented and highly successful Michael Mills, the series was based on the short stories of H.F. Ellis, which had appeared in *Punch* from 1938 and were adapted for television by Basil Boothroyd.

Arthur Lowe, in the sunset years of his career, took on the role of mathematics schoolmaster A.J. Wentworth in this sweet series, set in the 1940s in an English public school. Amid ink nibs, chalk, academic gowns and boys that looked like Harry Potter, the programme was littered with small roles for famous faces. John Bird appeared as Major Faggott, Michael Bevis was Gilbert and Harry Andrews played the part of snobbish headmaster Rev. R. Gregory-Saunders – known as 'Squib' by the boys. The staff at the fictional Burgrove Preparatory School in the town of Wilminster try to control some typically exuberant and unruly boys. A.J. Wentworth has the task of dealing with the boys of Form IIIA, something that H.F. Ellis was able to write about with clarity as he had been a schoolmaster himself.

Filmed on location at Box Hill School near Dorking in early 1982, the series featured Maddie as Mrs Hillman. Playing the part of a parent was rather appropriate, given that Maddie was now a mum herself. She has fond memories of the filming.

> 'Arthur Lowe was clearly not well at the time and struggled here and there but he was as polite and lovely as ever and you could see that this was a role that suited him well. He sort of bumbled along with shades of Captain Mainwaring, not really aware of what the boys were up to, but they held him in deep respect. It was a charming series and deserved more praise than it received – but I can say that about so many things really. The British public did not know how lucky they were to have such talented people able to perform such wonderful pieces for them.'

Soon after filming was finished, Lowe suffered a stroke following an interview on the BBC show *Pebble Mill at One*. He sadly passed away on 15 April 1982, and the series was shown posthumously in his honour during the summer of that year.

Arthur Lowe's funeral was a small affair, with just over a dozen people present. The newspapers reported that Lowe's wife, Joan, did not attend. However, this was not the result of some marital disagreement – far from it. Arthur Lowe's biographer, Graham Lord, later wrote that the couple both lived by the creed that 'the show must go on', agreeing that whichever partner survived, they would not attend the other's funeral, but instead would see a play on the day. Joan indeed went to see a play that they had once both been cast in. Arthur Lowe's ashes were scattered at Sutton Coldfield crematorium.

The stoic Harry Andrews, very appropriately and movingly, read an extract from the lines Lowe had spoken in *A.J. Wentworth B.A.* The entire series of this charming programme is now available on DVD.

After such a hectic and successful year, it was now Maddie Smith BA (Hons) that would need to once more decide on her future but, as her whole life demonstrates, it was fate that would make the decisions and 1983 would begin as 1982 had ended, with a nice and unexpected surprise – an offer of a reunion with the cast of *All Creatures Great and Small*, the BBC having decided to reprise the popular show with a Christmas special.

# Chapter 14

# The Two Masks of Drama

'There is always going to be pain. There is always going to be pleasure. But what is not always going to be there is balance. That is a personal decision.'

Frederick Lenz, writer and spiritual leader

Although Maddie has faced great sadness and tragedy in her life, these have been so personal that she decided they were, for the most part, not going to be a part of this book. During the 1980s, as a mother and later single mother, Maddie continued to do what she has always enjoyed, and that is to perform – that has been the pleasure of her life and she has made a conscious decision to keep doing this as long as she can. That is her 'balance'. Ahead of her were many opportunities to move into children's television as well as maintain her involvement in the theatre. She reached out to grab them as they came her way. Ahead in the coming ten years were two places of extreme pleasure and joy and another of deep and crippling sadness – the two faces of drama exerting their influence through comedy and tragedy.

## 'The Goat Lady' in *All Creatures Great and Small*, Christmas, 1983

Christmas specials were guaranteed to play their part in the ratings war between the BBC and the ITV networks. Putting a biro circle around the *Morecambe and Wise* or *Two Ronnies* Christmas specials in the double-issue *Radio Times* or *TV Times* were all part of the festive preparations, as important as a pillow case at the bottom of the bed for presents or leaving a carrot, mince pie and glass of milk for Santa and Rudolph in the fireplace. The *All Creatures* series had ended in 1980, but such was the enduring popularity of the show that the BBC attempted, with some difficulty, to bring the entire cast back together for a festive one-off special. This was not easy, as everyone was busy, especially Robert Hardy and Peter Davison.[1]

The episode involved James Herriot returning from the war, but bringing with him his experience's psychological after-effects. Nothing is quite the same, and nor is Maddie's character. For instead of rekindling the romance between Tristan and Angela Farmer from earlier episodes, Maddie was cast in a new role as Anne Grantley, the 'Goat Lady' of Yorkshire.

Maddie's reunion with Robert Hardy was predictably a warm and happy one.

> 'Robert Hardy was simply the person that he was on the screen. His role could have been written for him; it was a genius piece of casting that probably made the series the success it was. A lovely positive man with a most unusual voice – always full of energy. And the three lads – as I called them – worked so well together. They were like the Three Musketeers. There was never a cross word, lots and lots of laughing and some very serious professionals who knew what they were doing.
>
> 'The location scenes were filmed in horrific weather, so much so that I was made up in a little school room and filmed outside on my own – everyone else had gone home.'

The acting was of course perfect, taking viewers back to a simpler world where personal relationships and values were more important than fast cars and holidays abroad, where small sandwiches and afternoon tea were *de rigueur*, pampered dogs were called Tricky-Woo and chauffeurs stood tall behind their owners with a grey uniform and worn-out faces. *All Creatures Great and Small* remains one of the very best pieces of costume drama that the BBC ever produced.

Tristan Farnan is beguiled by Anne, whom he first sees at the village market. He asks Christopher Timothy (James): 'Who is that divine creature?' Anne lives with her goats high up in the fells, and their scene discussing goat droppings and bacteria is littered with moments of humour. There are a few wide-eyed 'Gollys' from Maddie in her role as porcelain-complexioned Anne, with her beautiful hair. Against a background of rolling green hills and farmland, time seems to pass by slowly between them. It seems like Tristan may have finally found his 'Miss Right'.

> 'I loved working on this. I had my English degree behind me, I was back acting which, gave me such a renewed sense of joy, and it was perhaps time for me to follow Anne Grantley's lead in the episode, and start my own family.'

The Christmas special was a huge success, with viewing figures far above what the BBC had expected. Maddie's face was once more familiar, a comfortable fit for casting directors, and 1984 looked like it was going to be a busy year – as it turned out, for all sorts of reasons, it was.

## *The Passionate Pilgrim*, 1983–1984

Just after the recording had taken place for *All Creatures Great and Small* in 1983, another offer came along. This time it was to play alongside Tom Baker and the national treasure that was Eric Morecambe in a comedy that Eric – and only Eric – could play in his particular style.

> 'Oh heavens, what a genius. Eric Morecambe was fabulous. Everything that you imagine and more. He never stopped practising his tricks with his glasses or sending people up. He was uncomplaining. Tom Baker was star-struck and wouldn't let Eric go to bed. He was so in awe of him and they sat in the bar until the early hours. We stayed in the Spa Hotel Tunbridge Wells and travelled out to Hever [Castle], and we were at it all day long. Hever was in bad state of repair at that time, so they probably managed to hire the location quite cheaply – not like it would be today! Our director was Charles Wallace, an Australian, who was very kind throughout filming what is a gentle and funny little film, very much in the Eric Morecambe style.'

The *Passionate Pilgrim*, a short comedy film of under 40 minutes, was shown in 1984. There were very few speaking parts, the programme being completed in mime, perfectly narrated by the erudite John Le Mesurier.[2] This little film is noteworthy for a number of reasons. Firstly, it was the final role played by Eric Morecambe, who was already ill. Secondly, Eric was not with his partner, Ernie Wise, which made this a very rare piece of work. Finally, it would be almost the last piece of work by John Le Mesurier, who was also quite unwell.

*The Passionate Pilgrim* was written and directed by Charles Wallace, who had created *Betjeman's Britain* with Peter Cook and Maddie Smith back in 1980. An experienced hand, he worked across all fifteen of the original ITV franchises, as well as with musicians Gerry Rafferty and Mike Oldfield. The quirky concept of this little film appealed to his sense of fun. Tom Baker was invited to play the part of a knight called Sir Thomas of Uppingham (those 'Carry On' film character names just would not die) in a collection of twenty poems in the style of Shakespeare (although only five are directly attributable to The Bard), dealing with love, desire and the complexity of emotions that make up any relationship.[3] The film added a comedic slant, in which both Tom Baker's knight and Eric Morecambe's lord vie for the attentions of a beautiful girl.[4] Maddie, performing in a castle that had once been the family home to the Dukes of Norfolk and Anne Boleyn, was dressed in stunning medieval costumes, waiting to see if the brave knight could break into the castle despite being sprayed by the lord with an aerosol can of 'Knight-Rid'. It was light-hearted fun, typical of Eric Morecambe's talent for visual comedy.

One of the first opportunities for new work for Maddie in 1984 came with an offer to join the Cambridge Theatre Group to tour and perform *Canaries Sometimes Sing*. This was a short play by Frederick Lonsdale, which had been a popular hit in London in 1929 and also a successful film in 1931. Rehearsals began almost straight away in early January 1984. It was a small cast of only four players, with a witty, fast-paced script about two couples unhappy in their marriages. The first performances came in February and March 1984. In a rare insight into her true personality, Maddie at last let down her guard, stood up in the little dark room at the top of The Bookshop in East Grinstead where we had been meeting every month for over six months, and started acting. It was a glorious moment, unscripted and spontaneous; Maddie clearly could not help herself. And there she was, at last, free of all the smoke and mirrors, the thing that I had been trying to find out all this time, just who was Maddie Smith.

> 'I played Elma, and this was the best part I ever played. Elma was me – a minx, always sidling up and causing trouble, plotting and listening to conversations for ammunition.'

This coy character suddenly emerged in front of me, looking over her left shoulder with fluttering eyelashes, arms and hands clasped tightly to her sides as she swivelled back and forth in full artistic motion. Her protection in life has been to be all things to all people, never attracting attention but always there: sweet, pretty, devoid of malice. She had learned how to cope with her natural beauty, which was both a gift and a curse. The coping strategies of a lifetime suddenly fell away, and a playful, sweet and genuine woman emerged like a butterfly, casting off the cocoon that guarded her throughout her life. For a few seconds I was her audience, given a privileged performance lasting all of ten seconds.

The part of Elma gave Maddie a chance to step back onto the stage for the first time since *Have You Anything to Declare* in 1980. It would have been so much easier for her to have just rested then, changed career and found something more reliable by way of an income. But this was not the way for the Maddie who I had now come to know.

> 'I have always regretted not having added the extra year to my degree to train as a teacher at Goldsmiths. It was the final year in which it was not necessary to have maths O-level, which I had voluntarily given up at school – something that should not have been allowed to happen – but I still wanted to perform. It was the love affair that would not die.'

The passion to act was as strong in 1984 as it had been in 1967, when she was a child and still at school.

In July and August 1984, Maddie reunited with Frankie Howerd in a stage version of *The Fly and The Fox* at the Churchill Theatre in Bromley. Adapated by Barry Took and Alick Morrison, a strong cast was assembled, which also included Ken Wynne. Maddie felt that Ken – a name now largely long forgotten – was simply the funniest man she had ever met.[5]

> 'When Ken was on form, the audience could laugh so hard that the rafters felt like they were shaking. His timing and facial expressions were just unique. Ken and I had been in the cast for *Shut Your Eyes and Think of England* when, during one evening performance, one of his contact lenses popped out. No one realized this to begin with, and then Ken started delivering his lines from all fours as he crawled around like a deranged madman on the floor. Gradually we all twigged what had happened and, one by one, we all started doing the same. The audience must have thought we were all going mad – unless, in the words of Alec Guinness, they were Japanese of course – and Ken then began laughing at himself. Oh my god it was infectious, and the whole stage could have ended up in chaos as we started to chuckle. I thought Ken was making this into a new part of the play and, just then, he leapt up and carried on with his original lines as if nothing had happened, having popped the lens back in. It was hilarious and he was a true pro – the show must go on after all.'

## *The Steam Video Company*, 1983–1984

Sometimes I wonder how Maddie crammed everything in to her life, but then she reminds me that lines could often be learnt and filmed within a few days, from inception to creation. This meant there was actually quite a lot of free time, unless she was on the stage daily in a full theatre production. It is thus not surprising that Maddie managed to fit in recordings for yet another television comedy production very late in 1983.

The brainchild of writers Andrew Marshall and David Renwick, *The Steam Video Company* was given a six-episode series by Thames Television. The original concept was to put the modern age of video in counterpoint with the golden age of steam – hence 'Steam Video'. Each episode was a parody of the low-budget horror movies of the 1960s and early 1970s, with non-stop jokes and ridiculous sketches, some of which fell flat while others were brilliant and would have been at home in the best episodes of *Monty Python*. Maddie featured in the sketch 'Bike Across The Rockies' with Jimmy Mulville, while in the same episode Barry Cryrer, in best hammed-up Jewish accent, appeared in 'Moses Schmoses' – you get the idea.[6] Bob Todd seemed to turn up everywhere, and as soon as he arrived laughter erupted. As it did with Barry, who doubled as Groucho Marx, complete with cigar and pith helmet, and lines like 'If I could stoop that low, I wouldn't need the talcum powder'. Maybe one needs to watch it to understand it. Maddie's facial expressions certainly suggest that she was trying very hard to keep up with the machine-gun banter of these highly talented comedians.

Maddie's character had apparently written a book about breeding rabbits, called *How to Make a Fast Buck*, and when asked by the dry and droll William Franklin (clearly needing to pay his electricity bill), 'Is it in Penguin?', she responds, 'No, it's in English.' Need I go on?[7] But despite the jokes, this short series was and is now considered a comedy classic. Transmitted from 19 January to 23 February 1984, a lasting image – for which some really ought to receive counselling – is seeing Bob Todd descend from above, dressed in a large and poorly fitting spider costume while uttering some unintelligible lines of dialogue. It is at one and the same time confusing and yet hilarious.

## Moliere and Terry Scott, 1984

There were even more roles in 1984, both on television and on the stage. In March and April of that year this included rehearsing with the household name that was Terry Scott. Terry was loved by the British public for his harmless brand of comedy, and *Terry and June*, with co-star June Whitfield, had been a hit since it began five years earlier in 1979. However, Terry harboured a desire to act in more classical roles and had agreed to work on a production of Moliere's *The School for Wives*.

> 'Terry was adorable and just like his television characters – funny, kind and gentle. But his mind was always racing, and he talked and chattered so fast it was hard to keep up with him. The play began in May 1984 at The Yvonne Arnaud Theatre, where I had many happy memories from playing there in *Blue Comedy* all those years previously. Our director was the very able and respected Roger Redfarn.
>
> 'The costumes were wonderful, and Terry wore his black tricorn hat and I my low-fronted embroidered dresses – with a corset. However, I was now pregnant! I tried to carefully loosen the cords, but director Roger kept coming up to me, delicately asking if I could perhaps tighten my corset up … it clearly was obvious. It was a tricky situation, as I had tried to keep my secret quiet for as long as I could.'

Being on stage with Moliere in the early summer of 1984 was soon followed by an appearance in a mini-series of Charles Dickens' *The Pickwick Papers*, Maddie taking the role of Miss Nupkins in episode seven. This was a chance for a reunion with Carl Davis, whose musical talents had expanded across film and television since *The End of the Pier Show*. Maddie played opposite Nigel Stock as Mr Pickwick and the magnificent Patrick Malahide as Mr Jingle in an episode that aired on 17 February 1985.[8] Maddie had to wear a specially adjusted costume for *The Pickwick Papers* because of her pregnancy, carrying on acting until a couple of weeks before the birth.

> 'At that time Patrick was doing a one-man show at the Royal Court Theatre as the dying George III, and it was one of the finest performances from any actor that I have ever seen.'

Maddie's beloved daughter, Emily – 'the best present I ever had' – was born just two weeks after recording her part in *The Pickwick Papers*. David, along with Maddie's father Robert and mum Ursula, were overjoyed.

## 'Regets, I've Had a Few, but Then Again ...'

From the outside looking in, one can be forgiven for feeling that the whole acting profession lives in a world of loveliness. Fellow actors are 'lovely', directors are 'wonderful' and writers are 'amazing' – the list of superlatives is almost exhausting. So when I probed Maddie further and asked what regrets she had, it was because the masks of comedy and sadness have an equal billing in most lives. In Maddie Smith's case, it is not that there are so few regrets that they are too few to mention, but rather that they are too painful.

Certainly, the relationship with her father, Bob, is something that she has grappled with all her life. Maddie still bears the emotional scars of a childhood wrecked by guilt, illness and trauma, yet tempered with affection, deep understanding and empathy. As Maddie often tells me, she is her father's daughter. School days are painful memories, as is the longing for recognition for a career that did actually hit the heights – one does not appear on the West End stage for a year with Sir Alec Guinness, followed by another year with Sir Donald Sinden and then yet another in *The Mousetrap*, if one cannot act. But these pale in significance compared to the tragic loss of a loving partner and the humiliation of being treated like a fool.

Maddie's partner in life, David Buck, co-starred in thirteen episodes of *Sherlock Holmes* for radio, and in addition wrote new material for radio and for the stage in the early 1970s. It was his passion to be creative – and he was talented. Those early plays for radio had established his name, and it was his gift that kept on giving in terms of new commissions. Now that he was a family man, they were sorely needed.

*The Image of God* was his own version of the 'Mystery Plays', running from 20 March to 3 April 1980, directed by the genius that is Martin Jenkins. From this flowed a whole series of other works for radio. David worked long hours and had a brilliant eye for detail, which made his work very appealing to the BBC. David scored a major success when he adapted eighteen Raffles adventures for radio, which were broadcast over three series in 1985, 1992 and 1998. In 1983, David wrote *Barnsdale Wake*, which was aired on16 January 1983, starring Dennis Quilley and Julian Glover. This was followed in April 1984 with a BBC Radio 4 presentation to celebrate Shakespeare's birthday. Entitled *The Actors Are Come Hither*, David compiled a series of readings from the Bard that were read out by a distinguished cast that included Timothy West, Dorothy Tutin and Ian McKellen. Thanks to such work, David was respected and widely known throughout the profession.

In 1984, while Maddie was recording *The Pickwick Papers* and on stage in Moliere with Terry Scott – whilst also trying to loosen her corsets as she coped with her pregnancy – David surpassed his previous efforts when he adapted for radio *Her Privates We* by Frederic Manning. Admired as 'one of the very finest accounts in the vernacular of the lives of ordinary soldiers in World War One', David's adaptation was aired to great acclaim on 20 August 1984.

As Maddie looked after 2-year old Emily in 1986, David Buck next produced *Conflict of Doves*, a Monday night play for Radio 4 that was an interesting tale set against the Berlin Olympics of 1936. He then wrote *The Robe* as a Radio 4 six-part serial in 1987. David was prolific – as prolific as a man who could foresee his own end. His greatest achievement, however, was adapting Robert Nye's *Falstaff* as a one-man show for radio, directed by John Tydeman – a friend, contemporary from Cambridge and head of BBC Radio drama.

> 'Bill Kenwright, a former actor himself, very kindly took *Falstaff* and put it on at the Fortune Theatre in London, and for David, this was ascending Mount Everest in his career. He was wonderful as Falstaff and the final line in the piece is "Remember me".'

On 8 July 1988, Maddie and David took a trip to Glyndebourne to watch an opera when David noticed something strange about his driving. It was difficult for him to keep the car straight on the road, and he developed a terrible headache. The pain continued for a few days and, when he sat with his head in his hands and told Maddie that he would not wish this on his worst enemy, Maddie called in a doctor, who dismissed the pain as depression. A few days later, David was driving to Glastonbury to complete some filming with Susan Penhaligon. Richard and Annie Briers' daughter was working as an assistant and detected that something was wrong with David. David managed to get home, where he just sat in a chair for twenty-four hours. His black tuxedo hung over a chair for almost a week, not put away from the Glastonbury trip.

'I drove David to Charing Cross Hospital, but they told him they could not see him and sent him home. But David knew he was ill and told me to go home – he was going to stay until they did see him. Sure enough, the next morning the telephone rang in the hall. I was in the garden pottering around and mowing the lawn, and a doctor on the other end told me that he considered me to be a very well balanced young woman by the way I had acted the day before, and that I needed to know that David was seriously ill with only six months to live. With my permission, they were going to operate straightaway. I was too devastated for words, and still am.'

Nothing is predictable in this largely happy and inspiring tale of a woman who just kept going – and still does. In a dramatic twist of love and affection, David and Maddie still had one more performance to give. At 1.00 pm on 7 August 1988, five months before the end of David's life, Maddie and David were married in the chapel of Charing Cross Hospital, where David was receiving intensive treatment.

'This date was chosen as we had to do this before he began receiving daily radiotherapy.'

Maddie and David had both realized that the ceremony needed to happen sooner rather than later. Seeing the hospital chaplain passing David's bed, Maddie asked him if he would perform the ceremony, which took place within a few days.

'This was easily the worst month of my life. We had also just moved house and then this [happened], but this exquisite service was provided by the hospital – staff, catering, music and everything – they were incredible at Charing Cross. On 2 August, my birthday, I had to go to Westminster Abbey to the sanctuary while a piece of paper, a dispensation, was prepared to allow me to get married without banns being read.

'The day began in my father's garden on a very hot day – Dad poured water from a watering can on Emmy's head. Then he drove us all to the hospital. The John Piper stained glass panels either side of the altar, one of which is the tree of life, were just gorgeous that day. The only witnesses were my very good friends Dr and Mrs Gavin and Sarah Webb-Wilson and my parents – my father gave me away and 3-year-old Emily, who was bridesmaid, was enchanting in her little dress on the day, getting completely drunk on champagne which she helped herself to as if it were water; hilariously to us all, she ended up lying on the floor with her legs stuck up in the air like a green and red beetle.'

Driven on by the needs of Maddie and Emily, David continued to work and towards the end of 1988 even performed for one of the last times in the cast of his adaptation of *The Dead Drummer*, one of the *Ingoldsby Legends*.

> 'David was allowed out of hospital for this performance. David said to me from his bed that "you do not have a choice, you have to get me out of this hospital bed to record this part", and I begged them to allow him to do this. The BBC sprang into action to receive him, and the hospital provided transport for my dying husband to BBC Radio Portland Place and back again to his bed. David had only just received surgery for two tumours and had a split like the parting of the Red Sea at the back of his head. By chance, this episode was aired on radio on 25 January 1989 – two days later David would pass away in The Princess Alice Hospice in Esher. He was so brave.'

It was startling to sit listening to Maddie while researching for this book – where I tended to listen and try to imagine a time when I might be able to ask a question – to suddenly be told: *'Oh, by the way, it is my wedding anniversary today.'* Startled as I was, I was unable to seize the moment to actually ask anything, and Maddie picked up the reins before I could draw beath. *'Yes, I married David today back in 1989 – he had been given only six months to live you see.'* No matter how easily bruised or how vulnerable Maddie can be, her ability to cloak herself with the defence that all good actors possess – the mask of tragedy that defies emotion in the face of an audience – showed itself at that very moment. I was full of respect, both for what she had done and how she had never forgotten. Maddie and I always met at 1.00 pm, and that day was 7 August. No tears, just admission and memory.

These are memories that never disappear – both the good and the painful – and although 'stoic' is, in the contemporary world, a much-used and even more misunderstood word, Maddie has always displayed the sense of detachment and lack of complaint about her life that would please any Greek philosopher. If what happened to David forms part of her regrets that are too few to mention, then so does an incident of professional discourtesy that affects her even today, from as far back as1992, just after Maddie had completed her year-long run in *The Moustrap*.

The *theatre de l'absurde* was a largely European movement for playwrights that developed in the 1950s and was designed to open up new ideas of existentialism, where man reacts to a world that has no apparent meaning and invisible, perhaps controlling, forces dominate their lives. In the English tradition of such plays, it is James Saunders that stands out as one of the foremost exponents of this style of expression. Saunders' work had already received numerous accolades in the early 1960s, and one of his plays – *Making it Better* – was successfully performed at the Hampstead Theatre between February and March 1992, the Richmond Theatre in early October and was due to open at the Criterion Theatre in London on 21 October 1992. This was another play supported by Michael Codron, the London theatre impresario.

Since David's death three years earlier, Maddie had been a full-time mum to Emily. It was not a case of having little time for her career and to work – there was no time. Emily was a busy, demanding and energetic little girl, now aged 6, and Maddie was both exhausted and penniless. The regularity of income from *The Mousetrap* had ended; this was the fallow period of her career. In order to make ends meet, Maddie was willing to take on almost any role, so accepted the part of understudy to the female lead in *Making it Better*, the talented Jane Asher. Along with a very young Rufus Sewell, Jane Asher was one of only four actors in the play, a new comedy 'wittily describing the painful search for loyalty in people and politics'.

> 'The understudy is a vital part of any theatre community and meant to be respected as such, but I speak for understudies everywhere when I say that, unfortunately, not everyone regards the understudy with the degree of respect that he/she deserves.'

Rehearsals were going well and Maddie did as was expected of her; she sat close to but away from the main performers, tracing their lines and acting in her head, ready, should she ever be needed, to stand in and pick up from the exact moment required in the play. Banter during any rehearsal is all part of the flow of learning the part, and it was an off-the-cuff remark from Rufus Sewell that he looked forward to playing Shakespeare that caused Maddie to innocently pipe up from her chair that she felt Rufus would make a wonderful Hamlet. No one expected what happened next. Perhaps it was the stress of the moment, maybe something else going on his life or just plain inexplicable rudeness, that caused the director to explode at Maddie.

> 'He suddenly screamed at me. "You are an understudy. Your job is to sit in the corner and keep quiet."'

All around there was a stunned silence at this unexpected outburst of temper, which reduced Maddie to tears and caused clear embarrassment to everyone within range of the director's expletives. She felt like walking away, but swallowed it, her sense of professionalism prevented her from doing so. Maddie retreated back into that invisible shell of timidity and guilt that she had always carried with her since she started work aged 16 all those years before. She still feels very hurt by the incident.

> 'That was just a terrible experience for me. I had never been humiliated like that by anyone – even when I had made the mistakes that even the best of us make, but this time I had not made a mistake, merely spoken up, and that made it all the more unfair. I have regretted the incident ever since – even after all this time, I just have a desire to make up with this man, even though I really had not done anything wrong. He would not speak to me then, nor would he speak to me when we met years later at a funeral. I went up to him and asked if we could be friends – after all, a lot of water had passed under the bridge since 1992. But time did not seem to have softened him at all. He just said that he had people he wanted to see and turned his back on me, just snubbed me and walked away. I felt like a leper. This was a unique experience, as all other directors have been kind, encouraging and supportive to me throughout my career.'

The entertainment business is full of talented people. Like all those for whom creativity is the driver, it sometimes comes at a cost, working with all sorts of emotional souls who work at different levels of stress. Maddie survived this experience, but as her father had once warned her, she was too soft to be a nurse and perhaps she was almost too soft to be an actress. Yet to her great credit, she has battled through all her life, and still survives the slings and arrows that pass her way.

## Chapter 15

# *The Mousetrap* and the End of Act I

> 'Out of my weakness and my melancholy,
> As he is very potent with such spirits,
> Abuses me to damn me. I'll have grounds
> More relative than this. The play's the thing
> Wherein I'll catch the conscience of the king.'
>
> Hamlet Act II ii

Every now and again, a play comes along and hits the West End like a whirlwind that captures the imagination of the British public; the media erupts and the public scramble for tickets to view the new phenomenon. Yet it was certainly not like this when *The Mousetrap* opened at The Ambassadors Theatre in the West End on 25 November 1952.[1]

Originally, Agatha Christie had written a short radio play as a birthday present for King George V and Queen Mary, and it was first broadcast on 30 May 1947 with the title *Three Blind Mice*. Drawing her creative idea from the tragic story of Dennis O'Neill, whose premature death at the age of 12 in 1945 had led to a complete revision of all fostering provision in the United Kingdom, Christie gave the rights to the play to her grandson, Matthew Prichard, as a birthday present. This has to have been one of the best birthday presents ever. Christie, being a shrewd businesswoman, added a whole series of clauses, such as that no film adaptation could be made until the play had closed on the West End stage for at least six months and that only one production of the play could be performed annually outside of the West End. One can only wonder if Agatha Christie foresaw that *The Mousetrap* would be the longest-running play in the world, having its 30,000th performance in March 2025?

There was, however, already another play in existence called *Three Blind Mice*, written by Emile Littler, who insisted that Christie's play be renamed.

It was her son-in-law who suggested the revised name of *The Mousetrap*, basing this on a line from Shakespeare about a play within a play which was designed to catch the conscience and the eye of a king.[2]

To sustain the vibrancy of this long-running play, the cast has been regularly renewed, with hundreds of actors playing one of the small number of parts. Maddie was given her opportunity to audition in November 1989. Leaving Emily with her granny, it was a cold November day – one of those days that always seems colder and wetter than it actually is if you are walking the streets of London – when Maddie arrived to audition for the part of Molly Ralston, which had first been played in 1952 by the gorgeous Sheila Sim.

> 'Mousetrap is Cluedo on stage. Ill-assorted, unpleasant characters are thrown together in a creepy guesthouse. United against their will by a snowfall, their emotional lives are laid bare to the audience, and there ensues a murder most foul. My character, Molly, is an innocent, with a husband scarcely more knowing than herself. Together they mismanage Monkwell Manor, the grim guesthouse that is the focus of the set.'[3]

The now Maddie Buck could not contain her joy when she was offered the part, knowing that she would be back on stage in the West End for a year. In addition to the thrill of performing, she would also have a regular income for her and Emily to lean upon. This was a ray of sunlight in a year that had begun with David's death in January. Grief was slowly giving way to the hope that 1990 and the months ahead would be more positive. Maddie, with the help of mum Ursula looking after Emily, first of all rehearsed and then stepped out once more on the stage to begin a year-long contract at St Martin's Theatre.

The opening night for the new cast could not have gone better. Indeed, the whole ensemble worked seamlessly together, every performance a joy until a few months into the run.

> 'My on-stage husband was played by Giles Ralston. One night I noticed that he looked really odd. His face was a beetroot colour and he looked as though he was boiling over. In our key scene together, where I was busy accusing him of scuttling off to London, evidenced by my finding a copy of the *London Evening Standard* in his pocket, I threw down the newspaper onto the table, shouting, "I KNOW you are lying!" Instead of doing what he had always done, Giles instead slumped down and cradled himself into the

> plaster mantlepiece and started declaiming speeches from *Hamlet*, crying out for his imaginary lost love, Helena Bonham Carter, who had once played Ophelia.
>
> 'Giles was very evidently raving, poor chap, and the audience were not sure whether this was part of the play. With no choice, I left him whimpering on stage, and dashed into the wings, softly crying "HELP ME!!"'[4]

Quite what had happened to him at that moment we will never know. It could have been an illness with a fever, or more likely a breakdown. But either way, Maddie received little help from the wings.

> 'The company manager should have responded by bringing down the curtain on proceedings. Instead, he flapped his long arms, said "Don't bother me now!" and disappeared into Dressing Room Number One. There, Pamela Lane, former first wife of playwright John Osborne, was always waiting with a chilled bottle of Chardonnay.[5]
>
> 'Now in frantic despair, I called my elderly friend and fellow cast member, the late Paul Imbusch, from his second-floor room. Paul was always bad-tempered before the show but, by now, his foul mood had dissipated and he was game to have fun. He relished his role as *The Mousetrap*'s red herring, Mr Paravacini. Our verbal spats were loud, but apologies came in the shape of cream cakes and port - good for the throat of course.'

Perhaps the audience on that night was another of those crowds that Alec Guinness had claimed were 'all Japanese', as no-one noticed that one of the actors was going through a complete breakdown on stage, perhaps believing this was how English plays unfolded. In any event, Paul and Maddie strode back on stage and invented some ludicrous dialogue, and the curtain was brought down – to sustained applause and a huge measure of relief.

> 'To make matters worse, as if that were possible, understudy Simon was down the road in the Two Brewers Pub in St Martin's Lane - an understudy is allowed to relax once the cast actor has made their first entrance. Luckily for everyone, Simon had not had time to drink too much, was quickly fished out of the pub and ran back to the theatre rather fast, to be told "you are on mate!" So, I had a husband at last and we went on as though nothing had happened.'

Such are the lives of those who create dreams in our lives when they often have nightmares in their own. Apparently, Maddie tells us, Giles had said 'goodnight' to a very surprised stage-door lady as he left halfway through the performance, hopped into his car and drove to Wormwood Scrubs prison, where he left the car and wandered the streets before being taken into custody. Poor Giles was treated for depression and 'returned to *The Mousetrap* exactly one month later, as though nothing had happened'.

As has been seen, Maddie Smith has the mind of a computer server on full-charge and rarely – if ever – forgets any detail. It is a talent that has served her well throughout her stage, television and film career. It also allows us another peek behind the scenes of *The Mousetrap*, where actor Nicholas Smith – of Mr Rumbold fame in *Are You Being Served* – had a habit of walking around the dressing rooms on matinee days dressed only in his underpants.[6] It was not a vision of beauty, as Maddie explained in her 2022 article for *The Oldie*: 'He was a lovely chap but virtually nude was not a pretty sight.'

In the 1990 run of *The Mousetrap*, the part of Miss Casewell was played by Cheryl Kennedy. Another convent school girl, Cheryl and Maddie hit it off so well that it made a year seem to fly by in weeks.[7] Audiences for the production were good. Maddie loved her part and looked forward to every performance, and of course the applause for a job well played – it was an almost perfect year.

## The curtain falls on Act I

*The Mousetrap* ended on a Saturday night. No cast members were allowed to play their parts for more than twelve months, and Maddie needed a rest, as did Granny Ursula, who was exhausted by little Emily. Maddie's daughter was becoming a young person and needed more of her mummy's time. There were also matters to deal with at home, where her father, Bob, had fallen ill again, and it was at this point in 1991 that the full-time acting career of Maddie Smith took a bow, to the applause of her final lines in *The Mousetrap*. Maddie drove home, went to bed and woke up on a Sunday morning realizing that one long act of her life had finished. She now needed time to pause, bring up Emily and then write the next act. She had known this moment was coming and had prepared for it. The next thirty years, between then and the creation of this book, have seen a whole series of other adventures in what we might call Acts II and III of her life, but to cover those is not the purpose of this book.

> 'I really wanted to become a full-time mum and the time seemed right. My own mother had been amazing and looked after Ems for a whole year, feeding her, entertaining and teaching her, plaiting her hair for school and taking her to and from school, and I had also been teaching poetry and reading in reception classes at Emily's school. I would then pop home and speed off for another evening performance. It had all become too much and, although the adrenaline drove me on and I loved it, I knew I had been lucky and my mum could not go on forever.'

The curtain thus came down on Act I of Maddie Smith's life when her contract for *The Mousetrap* ended. Since that time, Maddie has indeed written a number of new scenes in the play that is her life and career, with Emily beside her all the way.

During the mid-1960s, Maddie entered a world that was changing unbelievably fast, reconstructing itself after the horrors of the Second World War. She took those first tentative steps aware that she was attractive and had something unique about her, but was not quite sure what that was and could never in fact see it for herself. This self-blindness has remained with Maddie all her professional life. What her father had noticed in 1963 was quite unique, as those very early photographs taken by Fred testify. Like a Greek statue, it was not sex appeal, it was beauty – a beauty that Maddie has had to cope with her entire life.

As a very in-demand model and actress, surviving the 1960s – with its haze of drugs, parties, sexual liberation and unbridled freedom – was in itself an achievement. As this book has revealed, many did not make it out of the decade and into the equally amazing 1970s. The fact that Maddie maintained her shape as a person is testament to her incredibly strong personality, which has kept her going and avoided the many traps along the way in what can be a cut-throat industry. Maddie went on to build her career in the 1970s to a point where she was recognized everywhere, then continued her progress and was never out of work in the whole of the 1980s. Along the way, Maddie has met hundreds of talented and wonderful people, and her memories reveal so much about the characters and world in which she worked. But Maddie never lost her love for the theatre, indeed for acting in all its forms, and to this day has a schedule of appearances to fulfil for fans of Dr Frankenstein and the Hammer horror films, and of course for the millions of followers of the James Bond movies. She is still out there playing to audiences, with her genuine and loving nature, as we move through the 2020s.

Maddie discovered from an early age that beauty is a double-edged sword, finding a way to survive without losing her way. She learned coping strategies in her sometimes-troubled childhood, and then how to guard herself as she grew up and encountered one piece of good luck after another. She always looked to older men for their reliability, wisdom and safety, finding the right ones who recognized her vulnerability and genuine heart. Just as she is quick to say about everyone she meets, Maddie Smith is also a lovely person.

Maddie has been far too busy for the past sixty years to finish reading the story of *The Brothers Karamazov*, the book that helped launch her career in modelling all those years ago when she hid in the basement of Biba. But she continues to write her own story in front of audiences – and where there is no audience, she creates one, for, after all, the play's the thing.

# Notes

**Chapter 1**

1. Many of the buildings form Maddie's childhood still remain in Forest Row, and she can still match contemporary photographs with where she grew up.
2. Special thanks are due to the Parish Secretary for providing information on the church.

**Chapter 2**

1. Pel, Martin, *The Biba Years, 1963–1974 (*V&A Publishing, 2014).
2. Lewis Morley would later emigrate to Australia in 1971 and lived in Sydney. He created a retrospective at the National Portrait Gallery in 1989 and his autobiography, *Black & White Lies*, was published in 1992. Morley died in September 2013, aged 88, and his archive was donated to the National Media Museum in Bradford.
3. The Fashion & Textile Museum, *The BIBA Story 1964–1975.*
4. *Ibid.*
5. Not many people know this, but it was Biba that manufactured and sold the first cosmetic range for Black men.
6. 'What happens when a photogragpher plans to shoot swimsuits outdoors and it rains?', anonymous article in *V&V Collections*, 1963. John Cowan was born in 1929 in Gillingham and became one of the most sought-after fashion photographers of the 1960s. He passed away in September 1979 in East Hagbourne, Oxfordshire.
7. *The Brothers Karamazov* had taken Dostoevsky nearly two years to write, but it would take over twenty for Maddie to read!
8. Donald Silverstein was another London great in the world of photography in the 1960s. Born in 1934, Silverstein opened his London studio on Riding House Street, near Carnaby Street, and the new Biba catalogue was one of his first major fashion projects. In 1967 he would create one of the most famous sets of portraits of Jimi Hendrix. He died far too young in 1975.
9. Robert Amram (b. 1938) began his film career in the 1960s, and wrote and directed *The Mini Affair* in 1967. He won two Academy Awards in 1972.
10. From The Pirate Radio Hall of Fame, 'Disc-Jockeys D'.
11. *Oxford Dictionary of National Biography 1928–1997,* Evelyn Florence Kark nee Gordine, known as Lucy Clayton.
12. In the 1960s, New Bond Street became one of the most vibrant areas of London, with new developments, nightclubs and music that thronged the street, in contrast to the downtown Dubai of today.

**Chapter 3**

1. Mick Jagger also lived in Cheyne Walk.
2. Frankie's Nightclub was just coolness personified. It was one of the hardest places to get into.

3. Dandie Fashions was a joint venture between Guinness heir Tara Browne (1945–1966) and fashion entrepreneur Freddie Hornik (1944–2009). Tara was buried on the family Luggala Estate near Loch Tay.
4. Burt Bacharach (1928–2023) was already an established songwriter, and his songs of the Sixties inspired a love of fast cars, jet travel, sports cars and sleek bachelor pads, watching the girls go by.
5. Donald Cammell (1934–1996) was a precociously talented Scottish painter, screenwriter and director. With a cult reputation, the well-known, popular, Bohemian and wild Donald Cammell is an iconic figure in the history or the 1960s in London. His tragic and unusual death in 1996 marked the end of an obsessive existence.
6. Anita Pallenberg (1942–2017) was a style icon and 'It Girl', and had been born in either Hamburg or Rome (depending on which source you believe) before arriving in London and pursuing her romantic relationships with two members of the Rolling Stones.
7. Brian Jones (1942–1969) was the founder of the Rolling Stones and a stylistic and musical icon of the 1960s. He was found dead in his swimming pool, and although the police decided that it was death by misadventure, there was subsequent evidence that it may have been murder.
8. Donald Cammel died of a self-inflicted wound on 24 April 1996 in Hollywood.
9. Michael Cooper (1941–1973) is a central figure in the record of London society in the 1960s. His short, creative life deserves an updated exposure in a new book. He died by suicide.
10. Sharon Tate (1943–1969) was an American actress whose life was tragically cut short by her murder by Charles Manson and his cult followers.
11. Warren Beatty (born 1937) is married to Annette Bening and his sister is Shirley MacLaine. At the time Maddie met him, Beatty was aged 31, handsome and a Hollywood A-list star.
12. Prudence Glynn (1935–1986) was a British fashion journalist for *The Times* and also an author, and was pivotal in the coverage of the huge changes in the fashion industry that took place from Fifties' couture formality into the youthful Swinging Sixties.

**Chapter 4**

1. Sir Mick Jagger (born 1943) is a British rock musician who has been a dominant figure on the world pop scene since the early 1960s. When Maddie met Mick, he was already a national celebrity and some of the Rolling Stones' most successful songs had been in the charts.
2. Marianne Faithful (1946–2025) was born in Hampstead and rose to fame in both Britain and the USA, having been discovered by the manager of the Rolling Stones, Andrew Oldham.
3. Andrew Loog Oldham (born 1944) is a British record producer, impresario and author whose flamboyant style promoted the Rolling Stones to chart success between 1963 and 1967. Oldham's father was a United States Army Air Forces officer who was killed when his B17 bomber was shot down over the English Channel.
4. Movie Locations.com: '*Performance*', 3 June 2025.
5. Schofield, Matthew, '*The Ballad of Tam-Lin*', from *Between the Cracks You Sometimes Find Gold*, November 2011.
6. Ava Gardner (1922–1990) was a world-famous actress and Hollywood leading lady. By the time she was offered the part in *Tam-Lin*, Ava's list of film credits was substantial.

7. Stephanie Beacham (born 1947) first appeared on television in 1967 and was very new to acting, with *Tam-Lin* being only her second film.
8. Roddy McDowell (1928–1998) was a British-American actor whose career spanned over sixty years. *The Ballad of Tam-Lin* in 1970 would be his first and only venture into directing.
9. Ian McShane (born 1942) is a Lancashire lad who studied at RADA with Anthony Hopkins and John Hurt.
10. Kip Gowans (1930–2011) was a Cumbrian-born assistant director who met his future wife, Lee Remick, while working on a film called *Hard Contract* in 1969. They married the following year in 1970 and remained together until her death in 1991, aged 55.
11. Sean Connery (1930–2020) was the first actor to play James Bond in motion pictures. He would make a total of seven Bond films between 1962 and 1983.
12. Thornton, Michael, 'The Drunken Night Ava Gardner confessed all to me', *Scottish Daily Mail*, May 2000
13. Dudley Moore (1935–2002) was a musician, comedian, actor and composer, rising to prominence as a leading celebrity within the boom in British satire in the early 1960s.
14. Smith, Maddie., 'How Peter Cook Made Me Fall in Love with Laughter', *The Oldie*, 2012.
15. *Ibid*.
16. Bernard Cribbins (1928–2022) worked and performed in the entertainment industry for over eighty years and across all mediums – theatre, film, stage and radio.
17. Elen, Richard G., 'Thames Television', *Screenonline*, 20 May 2007.
18. 'Cribbins 1969', *The British Comedy Guide*.
19. Bob Todd (1922–1992) was a comedy actor who was best known for his roles as the straight man to Benny Hill and Spike Milligan.
20. Carmel McSharry (1926–2018) was an Irish character actress who played a wide range of parts in numerous popular television series of the 1960s and 1970s.
21. There would be two series in all, the last episode airing on 20 October 1970.

**Chapter 5**

1. Hammer Film Productions Ltd was most productive between 1950 and 1980. Classic horror film stars such as Vincent Price, Ralph Bates, Peter Cushing and Christopher Lee all owe part of their fame to working for Hammer films.
2. *Taste The Blood of Dracula* was directed by Peter Sasdy, who would go on to direct numerous other Hammer films.
3. Roy Kinnear (1934–1988), a product of RADA, was one of the most talented character actors of his generation, a gift that has been inherited by his son, Rory. Roy was loved by everyone that worked with him, and his television and film credits are too many to mention.
4. Peter Sallis (1921–2017) was an English actor in the finest tradition of the theatre, stage, film and television. A graduate of RADA, Peter had an impressive stage career during the 1950s and was a well-known and trusted actor well before his rise to national fame as the voice behind Wallace & Gromit and his role as Clegg in *Last of the Summer Wine*.
5. Christopher Lee (1922–2015) is considered one of the greatest actors of his time and was awarded both a BAFTA Fellowship in 2011 and BFI Fellowship in 2013.
6. www.Hammer-graveyard.org.uk.
7. Geoffrey Keen (1916–2005) should have gone to the LSE to study economics but had a last-minute change of heart and decided to enter RADA. He was already a member

of The Royal Shakespeare Company by 1939, having won a gold medal for acting. Cast as mostly establishment figures in pinstripe suits, Keen became a well-known face in six James Bond films between 1965 and 1972.

8. Ralph Bates (1940–1991) was a British actor who starred in horror films, dramas and sitcoms. A dual British-French national, Bates was bilingual and highly talented, winning a drama scholarship to Yale in the USA.
9. Sheridan Le Fanu (1814–1873) was an Irish writer and one of the greatest ghost story writers of the Victorian period.
10. Benson, E.F., *Sheridan Le Fanu* (Classic Horror Writers, New York, 1994), pp.48–49.
11. Roy Ward Baker (1916–2010) is known for his direction of Hammer films as well as many others. Baker worked in Hollywood before returning to the UK and directing numerous popular television programmes in the latter part of his career.
12. Ingrid Pitt (1937–2010) was elevated into a cult figure within the Hammer film community with her numerous roles as a calculating, bloodthirsty beauty. She also became an author in later life and lived in Argentina while she wrote about the Peron era. A restless but engaging spirit and fiercely independent, Ingrid's autobiography was called *Life's a Scream*, which was published by Heinemann.
13. Peter Cushing (1913–1994) had a career that spanned the decades. From Kenley in Surrey in 1913 through to Grand Moff Tarkin in *Star Wars*, Cushing would make over 100 films as well as perform on television, radio and the stage. Cushing's fan base today is stronger than ever, with followers from all over the world.
14. Higham, Nick, *BBC News*, 11 August 1994.
15. George Cole (1925–2015) was best known for his role as Arthur Daley in *Minder*, but his true abilities cover a huge repertoire of appearances that began with his first film, *Cottage to Let* (1941), where he played opposite Alastair Sim aged only 15.
16. Kate O'Mara (1939–2014) made her stage debut in 1963. Her career sparkled throughout the Seventies and Eighties in both the UK and the USA, where she played the scheming sister of Alexis Colby in *Dynasty*. Kate would write explicitly and shockingly about her experiences on the casting couch in the book *Vamp Until Ready: A Life Laid Bare*, which was published in 2003.
17. *Time Out* Film Review, 10 September 2012.
18. Weiler, A.H., 'Vampire Story with a New Angle Appears at the Penthouse', *The New York Times*, 4 February 1971.
19. Susan Fleetwood (1944–1995) was the elder sister of musician and actor Mick Fleetwood of Fleetwood Mac fame. The daughter of an RAF officer, she trained at RADA and was a gifted actress, receiving acclaim for her roles in some of Shakespeare's more challenging roles. Peter Hall asked her to join the National Theatre company in 1977. She passed away from ovarian cancer in 1995, aged only 51.
20. Forbes, Bryan, pp.221–222.
21. John Hurt (1940–2017) had a distinctive voice and presence and starred in numerous film masterpieces, such as *The Elephant Man* and *Midnight Express*.
22. Anne Rawsthorne played a key part in the world of the London theatre from the 1950s to the 1970s. One-time company and stage manager, Anne would become general manager at the Queens Theatre (now the Sondheim Theatre) on Shaftsbury Avenue and work across many London theatres. She was a forgotten but vital part of London theatrical history.

23. Paul Eddington (1927–1995) attended Sibford School in Banbury, a boarding school affiliated to the Religious Society of Friends (The Quakers). The motto of the school is 'Truth and Honour, Freedom and Courtesy', and Eddington lived his life by those precepts.
24. Charles Marowitz (1934–2014) was a critic, director and playwright who collaborated with Peter Brook at the Royal Shakespeare Company and later founded the Open Space Theatre in London. His experiences in the theatre in London were recorded in his book *Confessions of a Counterfeit Critic*, published by Methuen in 1973.
25. Donald Albery (1914–1988) was a pivotal influence on London theatre in the 1960s. His willingness to support adventurous plays saw Samuel Beckett's *Waiting for Godot* make it onto the London stage, and he also produced *Beyond the Fringe* when it played in London and New York in 1962.
26. Maureen Riscoe (1921–2003) was born in London and always harboured a desire to be an actress, but instead moved into casting, where she made her name initially with Yorkshire Television. Maureen was a lively and happy character with many tales to tell.
27. Tim Brooke-Taylor (1940–2020) was best-known for his work with *The Goodies* but he was far more versatile than television comedy, having begun his career at the University of Cambridge Footlights. Brooke-Taylor began teaching before success on the stage, and never looked back. He was a long-time stalwart of the BBC Radio 4 comedy programme *I'm Sorry I Haven't a Clue* before becoming a casualty of COVID in 2020.
28. Sue Lloyd (1939–2011) was from Aldborough in Suffolk and won a scholarship to the Royal Ballet School in 1953. Moving on to dance with Lional Blair's troupe, she was one of the last two debutantes to be presented to the Queen at Buckingham Palace in 1958 in the final ceremony.
29. Ronald Lewis (1928–1982) played leading roles in numerous films in his short career. Born in Wales, he had handsome features, enrolled at RADA and won a scholarship in his first year as the most promising student. His suicide from an overdose of alcohol and barbiturates was a shock to the profession.
30. 'South Sea Bubble', *Variety* magazine, 11 April 1956, p.62.
31. Rowan Dore (1951–2007) was a sociable and hard-working journalist according to those who knew him. He worked for the Press Association and *The Argus* in Brighton for many years before a combination of depression and financial worries led to his suicide at his home in Rottingdean, East Sussex.
32. *Diamonds Are Forever* was the film that saved the Bond franchise, Sean Connery managing to turn the productions into profit.
33. Richard Gordon (1921–2017) had been a ship's surgeon and anaesthetist before moving on to write many novels and screenplays for television and film. Gordon studied at Selwyn College, Cambridge, and at St Bartholomew's Hospital.
34. David Askey (1929–1999) was a highly respected television director. Askey directed the first of the 'Doctor' series, *Doctor in the House*, and was tasked with directing both a second and third series in 1971 and 1972. Askey went on to direct such TV gems as *Wodehouse Playhouse*, *Bless Me Father*, *Sorry* (starring Ronnie Corbett) and Rik Mayall in *The New Statesman*.
35. Ernest Clark (1912–1994) was a formidable acting talent, but few people are aware that he was also the holder of the Military Cross. Clark remained in the army for a while after the Second World War, then decided to try his hand at acting, which he had done

before the war. Clark was at his best playing authority figures, being able to maintain a frown even in the most hilarious of situations in the 'Doctor' series.

36. George Layton (born 1942) is another product of RADA, where he won the Emile Littler Award, and played numerous roles across film, television and on stage. Layton became one of the main presenters on *That's Life* with Esther Rantzen, and was seen regularly on *Minder*. George is the author of three books of short stories.
37. Barry Evans (1943–1997) was educated at orphanage boarding schools before winning a scholarship to study at the Central School of Speech and Drama. Evans was considered to have a precocious talent, and during the 1960s he was never without work. A sparkling film career beckoned, but he suffered from depression and was found dead at his home in Claybrooke Magna, Leicestershire, having suffered a heavy blow to the head. He was only 53.
38. 'Back to Stardom via the Dole Queue', Barry Evans, *TV Times*, 1977.
39. Arthur Lowe (1915–1982) was a British actor who appeared in television, film and stage plays, and remains best known for his role as Captain Mainwaring in *Dad's Army*.

**Chapter 6**

1. Bill Cotton (1928–2008) was a television producer and executive, and became the Controller of BBC1 between 1977 and 1981.
2. Ronnie Barker (1929–2005) was a writer, comedian and actor with some of the best television comedy to his credit, such as *Porridge, Open All Hours* and *The Two Ronnies*.
3. James Gilbert (1923–2016) was Head of Comedy at the BBC from 1973–1977, then Head of Light Entertainment from 1977–1982.
4. 'Jimmy Gilbert, BBC Producer who presided over a golden age of light entertainment', *Daily Telegraph*, Obituary, 8 June 2016.
5. 'Obituary for Ronnie Barker', *Entertainment*, October 2005.
6. 'The Two Ronnies – What a Fine Pair', *The Oldie*, 7 November 2023.
7. *Ibid.*
8. *Ibid.*
9. *Ibid.*
10. *Ibid.*
11. Maddie Smith, 'King of Hearts – The Charm of Richard Harris', *The Oldie*, October 2023.
12. *Ibid.*
13. *Belfast Telegraph*, 2017.
14. *Ibid.*
15. Maddie Smith, 'King of Hearts'.

**Chapter 7**

1. Michael Mills (1919–1988) served as Head of Comedy at the BBC between 1967 and 1972. He was instrumental in reshaping the BBC's approach to commissioning new comedy.
2. Ned Sherrin (1931–2007) was an author, director and broadcaster. Originally trained as a barrister, Sherrin worked for ITV before moving to the BBC.
3. Talbot Rothwell (1916–1981) wrote twenty of the thirty-one 'Carry On' films.
4. Royce Mills (1942–2019) was a gentle presence on any set and a very accomplished theatre, television and film actor. *Up Pompeii* was his first film, but it was soon followed by numerous others, including working with Mel Brooks.

5. Obituary, *The Independent*, 3 May 1995.
6. Michael Hordern (1911–1995) had a career that spanned seven decades and appeared in over 160 films, as well as more than 100 theatre productions.
7. Frankie Howerd (1917–1992) was one of the leading stand-up performers of his time. His characteristic catchphrases and improvisation made him a household name.
8. Patrick Cargill (1918–1996) had been a commissioned officer in the British Indian Army before returning to the UK after the Second World War. A very versatile actor, Cargill performed on the West End stage as well as in theatres across the UK, and was a well-known personality on British television and for his film roles.
9. *The Irish Independent*, June 2014.
10. Barbara Murray (1929–2014) starred in a number of films and was a very well-known television actress, appearing in *Danger Man*, *Dr Who* and *Albert & Victoria*.
11. Bill Fraser (1908–1987) was a Scottish actor with successful film, television and stage careers, winning the Laurence Olivier Award for Best Comedy Performance in 1986.
12. Adrienne Posta is a highly talented singer, film and stage actress and television personality, who was most active in the period 1957–2010.
13. Graham Stark (1922–2013) was a close friend of Peter Sellers and appeared in many film and television programmes. Graham's first film role was in 1939. He became a writer and director, and was adept at French accents.
14. Alfie Bass (1916–1987) was born in Bethnal Green, East London, and was the youngest of ten children to Russian-Jewish parents. His first acting jobs came in the 1930s, and he worked with Michael Caine in *Alfie* (1966).
15. Marty Feldman (1934–1982) was mostly known for his large, pronounced eyes, which helped gain him roles in some of the best comedies of the twentieth century.
16. Bill Pertwee (1926–2013) was a British actor and comedian from a family of British stars of the 1970s. A popular cast member across television, radio and theatre, Bill was also a prolific contributor to radio.

**Chapter 8**

1. Robert S. Baker (1916–2009) was a British film and television producer, as well as a director. A former British artillery officer, he was a combat cameraman in North Africa during the Second World War.
2. Tony Curtis (1925–2010) was a huge Hollywood star from the moment he began acting, enjoying great success in over 100 films during his career.
3. Ninety per cent of those invited to play roles in *The Persuaders* only worked in one episode, so the turnover was huge.
4. Anouska Hempel (born 1941) is a New Zealand actress and former model who is now married to Lord Weinberg. She is most famous perhaps for her interior design work.
5. Peter Wyngarde (1927–2018) was best-known for his portrayal of Jason King, but he also had a very long list of theatre credits to his name.
6. Gaughan, Gavin, 'Peter Wyngarde Obituary', *The Guardian*, 18 January2018.
7. Monty Berman (1913–2006) was a noted British cinematographer and producer who worked closely with Dennis Spooner on *The Champions* and *Department S* in the 1960s.
8. Bank House Books, 2009.
9. peterwyngarde.UK, The Official Website.
10. Hugh Burden (1913–1985) was both a playwright and actor who featured in numerous films between 1937 and 1975. A gently spoken man, his face was well-known by British cinema-goers and played opposite Alec Guinness in *The Malta Story* in 1944.

11. Willoughby Goddard (1926–2008) was a portly character actor who featured in numerous television programmes and films, including *The Charge of the Light Brigade* (1968), *The Wrong Box* (1966) and as Cardinal Wolsey in *God's Outlaw* (1986).

**Chapter 9**

1. Antonia Barber (1932–2019), a graduate of UCL, was a writer of books for children and adults and lived in Kent and Cornwall.
2. Lionel Jeffries (1926–2010) was a talented and much in demand British actor, known mostly for his work in films, although he also became a successful director. A graduate of RADA, Jeffries was most famous for his role as Caractacus Potts in *Chitty Chitty Bang Bang* (1968), but he was also prominent in *Two-Way Stretch* in 1960 with Peter Sellers and played opposite Margaret Rutherford in *Murder Ahoy!* (1964). His major directorial success was with *The Railway Children* in 1970.
3. Diana Dors (1931–1984) was a British blonde bombshell, very much in the mould of Marilyn Monroe. A graduate of LAMDA, she often appeared in cabaret and was a wonderful singer. Diana was also a popular chat-show guest and television actress. Her fame spanned the period between post-war austerity and social conservatism and the new age of social liberalism and freedom of the 1950s and 1960s.
4. Laurence Naismith (1908–1992) was without doubt one of the most popular and talented supporting actors in the British and American film industry, with a career that spanned the period between 1948 and 1972. His films included *The Happiest Days of Your Life* (1950), *The Million Pound Note* (1954), *The Dam Busters* (1955), *Richard III* (1955), *A Night To Remember* (1958), *Sink the Bismarck* (1960) and *Diamonds Are Forever* (1971).
5. James Villiers (1933–1998) was a renowned and respected British character actor whose career encompassed numerous film and television appearances.
6. Alan Lake (1940–1984) was the third and final husband of Diana Dors and an accomplished television actor in his own right. On 10 October 1984, five months after Diana had died and sixteen years to the very day since they had first met, Alan drove his teenage son to the local railway station, returned home and committed suicide by shooting himself.
7. Lynne Frederick (1954–1994) had a very controversial life, and even more controversial death. Her reputation has remained contentious ever since the death of her husband, Peter Sellers, and the inheritance that he left her. After a sparkling but short career, where Lynne was regarded as a highly talented film actress really going places, her marriage to Sellers changed her life. Lynne Frederick has almost cult status between those who hated her and those feeling she has been misjudged and poorly treated.
8. IMB.Com/TheAmazingMrBlunden/trivia.
9. Vallance, Tom, 'Obituary: James Villiers', *The Independent*, 21 January 1998.
10. Graham Crowden (1922–2010) was at his best playing eccentric characters, be they doctors, scientists or teachers. Born in Edinburgh, Crowden rose in his profession to play numerous significant roles in such television successes as *Porridge*, *Rumpole of the Bailey*, *Dr Who* and *A Very Peculiar Practice.*
11. David Lodge (1921-–2003) graced many films during the period 1954–1989. The prolific Lodge was a superb supporting actor in dozens of films and was a familiar face on British television. As a great friend of Spike Milligan and Peter Sellers, Lodge appeared in many of their films and other programmes.

12. Gabrielle Chevalier (1895–1969) fought and was decorated during the First World War and went on to become one of France's most highly regarded novelists.
13. Saul, Marc, *Television Heaven*, 20 December 2021.
14. Nostalgia Central, 'Clochemerle'.
15. Wendy Hillier (1912–2003) had already established a long and varied career spanning sixty years and was nominated three times for an Academy Award, winning Best Supporting Actress for *Separate Tables*. She was also nominated for two BAFTAs, two Golden Globes and a Laurence Olivier Award.
16. Joel Hirschorn, writing his 1984 compilation *Rating the Movie Stars*.
17. Cyril Cusack (1910–1993) was born in South Africa. Of Irish ancestry, he came to be seen as one of Ireland's most outstanding actors – reaching number fourteen in one poll. Cusack performed Shakespeare for much of his early career, going on to join the Royal Shakespeare Company in 1963. His son-in-law is Jeremy Irons.
18. Saul, Marc, *Television Heaven*, 20 December 2021.
19. Roy Dotrice (1923–2017) was a member of the RSC and played numerous roles in the theatre, including long runs in the West End. Dotrice was a popular radio voice in numerous roles, including *The Men from the Ministry*, and on television he was seen in *Space 1999* and the 1980s series *Beauty and the Beast*.
1. Moore, Roger, *Roger Moore as James Bond 007* (Pan Books, 1973).

**Chapter 10**

2. Guy Hamilton (1922–2016) had won the DSC during the Second World War. His first job was working under Alexander Korda as Third Assistant before embarking on directing his own films from 1952 onwards. His fourth film was *The Colditz Story* in 1955, which was a great success, and he was thereafter never without work.
3. Moore, Roger, *Roger Moore as James Bond 007* (Pan Books, 1973), p.22.
4. BBC News Report, 'Bond Director Guy Hamilton dies aged 93', 21 April 2016.
5. Moore, Roger, *ibid.*, p.168.
6. *Ibid.*, p.168.
7. Bernard Lee (1908–1981) had a film career that began in 1934 and lasted through until 1979. Trained at RADA, Lee was often an authority figure in films, although he played numerous other roles. He was commissioned as a second lieutenant into the Royal Sussex Regiment on 13 September 1941.
8. Lois Maxwell (1927–2007) was best known for her roles as Moneypenny in the first fourteen Eon-produced Bond films.
9. Moore, Roger, *Roger Moore as James Bond 007* (Pan Books, 1973), p.170.
10. Luisa Mattioli (1936–2021) was an Italian actress and third wife of Roger Moore.
11. www.jamesbondlifestyle.com/hamilton/pulsar2.
12. www.christies.com.
13. George Martin (1926–2016) was an English record producer, composer, conductor and musician. He was often referred to as the 'fifth Beatle'.
14. The song was nominated for an Academy Award for Best Original Song, but lost out to 'The Way We Were'.
15. Jones, Portia., *UK Movies*, Yahoo interview, 27 July 2022.
16. *Ibid.*

**Chapter 11**

1. Alan Bennett (born 1934) has won four BAFTA awards in his hugely influential career as a writer, author and screenwriter. Many of his plays have been adapted into films, such as *The Madness of King George* and *The History Boys.*
2. Proscenium, *Habeas Corpus* by Alan Bennett, June 2005.
3. Billington, Michael, 'Habeas Corpus', *The Guardian*, 11 May 1973.
4. Ronald Eyre (1929–1992) was born in Yorkshire and became one of the foremost directors for cinema, opera, television and the theatre. He was the godfather of actress Emma Thompson.
5. Maddie Smith, 'Alec Guinness was good for me', *The Oldie*, July 2024.
6. Michael Codron (born 1930) is a theatre producer best known for productions of the work of Harold Pinter and Tom Stoppard. He was presented with a Laurence Olivier Award for Lifetime Achievement and is a part-owner of the Aldwych Theatre in west London.
7. Alec Guinness (1914–2000) is a giant of English film and theatre. He won an Academy Award, BAFTA, Golden Globe and Tony Award, and was knighted in 1959.
8. Margaret Courtenay (1923–1996) was a member of the Royal Shakespeare Company and is best known for her roles in numerous films and theatre productions.
9. Phyllida Law (born 1932) has worked across film, television and theatre. She set out as a stage designer before deciding to become an actor instead.
10. Andrew Sachs (1930–2016) worked well into his 80s. Although best known for his role as Manuel in *Fawlty Towers*, he was a prolific stage, radio and television actor.
11. Wendy Shutler began acting in 1963 and worked at The Little Theatre in Bristol. She is an author and poet as well as an accomplished and versatile actor.
12. John Bird (1936–2022) was primarily known for his work as a satirist with John Fortune, but also had an acting career that lasted over fifty-five years. He was well known in film, television and theatre.
13. Roddy Maude-Roxby (born 1930) appeared in numerous films and was one of the nation's first performance artistes. He was in Walt Disney's *The Aristocats* as well as numerous other comedy programmes such as *The Goodies* and *Not Only … But Also.*
14. Patricia Hayes (1909–1998) was born in Streatham, London, and attended RADA, where she graduated in 1928. Active between 1940 and 1996, Patricia was a central figure of the profession and known for her work in many films and television prohrammes.
15. Maddie Smith, 'Alec Guinness was good for me', *The Oldie*, July 2024.
16. Play scripts for *Habeas Corpus*, 1972–1973, MS Bennett 99 Fols. 1-603, Bodleian Libraries.
17. Maddie Smith, 'Alec Guinness was good for me', *The Oldie*, July 2024.
18. *Ibid.*
19. Joan Sanderson (1912–1992) was a commanding figure on stage and in any role that she played. Trained at RADA, Joan appeared across many theatres in the West End and was an accomplished Shakspearian actor.

**Chapter 12**

1. Jonathan Elsom (born 1938) was born in New Zealand and appeared in numerous television series of the 1960s and 1970s, and was still being cast in films such as *Pirates of the Caribbean* in 2017.
2. David Buck (1936–1989) was a talented and sought-after actor, writer, author and radio producer. Born in London, he was the voice actor for films such as the *The Dark*

*Crystal* and *The Lord of the Rings*, as well as acting in and directing dozens of plays for radio. His most popular book, *The Small Adventures of Dog*, was published by William Heinemann in 1968.

3. Douglas Argent (1921–2010) was born in Kent and became a leading television producer and director. He produced major successes such as *The Liver Birds*, *Steptoe and Son* and *Fawlty Towers*.
4. Caroline Munro (born 1949) rose to fame through her appearances in some of the Hammer horror films of the 1970s and went on to have a successful career. Originally a model, Caroline also featured in the Bond movie *The Spy Who Loved Me* in 1977.
5. Caryl Brahms (1901–1982) was an English critic and novelist, and later developed her talents into writing scripts for radio, film and television. A talented musician who did not rate her own abilities, Caryl developed a close working relationship with Ned Sherrin and published numerous books.
6. Richard Briars (1934–2013) worked for over fifty years across radio, stage, film and television, and is mostly known for his portrayal of Tom Good in *The Good Life*. Richard narrated *Roobarb*, the children's animated television series, and was the voice of Fiver in *Watership Down*.
7. Patricia Brake (1942–2022) was actually Patricia Kennedy and was born in Bath. A member of the Royal Shakespeare Company, Patricia was an accomplished and versatile actress and appeared in both *EastEnders* and *Coronation Street*.
8. Jonathan Cecil (1939–2011) was the son of Lord David Cecil and was educated at Eton and New College Oxford, where he specialized in French. David was a prolific actor across television and the theatre but also narrated for radio, including many of P.G. Wodehouse's books.
9. Leslie Phillips (1924–2022) came to fame playing smooth and upper-class roles and was noted for his catchphrase 'Ding-Dong'. He was born in Tottenham in Middlesex and trained at the Italia Conti Academy of Theatre Arts. Well known for his 'Carry On' roles, his repertoire was extensive. He was appointed a CBE in 2008.
10. Jan Holden (1931–2005) was known for roles in light comedy as well as work in the theatre and television. She played roles in *The Saint*, *The Champions* and *Are You Being Served?* Amanda Holden is her great niece.
11. Mary Whitehouse (1910–2001) was a campaigner against social liberalism. During her lifetime she built a significant position as the moral conscience of the nation and government.
12. Obituary for Dave Allen, Wayback Machine, *The Stage*, 15 March 2005.
13. Andrew Gosling (1944–2016) was a British television director and one of the first to use blue screen. He was also the animation director for *Who Framed Roger Rabbit* in 1988. He directed Geoff Hamilton in *Gardeners' World* and lived on the island of Osea in Essex.
14. John Fortune (1939–2013) was an English writer, actor and satirist, best known for his television double act with John Bird. A dry wit, he was adored by his audiences and appeared in numerous television roles.
15. John Wells (1936–1998) was educated at Eastbourne College and St Edmund Hall, Oxford. A satirist right at the very start of the movement in the 1960s, Wells made cameo appearances in films such as *Casino Royale* (1967) and also played parts in *Yes Minister* and *Tinker, Tailor, Soldier, Spy*, and was an original writer for *Private Eye*.

**Chapter 13**

1. Barry Foster (1927–2002) was an English actor with an extensive career spanning fifty years.
2. Nicholas Henson (1945–2019) played a number of television roles and was a heartthrob for much of his career. He married Una Stubbs in 1969, although they were later divorced.
3. 'Nicky Henson, EastEnders and Fawlty Towers Star dies aged 74', *Evening Standard*, December 2019.
4. Cliff Owen (1919–1994) was a film and television director, working on two films with Eric Morecambe and Ernie Wise.
5. Trevor Howard (1913–1988) was a stage and screen actor and was cast in supporting and leading roles in dozens of British films. He was nominated for a BAFTA award four times (winning once), and was also nominated for an Academy Award.
6. Bumble Dawson (1908–1976) was known as Beatrice until her nickname defined her. She was nominated for three BAFTAs and an Academy Award. Dirk Bogarde once referred to her as 'one of the very best'.
7. Harper, Sue, *Women in British Cinema* (Continuum, 2000).
8. Joan Collins (born 1933) is an English actress, columnist and author. Winner of a Golden Globe and a Prime Time Emmy, Joan has a star on the Hollywood Walk of Fame. She has been married five times.
9. John Chapman (1927-2001) was a British actor, screenwriter and playwright.
10. Donald Sinden (1923–2014) featured in numerous films with The Rank Organisation and was highly regarded as a Shakespearian actor and television sitcom star.
11. Frank Thornton (1921–2013), although best known as Captain Peacock in *Are You Being Served?*, was an accomplished actor across many decades. He was very highly thought of for his largely supporting roles.
12. Peter Bland (born 1934) was born in New Zealand and is a poet and actor.
13. Patsy Rowlands (1931–2005), best remembered for her roles in the 'Carry On' films, was a versatile comedic actress.
14. Parnaby, Linda, 'Obituary for Donald Sinden', *The Irish Times*, 2014
15. 'In The Looking Glass', DoYouRemember.co.uk.
16. Francesca Annis (born 1945) is known for her television roles. She has received six BAFTA nominations, winning Best Actress in 1979.
17. Smith, Maddie, 'I Was Peter Cook's Caddy', *The Oldie*, 7 April 2023.
18. Jim Parker (1934–2023) was a BAFTA-winning composer.
19. Charles Wallace is an Australian producer, writer and director who has worked for all the major ITV companies.
20. Smith, Maddie, 'I Was Peter Cook's Caddy', *The Oldie*, 7 April 2023.
21. Smith, Maddie, 'How Peter Cook Made Me Fall in Love with Golf', *The Lady*, 2012.
22. Smith, Maddie, 'I Was Peter Cook's Caddy', *The Oldie*, 7 April 2023.
23. *Ibid.*
24. *Ibid.*
25. Brian Cox (born 1946) is a classically trained Shakespearian actor known for his work across film and stage. He has received two Olivier Awards and a Golden Globe. He is a highly talented and valued member of the acting profession.
26. Doig, Clive, 'Stories from a Life in TV', The Tech Ops History Site.
27. Jeremy Beadle (1948–2008) was an English radio and television presenter, writer and producer.

28. Sarah Greene (born 1957) is a former BBC television presenter, well loved and known for her role in *Blue Peter* during the 1980s.
29. Harry Andrews (1911–1989) featured in over eighty films during his career. He was a BAFTA nominated actor, best known for his portrayal of tough military officers and NCOs.

**Chapter 14**

1. Peter Davison (born 1951) made his debut in 1975 but shot to fame with his portrayal of Tristan Farnon in *All Creatures Great and Small.* Peter was the fifth incarnation of *Dr Who* and continues to work across radio and television.
2. John Le Mesurier (1912–1983) was an understated but highly talented and popular actor, whose work spanned over 120 films, mostly in a supporting role but always with a very noticeable presence.
3. Tom Baker (born 1934) was the fourth and longest-serving *Dr Who* in a career that spans the 1960s to the present day. A hugely versatile and talented actor, Baker was nominated for two Golden Globe awards and can also been seen and heard in *Little Britain*, where his quirky humour shines.
4. Eric Morecambe (1926–1984) was one of the most popular entertainers in British comedy history, and was nominated as one of the 100 Greatest Britons.
5. Ken Wynne (1920–2012) was a comedy actor who was popular in supporting character roles in numerous television series of the 1970s.
6. Barry Cryer (1935–2022) was an English writer and comedian, known across radio and television for his wit, good humour and quick-fire jokes.
7. William Franklin (1925–2006) was a versatile and popular performer across radio, stage, film and television. Erudite and calm, Franklin appeared in many popular situation comedies across the 1960s, 1970s and 1980s, and took over the role of narrating *The Hitchhiker's Guide to the Galaxy* from his friend Peter Jones.
8. Patrick Malahide (born 1945) is a popular, talented and versatile British actor whose first television performance came in *The New Avengers* in 1976. Malahide is well known for appearing in *Game of Thrones* between 2012 and 2016, as well as numerous supporting cast roles in films and on television.

**Chapter 15**

1. The production moved to St Martin's Theatre on 25 March 1974.
2. *Hamlet*, Act 2 Scene 2.
3. *The Oldie*, 26 November 2022.
4. *Ibid.*
5. Pamela Lane (1930–2010) was an English actress who was born in Somerset and was married aged 21 in a passionate and love-at-first-sight moment. Digby Day said of her, 'Lane wasn't a national name, but her outstanding talent and commitment throughout her long working life placed her at the heart and soul of our theatre.'
6. Nicholas Smith (1934–2015) was an English comedic actor who trained at RADA and appeared in the West End, at the Bristol Old Vic and on Broadway.
7. Cheryl Kennedy (born 1947) is an English singer and actress who was cast in numerous musicals, appearing in the West End in *Half a Sixpence* and *The Matchgirls.* Cheryl also appeared in numerous films, as well as *The Bill* and *The Professionals* on television.